Speaking from the Heart

New Feminist Perspectives Series

General Editor: Rosemarie Tong, Davidson College

Beyond Domination: New Perspectives on Women and Philosophy
Edited by Carol C. Gould, Stevens Institute of Technology

Claiming Reality: Phenomenology and Women's Experience
by Louise Levesque-Lopman, Regis College

Dehumanizing Women: Treating Persons as Sex Objects
by Linda LeMoncheck

Evidence on Her Own Behalf: Women's Narrative as Theological Voice
by Elizabeth Say Virgili, California State University, Northridge

Gendercide: The Implications of Sex Selection
by Mary Anne Warren, San Francisco State University

Is Women's Philosophy Possible?
by Nancy J. Holland, Hamline University

Manhood and Politics: A Feminist Reading in Political Theory
by Wendy L. Brown, University of California, Santa Cruz

Mothering: Essays in Feminist Theory
Edited by Joyce Treblicot, Washington University

Speaking from the Heart: A Feminist Perspective on Ethics
by Rita C. Manning, San Jose State University

Toward a Feminist Epistemology
by Jane Duran, University of California, Santa Barbara

Uneasy Access: Privacy for Women in a Free Society
by Anita L. Allen, Georgetown University

Women and Spirituality
by Carol Ochs, Simmons College

Women, Militarism, and War: Essays in History, Politics, and Social Theory
Edited by Jean Bethke Elshtain, Vanderbilt University, and Sheila Tobias, University of Arizona

Women, Sex, and the Law
by Rosemarie Tong, Davidson College

Speaking from the Heart

A Feminist Perspective on Ethics

Rita C. Manning

Rowman & Littlefield Publishers, Inc.

ROWMAN & LITTLEFIELD PUBLISHERS, INC.

Published in the United States of America
by Rowman & Littlefield Publishers, Inc.
4720 Boston Way, Lanham, Maryland 20706

Copyright © 1992 by Rita C. Manning

British Cataloging in Publication Information Available

Library of Congress Cataloging-in-Publication Data

Manning, Rita C.
    Speaking from the heart : a feminist perspective on ethics /
Rita C. Manning.
      p.   cm. — (New feminist perspectives series)
      Includes bibliographical references and index.
      1. Ethics. 2. Caring. 3. Feminism. I. Title. II. Series.
BJ1031.M29   1992
170'.82—dc20   91–44434 CIP

ISBN 0–8476–7733–8 (cloth : alk. paper)
ISBN 0–8476–7734–6 (pbk. : alk. paper)

Printed in the United States of America

 TM The paper used in this publication meets the minimum requirements of
American National Standard for Information Sciences—Permanence of
Paper for Printed Library Materials, ANSI Z39.48–1984.

To my grandparents,
Andrew and Margaret Kelly Phair

Contents

Acknowledgments

It is simply not possible to name all the people who have helped me with this project. I read versions of chapters one, two, four, six, and seven at various meetings of the Pacific Division of the Society for Women in Philosophy (SWIP) and received great encouragement and support as well as many valuable suggestions from my colleagues in SWIP. Several others read and commented on parts of the book: Michael Katz, Thomas Leddy, Barbara Maguire, and Julie Ward. Other extremely generous souls read the entire manuscript in one incarnation or another: Scott Cook, Dianne Romaine, Linda Williams, and Elizabeth Wolgast. All of these readers were also thoughtful and perceptive sounding boards for the ideas that went into the book. My students have also served as sounding boards over the years. In particular I want to thank Melissa Burchard, Kevin Keith, Joseph Nyugen, and Mary Ann Shukait for helping me think through many of the ideas in this book. San Jose State University has been very generous in funding my research with grants over the years which culminated in a paid sabbatical in 1990–1991. Joseph Murphy and Susan Neuhoff helped get the final draft typed. Claudia Close provided invaluable assistance in preparing the final manuscript. Finally, I want to thank my husband, Ronald Nusenoff, who pointed out many stylistic infelicities and incoherent remarks in every draft. I benefited greatly from the help and encouragement of all these people.

An earlier version of Chapter Four, "Just Caring," was read in October 1988 at a conference sponsored by the University of Minnesota, Duluth, "Explorations in Feminist Ethics," and appears in an anthology, *Explorations in Feminist Ethics*, edited by Eve Browning Cole and Susan Coultrap McQuin, published by Indiana University Press in 1991.

Introduction:
Hearing Voices

I began my career in philosophy as a moral philosopher whose primary interest was in ethical theory, and ethical theory rather narrowly conceived—as including only Kantian and consequentialist views. When I first taught a contemporary moral issues class in 1979, I spent the bulk of the time discussing ethical theories with some token applications thrown in at the end. From both a philosophical and a pedagogical perspective, this seemed the right way to approach the material. The students were relatively co-operative; if they were often bored and mystified by the relevance of ethical theory to their own lives, they hid it with good grace. This remained my practice, with a few minor alterations, until about 1984 when I taught medical ethics to forty-eight female nursing students. They were not cooperative. When I showed them how to analyze moral reasoning in terms of underlying principles, they said, "I don't do that when I think about moral matters." After I presented Kantian and consequentialist accounts, they asked, "Aren't there any other options?"

I initially dismissed their worries as evidence of their inability to think sufficiently abstractly. "Don't worry," I told them. "Just because you are unable to describe your moral reasoning in terms of principles doesn't mean you aren't doing it that way. After all, we're often inarticulate about things we do very skillfully. And the fact that you do reason morally shows that you do have that skill." Though I spoke with assurance, the seed had been planted. Perhaps there was some other way.

Later I read Carol Gilligan and I began to see my students' criticisms in a new light. Perhaps they were appealing to the care and responsibility model that Gilligan described. When I later read Nel Noddings's book on caring, I was initially very resistant, but her idea of care as morally central began to grow on me. It helped me to make sense of my students' descriptions of their moral experience, and it allowed me to better understand and justify my own moral experience.

Before the language of care became available I was a moral philosopher without a moral philosophy. When students asked me which theory I preferred, I jokingly responded that I was a Kantian for consequentialist reasons. But the truth was that I couldn't accept either of these alternatives. I was also confused about how to justify my own moral intuitions; I often caught myself saying, "This is what I believe, but this is what I think I can defend."

At a certain point, perhaps in virtue of my discovery of the language of care, I decided to trust my own intuitions. Tentatively at first, and then more and more confidently I began to evaluate my moral intuitions in terms of an ethic of care. I discovered that I could make sense of my intuitions, that my moral experience did hang together, and that the thread was caring.

This book grew out of these explorations. I started by taking a more critical look at ethics and moral philosophy. Here, as elsewhere in my work, my motivation and methodology was strongly influenced by feminist insights. Next, I turned to the account of care, trying to get clear about what it involved both as a morality, an ethic, and a metaethic.

At first it was very hard for me to admit that my earlier commitments in moral philosophy—to the centrality of theory, to the exclusion of all but Kantian and consequentialist accounts, to a strong version of moral realism—were misguided. At the same time, it was tremendously exciting and liberating to speak in my own voice for the first time. I felt I'd managed to overcome the schisms that had plagued me since discovering philosophy—between feminism and philosophy, between my own moral experience and moral philosophy.

When I began to listen more carefully to my own moral voice, when I began to develop this voice through reading and talking, mostly to other women, about care, I was no longer forced to choose between what I believed and what I thought I could defend. Instead I found myself able to speak both confidently and authentically in the voice of care. The title of my book reflects this, using the metaphor of speaking to refer to my emerging voice and the voices of women in general who have been silenced or lip-syncing too long. Describing the speaking as from the heart suggest two things: first, that the voice is personal and authentic, reflecting the integrity of the speaker; second, that this voice is not located in the heady realm of abstraction but centered in the earthy, emotion-infused world of human interaction.

Joyce Treblicot states as one of her dicta for feminist theorizing "I speak only for myself."[1] Although my account of care does begin with my own experience, I hope that I'm not merely speaking for myself but that what I say will reverberate with and clarify the intuitions of some of my readers.[2] The literary style of this book reflects my hopes. Sometimes I will adopt a style reminiscent of the absent author (who speaks universal truths from on high while unaware of the need to qualify), though I remind my readers that I am merely slipping into the background at these junctures. Often, I will begin discussions by telling stories, for I am convinced that our moral theorizing must be firmly grounded in our moral experiences.[3]

My project in this book is fairly ambitious: I shall challenge the received wisdom about moral philosophy. I do not reject the entire tradition; I think there is much to save, but, more importantly, I think that humility and a recognition that we are speaking from our own experience, limited as it is by time and place, is the appropriate attitude.

I shall be defending an ethic of care both as an adequate and as a feminist moral philosophy. Here I want to say what I take an ethic of care to be and why I see it as both an adequate and a feminist account.

Morality can be contrasted with ethics, where morality is seen as involving the actual beliefs and practices that we turn to when we must decide what we morally ought to do. Ethics, by contrast, is the study of morality. When we do ethics, we try to get clear about our moral commitments: Why do we hold this particular set? How does this set hang together? What does our moral language mean? What conceptual strategies are we using? We can further divide ethics into normative ethics, which I see as the underpinnings of a particular morality, and metaethics, the exploration of moral language and concepts. I don't see metaethics as neutral between conflicting moralities or normative ethics, though its connection to a particular morality or normative ethic is less intimate than the connection between a morality and its normative ethic.

When I talk about an ethic of care, I will usually be referring to what is standardly described as morality, a set of commitments and related practices, a way of being in the moral universe. But I shall also describe a related ethic, and though I am skeptical about a foundationalist moral philosophy, I do not despair about the possibility of answering the kind of ethics questions sketched above. Accordingly, this book includes both a statement and a defense of an ethic of care taken as a morality and a normative ethic, and an ethic of care as metamorality. Although I see my morality of care and my ethics of care as hanging together in a reasonable way, I do not think this is the only way to make sense of an ethic of care. One might, for example, see an ethic of care as based upon a firmer foundation than I defend here. In what follows, I shall use "an ethic of care" to refer to my grander project, which includes a morality and an ethics described above.

I describe this ethic as an adequate one since I don't believe that there can be one correct ethic, and I view the search for such an ethic as misguided. Rather, I think that an ethic grows out of one's lived experience, attachments, and sense of personal integrity. I see an ethic of care as growing out of a certain kind of experience and this book is an attempt to flesh out both the ethic and the perspective from which it arises.

I describe the ethic as feminist because it is compatible with what I take to be an underlying commitment of feminists, whatever their other differences, to the improvement of the status of women. Again, I don't think that every feminist need be committed to an ethic of care, although I think its grounding in the experience of many women requires that every feminist take it seriously. Finally, when I describe it as a feminist ethic, I do not mean that only feminists ought to take it seriously. Rather, I see the feminist enterprise of taking women and their experience seriously as incumbent upon everyone who desires to live a morally decent life. In this sense, an ethic must be feminist in order to be adequate.

An ethic of care involves a morality grounded in relationship and response. When we are committed to an ethic of care, we see ourselves as part of a network of care and our obligations as requiring a caring response to those who share these networks and to those whose need creates an obligation to respond. In responding, we do not appeal to abstract principles, though we may appeal to rules of thumb; rather we pay attention to the concrete other in his or her real situation. We also pay attention to the effect of our response on the networks of care that sustain us both.

I begin in Chapter One by discussing some of the feminist critiques of moral philosophy that motivated my search for a feminist alternative. I discuss specific feminist criticism there, but the general problem is that much of moral philosophy has historically been dominated by white males who were completely unaware that they were speaking from their own experience. When their guts rumbled, they thought they were in contact with the absolute. In fairness to these philosophers, insularity and power have the same effect on everyone; when we speak only to like-minded people, when our culture is defined by such like-minded people, it's natural to universalize our experience. And even in speaking from their own experience, the moral philosophers whose work comprised what used to be the canon were tremendously insightful and provocative. Feminist moral philosophy takes up where they left off, beginning with the moral experience of women and other marginalized groups.

In Chapter Two, I defend the anti-theory position and reject a robust moral realism. This is consistent with my belief that all moral theorizing begins with one's own experience. I go on to use my metaethical conclusions and the feminist criticisms in Chapter One as a springboard for developing an adequate ethic. There, I describe the criteria that any adequate and feminist ethic ought to have. I shall disappoint those readers who want to see these issues settled or at least more thoroughly thrashed out, but such desires often get in the way of doing other projects. If feminists spent all their time responding to all the traditional theories and all the standard criticisms, they would never do any distinctly feminist theorizing.

In Chapter Three, I turn to more empirical questions about the effect of experiences of gender, class, race, and parenting on moral reasoning. I included this chapter because I was initially inclined to agree with Carol Gilligan that males and females reason differently about moral issues, but I was a bit skeptical. I was also curious about what the care and responsibility voice sounded like. So, throwing caution to the winds, I respond to the Gilligan-Kohlberg debate about female moral reasoning by discussing a survey that I designed, administered, and analyzed. Along the way, I review some of the social science literature on gender-based differences in moral reasoning.

In Chapter Four, I describe the voice of care both as a morality and an ethic. I look at caring for persons in Chapter Five and caring for animals in Chapter Six. In these chapters I draw extensively on my own and others' moral experience, telling stories both to illustrate the perspective of care and to challenge the reader's intuition. My method in choosing a story to tell is to use one that either illustrates the ethic of care or provides material for applying this ethic. I often contrast the ethic of care with more traditional accounts by showing how they would differ in particular cases.

Finally, I return to the question of whether an ethic of care is truly a feminist ethic in Chapter Seven. I also respond to some possible general objections. There are two different kinds of criticisms of an ethic of care. The first focuses on it as a morality. The concern here is that if women and other marginalized groups take an ethic of care seriously, they'll be supporting the oppressive status quo. Though I admit that there is tremendous pressure on women and other marginalized groups to be society's care-givers, I don't think an ethic of care supports this division of labor. Instead, it can be the foundation of a powerful critique of the status quo.

The second kind of criticism focuses on the metaethics of an ethic of care as I describe it. There are two related objections here: an ethic of care is insufficiently grounded and insufficiently action-guiding. Though I agree that it is less grounded and action-guiding than some other moral perspectives, I don't think this is a problem. I shift the burden of proof here to those who insist that a moral perspective needs to have such a foundation or give such explicit guidance.

Though I develop a sustained thesis in this book, it is possible to get an understanding of the central thesis by reading chapters four through six. Chapter Two is the most straightforwardly philosophical, so, depending on your interests, you might want to read it first, last, or not at all. Chapter Three is primarily a discussion of the claim that moral reasoning is gender (and class and race) based, so if you are intrigued by this debate, you might want to read this chapter first. If you are already convinced of the truth or falsity of this claim and/or you wish to evaluate an ethic of care independently of its use, you might want to save this chapter for later.

Obviously, my task in this book is a challenging one, and I cannot address every aspect or every criticism of an ethic of care. What I hope to do is to draw a map with sufficient detail to encourage fellow travelers to discover new lanes and shortcuts and avoid some of the dead ends and circuitous paths that I am certain to take.

NOTES

1. Joyce Treblicot, "Dyke Methods or Principles for the Discovery/Creation of the Withstanding," *Hypatia* 3 (1988): 1–13.

2. Here, I use "intuition" in much the same sense as William Shaw advocates; that is, I am not referring to glimpses of morality from some transcendent realm, but to shared moral conventions based on experiences we share as fellow humans. See "Intuition and Moral Philosophy," *American Philosophical Quarterly* 17 (1980): 127–34.

3. Jeffner Allen combined stories and discussion in a moving and philosophically rich way in *Lesbian Philosophy: Explorations* (Palo Alto, Calif.: Institute of Lesbian Studies, 1986). I am grateful for her example.

Chapter One

Feminist Critique of Ethical Theory

Ever since the publication of Alasdair MacIntyre's *After Virtue*,[1] it has been open season on ethics. Ethics, as we've come to know it in the twentieth century, has been described as focusing too narrowly on actions,[2] as rigidly rule governed,[3] as too blissfully ignorant of social science,[4] and even as reductionist.[5] This criticism has been healthy and has led to some of the best work in moral philosophy in a long time. I propose to add fuel to fire by asking whether there is a distinctly feminist criticism of standard ethical theory.

Carol Gilligan's *In a Different Voice*[6] jolted me out of my dogmatic slumber. Soon I began to examine my many doubts about ethical theory and moral philosophy. In this chapter, I will share these doubts and set the stage for an examination of an ethic of care by focusing on four critiques of ethical theory motivated by feminist concerns. The first involves a feminist critique of the picture of the self. The second is a critique of moral reasoning. The third is a critique of the division of moral philosophy into "applied" and theoretical ethics. The fourth is an extension of Sandra Harding's critique of science in *The Science Question in Feminism*[7] to moral philosophy.

Before embarking on this critique, one first needs to say just what standard ethical theory is. This question is usually answered by pointing to Kantian and utilitarian approaches to deciding questions about what one morally ought to do. I'm not satisfied with this approach, both because it leaves out too much and because it is historically inaccurate. Neither Kant nor the early utilitarians Bentham and Mill were trying to develop the "ideal" way to decide what one morally ought to do. Kant was more concerned with trying to explain why our moral intuitions and judgments converged. Granted, his "explanation" involved outlining the metaphysical foundations of morality, but he did take it as a given that our sincere judgments would converge. Bentham and Mill, navigating in a world that did not see the essential wrongness of child labor, were concerned with mapping out a decision procedure, which could serve as an alternative to prudential calculations and which could be "sold" to the heartless capitalists.

Instead of focusing on the "big two," I propose to focus on three issues that cut across the great divide: the division between ethical theory and applied ethics, the picture of moral reasoning that the two traditions have been made to fit, and the picture of the self presupposed by each.

One might first ask what is to count as a distinctly feminist criticism. This inevitably raises the issue of what feminism is. I shall offer a tentative analysis of what feminist philosophy is and leave it to the readers to see if they agree.

Feminist scholarship, in philosophy as elsewhere, is committed to one or both of the following claims. The first is that women are the moral equals of men and that the oppression of women is wrong. The second is that our categories, the way we slice up the world, are not simply given but are influenced by the social context.

With regard to the first claim, the assumption is made by scholars that oppression can be addressed by scholarship. Here one might accept the radical view that scholarship (deeper understanding of the problem, its historical context, etc.) is sufficient to right the wrongs, or one might accept a more modest view that research programs can shed some light on problems that cannot be solved without the reflective understanding that scholarship provides.

The second claim is that our categories have been shaped by the patriarchal society in which we live. If this is right, then it might not be possible to overcome the oppression of women without at least looking at these "givens." Indeed it might not even be possible to talk about oppression in the accepted paradigms.

Contemporary work in feminist philosophy is going on in two arenas. One kind of work accepts the given paradigm and argues within it. The other attempts to look critically at the paradigm, or to create a new one. In what follows, I will be doing a bit of both.

I. THE SELF

Both Kantians and utilitarians assume a particular picture of the self. Michael Sandel calls this picture of the self the "unencumbered self." "The priority of the self over its ends means I am never defined by my aims and attachments, but always capable of standing back to survey and assess and possibly to revise them. This is what it means to be a free and independent self, capable of choice."[8] In the Kantian framework, this self is both the focus of moral concern and the moral agent. The standard criticisms of utilitarianism deny that the utilitarians take this picture as seriously as they might. John Rawls offers what he takes to be the last word, "Utilitarianism does not take seriously the distinction between persons."[9] Though utilitarians do not take this picture as conferring a special moral status on agents, they do accept it as a reasonable picture of what moral agents are like.

It is not clear whether this unencumbered self is supposed to be a description of actual selves or a normative picture. The lack of empirical data suggests that perhaps it is meant to be a normative picture. I am troubled by the consequences of it in either case; it leads one to adopt a particular style of moral deliberation, detached and "objective." (I will return to this criticism when I discuss the textbook model of moral reasoning in the next section.) It also influences our treatment of moral persons. If moral persons are free to choose among aims and ends, we needn't be overly concerned with roles and relationships. But feminists have identified traditional gender roles and relationships as oppressive precisely because they restrict the ability of women to choose and carry out aims and ends. This is an important criticism of the unencumbered self.

If it turns out that this is a correct empirical description of the self, then perhaps we should reevaluate our analyses of oppression. If it isn't accurate, then we should recognize its role in affirming the status quo. If it is meant to be a normative picture, even though it is not empirically accurate, then we should ask why we should adopt this picture, especially in light of the fact that it does provide support to those who would oppress women.

One could argue here that this is a double-edged sword. The unencumbered self as a normative ideal might require treating people as though they were autonomous or it might require organizing our social institutions so that people can achieve autonomy. These suggestions may be incompatible. At any rate, if we are to see it as a normative ideal, we need to argue for it. It is not sufficient to accept it because it has been presupposed by so much of standard moral philosophy.. What strikes me is that the question of whether it is a description or a prescription is never raised in standard moral philosophy.

If we consider the unencumbered self as an empirical description, we need to ask whether it describes both men and women, rich and poor, East and West, etc. As David Potter pointed out, Frederick Jackson Turner's model of rugged individualism on the frontier was deeply sexist.[10] Though the frontier experience did encourage individualism, competition, and egalitarianism among men, it denied women alternatives to marriage and hence encouraged quite another set of character traits for women. American liberalism is deeply influenced by this sexist frontier picture, but before we accept it as a picture of human nature, we need to ask if it captures the experience of women and other nonmale, non-Western groups.

Perhaps we need to look at alternative conceptions of the self and evaluate them both as descriptions of the self and as normative ideals. If they do not correspond to the experiences of women, we should discard them. Sandel offers just such an alternative, which he calls the "situated self." This is a view that is held by communitarians. "We cannot conceive ourselves as . . . bearers of selves wholly detached from our aims and attachment . . . certain of our roles are partly constitutive of the persons we are—as citizens of a country, or members of a movement, or partisans of a cause."[11] I am still thinking about this alternative, but it seems to me that it may prove a better description of women's and men's lives as well as a tool for critiquing the status quo.

Connected with the unencumbered picture of the self is a picture of moral reasoning. If I am free to choose my own ends unencumbered by social conditioning or roles, then I either choose arbitrarily or by appeal to some internal standard. If that internal standard is to have appeal to other similarly situated radically free selves, there must be some universal ground to which we can all appeal. Thus enters the textbook picture of moral reasoning.[12]

II. MORAL REASONING

I call this the textbook picture of moral reasoning for two reasons: first, because it is widely accepted by writers of issue-oriented texts; second, because I think it is the most widely held view of moral reasoning. In the textbook picture, the outcome is typically a judgment about what one ought to do, though it can also be a judgment about whether and how to fix blame. This outcome is arrived at by applying the appropriate principle or principles to the relevant facts.

In its full glory, the textbook picture is deductivist, mechanical, and foundationalist. It is deductivist when the principles are cast as universal prescriptions of the form "whenever these facts obtain . . . everyone ought . . . ." When the appropriate facts obtain, the individual ought to do what the general principle dictates. It is mechanical when one need only describe the facts correctly and pull out the appropriate principle for the judgment to follow automatically. It is foundationalist when the judgments are taken to be knowledge. If this is the case, then the principles must themselves be true. It is this picture of moral reasoning that has motivated attempts to justify the principles as true.

In its more modest manifestation, the picture is inductivist and relativist in one way or another. The picture is inductivist when the principles are seen to be merely *prima facie* or when the facts are deemed to defy complete and accurate description. It is relativist when the principles are seen to have less than airtight justification. When this is the case, alternative principles can also be justified. Both the strict and the loose picture share this essential feature: principles applied to facts yield judgments. Though there are many criticisms of this picture, I want to focus on one that is suggested by Carol Gilligan.

Gilligan addresses her criticisms to Lawrence Kohlberg's work in moral development. Kohlberg theorized that we go through distinct stages in moral development, culminating in the ability to apply universal principles to the facts, yielding judgments about what we ought to do. One's moral development can be measured by seeing what principles one appeals to. Gilligan has argued that women and girls do not fit neatly into any of Kohlberg's stages. She suggests that women do not typically use what I am calling the textbook picture; that is, no principles clearly emerge when analyzing responses of many females. If no principles emerge, the respondents can be classified on the Kohlberg scale only with some difficulty. In support of her thesis that females don't use the textbook model, she offers two responses to a moral dilemma, one from an eleven-year-old boy and one from an eleven-year-old girl.

> In this particular dilemma, a man named Heinz considers whether or not to steal a drug which he cannot afford to buy in order to save the life of his wife. In the standard format of Kohlberg's interviewing procedure, the description of the dilemma itself—Heinz's predicament, the wife's disease, the druggist's refusal to lower his price—is followed by the question, "Should Heinz steal the drug?"
>
> (Jake's response) For one thing, a human life is worth more than money, and if the druggist only makes $1000, he is still going to live, but if Heinz doesn't steal the drug his wife is going to die. (Why is life worth more than money?) Because the druggist can get a thousand dollars later from rich people with cancer, but Heinz can't get his wife again. (Why not?) Because people are all different and so you couldn't get Heinz's wife again.
>
> (Amy's response) Well, I don't think so. I think there might be other ways besides stealing it, like if he could borrow the money or make a loan or something, but he really shouldn't steal the drug—but his wife shouldn't die either. If he stole the drug, he might save his wife then, but if he did, he might have to go to jail, and then his wife might get sicker again, and he couldn't get more of the drug, and it might not be good. So, they should really just talk it out and find some other way to make the money.[13]

Gilligan offers an analysis of what is going on in both responses: Amy sees the parties as related, and the solution is to create a stronger and more responsive relationship between them. We can easily analyze Jake's reasoning by appeal to the textbook picture. His principle is something like: "Whenever there is a conflict between human life and money, the choice should be made in favor of life." Another possibility is that Jake holds two principles and a method for prioritizing them. The principles might be: "It is wrong to steal," and "It is wrong to deprive someone of a chance to live when you can give that chance." The second principle takes priority over the first. The facts are that Heinz's wife will die without a drug which the druggist wants to withhold from her in the interests of making a profit. The judgment is that it is all right in Jake's view to steal the drug. Amy's reasoning does not fit into the textbook picture at all. One might conclude that Amy has not yet learned to do moral reasoning. This is not a conclusion that Gilligan wants to embrace, because her research has convinced her that Amy's reasoning is fairly typical of females of all ages. What does this tell us?

One implication is that, as a description of moral reasoning, the textbook picture is biased in favor of males. If we are simply trying to describe how humans reason about moral issues, then this model is clearly deficient. But this is not the task that philosophers are typically engaged in. The task for moral philosophers is to impart a model of moral reasoning. (If moral philosophers should concern themselves with moral reasoning at all. I happen to think that they should, for reasons that will become apparent in the discussion of "applied" ethics, but my view may not be widely shared.) If this is so and if Jake's reasoning is closer to an ideal, then we should be perfectly willing to say that Jake's reasoning is better than Amy's. If Amy's reasoning is typical of female reasoning about moral issues, then the fault could be laid to conditioning. But before we can come to this conclusion, we should try to make some sense of Amy's reasoning.

Nel Noddings offers an analysis of moral considerations which we can apply here.[14] Noddings says that I ought to decide what I ought to do by asking myself what my ideal caring self would do in this situation. This involves recalling some incident in one's life when this ideal caring self emerged and asking what that self would do in this situation. Although I disagree with some of the implications that Noddings goes on to draw, I am convinced that she has an important insight. Her analysis also fits Amy's narrative. Amy is trying to see what the ideal caring selves of all the parties, Heinz included, ought to do. Jake applies general principles, Amy adopts a perspective. Noddings's view might be assimilated into some version of virtue ethics, or some other distinctly female or feminist analysis might be developed that fits with Amy's reasoning, but, in any case, if these attempts fit the reasoning of females better than the textbook model then we must look at them very seriously.

Another possibility, though not incompatible with Noddings, is that Amy simply values compromise and accommodation. She is searching here for a way for all the parties to compromise so that everyone is accommodated. She is unwilling to assume, as Jake seems so ready to do, that such a compromise is impossible.

Several things are going on in Amy's view. Gilligan is right that Amy sees creating better and more caring relationships between the parties as the solution. This requires that all the parties adopt the stance of "ideal caring selves," as Noddings puts it. Finally, Amy believes that compromise and accommodation are both possible in this case and would result in a stronger and more caring bond between the parties.

III. "APPLIED" AND THEORETICAL ETHICS

A third critique of ethics is that the division between theoretical and "applied" ethics and the subsequent denigration of "applied" ethics is pernicious and related to gender. Describing the making of moral judgments as "applied" suggests two things. First, it suggests that this is a simple matter and can be done in a straightforward way after the real work, justifying an ethical theory, is done. This assumes that the ethical theory can be worked out without any appeals to its consequences in real judgments. Second, it implies that the making of moral judgments is not as important or philosophically worthwhile as setting out theories. Both of these assumptions are controversial at best.

Let me start with the first. I don't think that it is at all clear just what an ethical theory is supposed to be, or even why the central focus of moral philosophy came to be called "ethical theory." One of my colleagues has suggested that the title of Sellars and Hospers's widely used anthology created this monster. Whatever the genealogy, we are left with a peculiar division within moral philosophy, between ethical theory and applied ethics. A second division exists between both of these and metaethics. I am totally puzzled by this latter division, as it seems to me that we can only debate the meaning of moral terms within theories, either about morality or about language. I do understand the value of asking about the foundations of theories, about their justifications, about the status of key concepts, but I'm not convinced that this enterprise can be done cleanly, without begging the question in favor of one theory or another. The reemergence of metaethics suggests that not everyone would agree with me on this issue, but I don't need to make this point in order to critique the division between theoretical and applied ethics.

To return to my question, why would anyone think that a theory, presumably about what one ought to do, could be worked out independently of its practical application? I suspect that part of the answer is that ethical theory is not widely conceived as a theory about what one ought to do. I do not mean to suggest that this conception would be especially controversial. I suspect that it would be given lip service in every course on ethical theory. What I mean to suggest is that moral philosophers seldom think of ethical theory this way while working away on the fascinating puzzles that arise when doing theoretical ethics. Perhaps this is a personal idiosyncrasy, but I did ethical theory for years without really asking what it was that the theories were designed to do. It was only after teaching ethics to cynical and disbelieving audiences that I began to think that it ought to give them some guidance about how to live. The cynical picture of the enterprise that emerges when one looks at what's going on in ethical theory these days is that of tinkerers filling in the gaps in one theory or another, of sharp minds discovering the crack in some other.

I don't share this total cynicism about the state of the art; some very good work is going on within ethical theory, but the more modest task, that of developing guidelines for living morally decent lives, is not being pursued aggressively enough by moral philosophers. This is an important part of ethical theory. It should be done by moral philosophers and should have the prestige of the other enterprises that are carried on under the banner of ethical theory. If this were to be seen as at least one of the tasks of ethical theorizing, then the impossibility of doing theory apart from normative ethics would be obvious. How could we develop decent theories about how humans ought to behave without seeing the theory in action? This kind of reflective equilibrium would be essential to the task.

The second assumption that I want to challenge is that making moral judgments is not as important or philosophically worthwhile as the other work in ethical theory. This assumption is closely related to the assumption just discussed—that theory and practice can be cleanly divided and separately worked out. If the conception of theory that I have defended—that theory should involve developing guidelines for living morally decent lives—is right, then the making of moral judgments becomes central. Theories are just ways of making such judgments. This conception of theory is the prevalent one in texts on applied ethics, though, as argued earlier, the model of moral reasoning there is often too mechanical.

So far, I have suggested that the division between applied and theoretical ethics cannot be defended, because if we see one important task of ethical theory as devising guidelines about how to live, we must look at our lives and the impact of such guidelines on our lives.

I now want to suggest that applied ethics is not taken as seriously by the profession as theoretical ethics. I think we all have a sense of the ranking of areas in professional philosophy. Though one could argue about the relative ranking of areas, I doubt that many would put applied ethics at the top. Nor would many see applied ethics as a more prestigious undertaking than theoretical ethics. The currency of the label "applied" supports my thesis. It probably did have an innocent beginning, but the way it has flourished suggests something more sinister.

"Applied" and "theoretical" have a fairly clear sense in science, and the popular wisdom is that the theoretical types are doing the real work. This view is not shared by experimentalists, nor is it shared by the Nobel committee which has been awarding its prizes, especially in particle physics, to applied work. Still, this division exists in science departments at universities all over the country. Since I don't think that one can do either theoretical or applied ethics independently, I am not persuaded that the label is justified by the role of applied ethics as application of theory to the real world. Other defenders of the label in ethics might suggest that it means only that this is an enterprise that cultivates an audience outside philosophy. I have no quarrel with this conception of the role of applied ethics, but I wonder why philosophies of science and aesthetics are not so described. The explanation of the currency of "applied" ethics is pernicious. It serves to label those who do it as less serious than their counterparts in theoretical ethics. This causes philosophers interested in such basics as a job and an audience to resist working in "applied" ethics. Obviously the temptation to work in this area is strong enough to cause many first-rate philosophers to write about concrete issues—some of the very best work in philosophy is going on in the pages of ethics journals, and journals devoted to concrete issues in particular, but those working in this area do so at a price.

To summarize, the division between theoretical and applied ethics is untenable, and the perception that such a division exists and the subsequent denigration of applied ethics is pernicious. Now I want to develop the feminist critique. This critique is admittedly sketchy and speculative, but it has some surface plausibility. In this critique, I shall focus on two possible and related reasons why work is denigrated: because women do it and because it is perceived as women's work. According to the *1984–85 Directory of Women in Philosophy*, more women listed normative and applied ethics as an area of interest than any other area. There are still far more men than women in philosophy, so there are more men doing normative ethics than there are women, but women are still more likely to work in this than in any other area in philosophy. This suggests the second reason why it is denigrated, because it is perceived as women's work. In a patriarchal society, women are seen as the care-givers and as the child-raisers. Men are seen as defenders of the intellectual realm, as the theoreticians, while women care for and about the emotional and the concrete. Is it any wonder then that when women entered philosophy in greater numbers than ever before that a division of intellectual labor occurred? The division of ethics into theoretical and applied fit into the patriarchal perception of the relative worth and interests of men and women. Another reason why applied ethics is seen as women's work is that it is closely connected to moral education. Proselytizing is just beneath the surface in discussions in applied ethics. The desire to educate the audience is apparent. Applied ethics is also very much at home in the classroom. When we get into moral education, we are getting perilously close to child-rearing, and that is women's work.

To support my suspicion that the theoretical/applied distinction in moral philosophy is gender based, it is instructive to look at how the distinction came to operate in other disciplines. When men began to see previously domestic areas as proper arenas for science, theoretical disciplines emerged. These disciplines were dominated by men, while the actual practice was dominated by women. It is instructive here to look at healing, child-birth, and child-rearing. Healing became medicine and medicine began to be organized into two camps, the doctors, who were primarily theoreticians and diagnosticians, and the nurses, who were primarily care-givers. Midwives gave way to obstetricians, grandmothers to experts on child-rearing.

Philosophy was once seen as a purely theoretical enterprise. Professors professed, and students watched and listened. Two things happened in the latter half of this century to change this: philosophy moved into state universities and colleges, and women moved into philosophy. As philosophy moved into state colleges and universities, philosophers were told that they were to teach, not to profess. Teaching, as we know, is women's work. Luckily, women began to enter philosophy in larger numbers, and a division of labor between men and women became possible. Men could continue as theoreticians, professing and doing the real work in philosophy, and women could teach and do the applied work, scurrying off with the insights of the men and valiantly trying to apply them in practice. Perhaps, this analysis is somewhat overdrawn, but I find it chillingly suggestive. In any case, we must be willing to subject our own discipline to the same scrutiny to which we subject others.

The feminist critique that I have given so far is incomplete. In any case, addressing the two criticisms discussed here would require some rethinking of moral philosophy. First, we need to rethink the division between theoretical and applied ethics. I've argued that theoretical ethics is not centrally concerned with developing guidelines for living morally good lives. If we begin to see this as a central task of moral philosophy, then we could bridge the gap. We might also see the transmission of moral ideals as the business of moral philosophy. This would require us to look seriously at moral development and strategies for moral education. This would shift the traditional emphasis away from rational adults to children, but there is no reason for philosophy to shy away from the education of children. That this has traditionally been seen as women's work is not a philosophically respectable reason for avoiding it. The current relative prestige of areas in philosophy ought to be reevaluated, and good philosophers should be encouraged to begin or continue to work in applied ethics and moral education.

The textbook model of moral reasoning ought to be reevaluated in light of the experimental evidence that females are far less likely to use it than males. First, we must get clear about exactly what kind of reasoning is being used by men and women. This requires us to look seriously at the work going on in moral reasoning, development, and education. If we agree that there are at least two distinctly different models, we must evaluate each model. If the "male" model appears to be superior to the "female" model, then we should bite the bullet and continue to teach and refine it. In carrying out the evaluation though, we must decide what it is that moral reasoning is supposed to do.

Perhaps we should take seriously the virtue tradition's claim that judgments about actions are not the only, or even the most important, judgments we need to make. If we think that a new model is required, we must reevaluate our traditional theories to see if they could fit the new model. I am not convinced that Kantian ethics is wed to the textbook model, though utilitarianism might be more dependent upon it. Our job ought to be to see if we can sketch a version of Kantian ethics and utilitarianism which will fit a new model. The virtue tradition might turn out to be a good candidate. Last, we must take seriously the attempts of feminist philosophers to sketch an alternative model.

We need to take a critical look at the picture of the self that is presupposed by standard moral philosophy. Is it an empirical description? If so, is it accurate? Is it a normative ideal? If so, should we accept it? Is it a better ideal than its alternatives? How can we achieve it? Answering these questions requires philosophers to take social science and feminist scholarship seriously. An empirical description ought to be consistent with the data about men and women. A normative ideal ought to make the "good life" possible for men and women.

In the final analysis, we may get by with some tinkering, but we may need to completely rethink our picture of moral philosophy. This is a good time for such rethinking, and some of it must be done from a feminist perspective if our theories are to take into account and to provide for all persons.

IV. THE MORALITY QUESTION IN FEMINISM

Sandra Harding, in a provocative recent book, *The Science Question in Feminism*,[15] has mounted a feminist critique of science. Some of her criticisms are fairly obvious—for example, that women have been denied the opportunity to compete with men in science—but some are both subtle and rich with insight, especially her description of an alternative feminist epistemology.[16] I think that we can profitably apply these insights to moral philosophy, so, in the spirit of this thoroughgoing text, I will turn my attention to academic moral philosophy and focus on the content of academic moral theorizing as well as the sociology of moral philosophy. Because I am not a social scientist, and because there is no formal evidence to speak of anyway, this section will be tentative and impressionistic. I apologize for the lack of precision, but hope that my account will motivate more systematic critiques.

Harding offers five feminist criticisms of science. First, she argues that there is a "massive historical resistance to women's getting the education, credentials, and jobs available to similarly talented men . . . [with] psychological and social mechanisms through which discrimination is informally maintained even when the formal barriers have been eliminated."[17] Second, "science is used in the service of sexist, racist, homophobic, and classist social projects."[18] Third, "the selection and definition of problematics— deciding what phenomena in the world need explanation, and defining what is problematic about them—have clearly been skewed toward men's perception of what they find puzzling."[19] Fourth, the "rigid dichotomies in science and epistemology . . . [are] inextricably connected with specifically masculine—and perhaps uniquely Western and bourgeois—needs and desires. Objectivity, subjectivity, the scientist as knowing subject versus the objects of his inquiry, reason versus the emotions, mind versus body—in each case the former has been associated with masculinity and the latter with femininity."[20] Fifth, there are alternative feminist epistemologies that can serve as the "basis for an alternative understanding of how beliefs are grounded in social experiences, and of what kind of experience should ground the beliefs we honor as knowledge."[21]

We can draft analogous criticisms of moral philosophy. The first is simple enough: that there is tremendous resistance to women's getting the education, credentials, and jobs available to similarly talented men in moral philosophy. The second would be that moral philosophy is used in the service of sexist, racist, homophobic, and classist social projects. The third is that the selection of problematics has been skewed toward problems of interest to men. The fourth would be that dichotomies embedded in moral philosophy reflect patriarchal conceptions of men and women. The fifth would be that an alternative feminist epistemology is available for moral philosophy. The first two criticisms are directed toward the profession, and the final two toward the content of moral philosophy; the third cuts across both. I will focus on each in turn, beginning with a sketchy look at the first three and lingering over the final two criticisms.

According to *The 1987 NEA Almanac of Higher Education*, there were 442 doctorates in philosophy awarded in 1983 and 1984. Of that number, 330 were awarded to men and 112 to women. If we assume that women are as potentially philosophically talented and inclined as men and that their career choices are influenced by non-gender-related outside factors (e.g., the economy, the relative status of professions) in much the same way as men, then we must assume that discrimination accounted for the difference. As Harding points out in her critique of science, much of the discrimination is institutional and virtually invisible. The corresponding disparities in the sciences (5,196 men versus 1,547 women) and mathematics (569 men versus 126 women) suggest that our culture discourages women from engaging in "theoretical" pursuits. The pattern tends to reinforce itself; women undergraduates see few female faculty in these areas. The evidence of more overt discrimination is anecdotal, but widely reported when female philosophers get together (especially at meetings of the Society for Women in Philosophy). Moral philosophy may be in better shape in this respect than the rest of philosophy. Again, my evidence is mostly anecdotal; though, according to the 1984–85 *Directory of Women in Philosophy*, women are more likely to list moral philosophy as an interest than any other area in philosophy.

The second criticism, that moral philosophy is used in the service of sexism, racism, homophobia, and the like, is more problematic. Perhaps I am too close to the subject to present a clear picture, but I like to think that moral philosophy is more likely to be used to combat these evils.

The third criticism is more complicated. First, we need to be clear about what counts as a problematic in moral philosophy. The concrete moral issues which moral philosophers address would count as problematics. Moral philosophers are often content to say something intelligent about these issues, pointing out the possible solutions as well as the drawbacks to each. Other discussions are more forceful, defenses of some particular position on an issue. In any case, the issues are provided by the larger society. Since we live in a patriarchal society with men setting the social agenda, one might expect the issues to be skewed in favor of those more interesting to men.

Issue-oriented moral philosophy can be roughly divided into two areas: professional ethics and social issues. Professional ethics includes issues of special concern to members of the corresponding professions. Some of the professions that have gotten special attention by moral philosophers are business, medicine, and law. Engineering and criminal justice (corrections and police work) are beginning to receive some attention. The bias in favor of "men's" interests is clear. These professions are dominated by men. Where are the discussions of professions with a preponderance of women? Teaching, for example, is not inherently less philosophically interesting than business. Social work, long dominated by women, receives almost no attention from moral philosophy, though it is a profession rife with moral dilemmas.

Social issues addressed by philosophers include abortion, nuclear war, apartheid, discrimination and equality, pornography, privacy, and property. These issues arise from the larger social context, and there are no issues here that are of interest only to men. Abortion, discrimination, and pornography are clearly of interest to women, though they are equally important to men. Both women and men are interested in avoiding nuclear war. Although women have historically been more active in antinuclear activities than men, and in spite of the fact that the issue concerns professions dominated by men—the military and military contractors—I would classify nuclear war as a gender-neutral issue. On the social issues side, moral philosophy seems to be doing reasonably well. The issues seem to be of general concern, and much of the work is being done by women.

Unfortunately, there is a whole area that is virtually ignored by moral philosophy—interpersonal ethics. Although there is some history to draw on (e.g., Aristotle's discussion of friendship), there is little work in contemporary moral philosophy on friendship and family. These are issues that arise in what is called the private sphere, a sphere that has been seen, in the Western tradition, as the province of women. Men were identified with the public sphere. Although the distinction is questionable, one can argue there that the problematics of moral philosophy concern the public sphere rather than the private. In this sense, the problematics betray a gender bias.

There are other problematics in moral philosophy that arise from within the field itself, though they too are influenced by the larger social context. One might make a case that these problematics are skewed toward the interests of men. In order to come up with a list of the problematics in moral philosophy, I followed the totally unscientific procedure of scanning the headings in *The Philosopher's Index* for the last six years (1985 through 1990) and came up with the following list: moral knowledge (moral realism), justice, rights, virtues, moral psychology, moral development, moral education, and history of moral philosophy. Appearing for the first time were "Gilligan" and "Caring." The citations under "feminism" (which is a rapidly growing section) include many articles on feminist ethics. I found this list to be encouraging. It included sections on issues that are of interest to transmitters of moral values: moral psychology, moral development, and moral education. Although I don't think that women are more suited to transmitting moral values, the fact remains that we are more often saddled with this task and are hence more interested in it.[22]

Harding's fourth critique of science is that the rigid dichotomies in science reflect masculine (and perhaps Western and bourgeois) values and interests. She mentions the following dichotomies: mind versus body, reason versus emotion, culture versus nature, subject versus object, objectivity versus subjectivity, the abstract and general versus the concrete and particular, and public versus private.[23] Harding argues that the insistence on these dichotomies serves to uphold the patriarchal status quo. These same dichotomies can also be seen in moral philosophy, although we could add an additional two: fact versus value and theoretical ethics versus applied ethics. I shall ignore the subject/object dichotomy as well as the objectivity/subjectivity dichotomy because it is not clear to me that moral philosophy reflects these dichotomies. I shall consider each of the other dichotomies in turn.

The mind/body, reason/emotion, and culture/nature dichotomies are all aspects of essentially the same dichotomy, so I will consider them together.[24] The mind is the seat of reason, and the emotions are seen as visceral, bodily reactions. When culture acts on nature, it is the intellectual transformation of the purely physical, the collective mind acting on the collective body.

Many feminist theorists have pointed out the historical identification of women with nature and men with culture.[25] Some feminists, notably Susan Griffin,[26] have agreed with the dichotomy and the identification of women with nature but have deplored the subsequent denigration of nature and things natural. Harding argues that a feminist critique of science must start by questioning the dichotomy itself. In the contemporary ideology of science, science is seen as the masculine enterprise of unveiling, and subsequently exploiting, nature, which is seen as female.[27] It is reasonable to assume that the dichotomy and the gender identification exist in moral philosophy as well, since it is no less immune than science to the social context. If women are identified with nature, then presumably men are identified with morality, which is one aspect of culture. The task of morality, on one reading, would be to conquer nature. Nietzsche argues that this

was precisely the task of prevailing morality. If nature is seen as feminine
and morality is an attempt to crush nature, then morality is profoundly
misogynous. I'm not convinced that all morality requires the repression
of nature, but I suspect that Nietzsche was not merely constructing a straw
man (woman?) argument. He writes:

> When one finds it necessary to turn reason into a tyrant, as Socrates did, the
> danger cannot be slight that something else will play the tyrant. Rationality was
> then hit upon as the savior; neither Socrates nor his "patients" had any choice
> about being rational: it was de rigeur, it was their last resort. The fanaticism with
> which all Greek reflection throws itself upon rationality betrays a desperate
> situation; there was danger, there was but one choice: either to perish or—to be
> absurdly rational. The moralism of the Greek philosophers from Plato on is
> pathologically conditioned; so is their esteem of dialectics. Reason-virtue-
> happiness, that means merely that one must imitate Socrates and counter the
> dark appetites with a permanent daylight—the daylight of reason. One must be
> clever, clear, bright at any price: any concession to the instincts, to the
> unconscious, leads downward.[28]

Here, Nietzsche is not rejecting morality per se, but a morality that
requires the rejection of the instincts, the emotions. He explicitly includes
Plato, Socrates, and Kant as defenders of this pernicious morality. He
describes an alternative morality:

> I reduce a principle to a formula. Every naturalism in morality—that is, every
> healthy morality—is dominated by an instinct of life; some commandment of
> life is fulfilled by a determinate canon of "shalt" and "shalt not"; some inhibition
> and hostile element on the path of life is removed. Anti-natural morality—that
> is, almost every morality which has so far been taught, revered, and preached—
> turns, conversely, against the instincts of life: it is condemnation of these
> instincts, now secret, now outspoken and impudent. When it says, "God looks
> at the heart," it says No to both the lowest and the highest desires of life, and
> posits God as the enemy of life. The saint in whom God delights is the ideal
> eunuch. Life has come to an end where the "kingdom of God" begins.[29]

Is Nietzsche right to reject all such moralities, and should feminists
join him in this rejection? If we agree that women are correctly identified
with nature, and we further agree that appeals to "reason" are simply veiled
attempts to reject the "female" in our natures, then we must agree with
Nietzsche.[30] I am not convinced, though, that women should rest content
with the identification with nature. Rather, I am in agreement with Harding
that the dichotomy needs to be rejected.

I now want to turn to the final critique, that moral philosophy assumes
an epistemology that pays no attention to how and whether beliefs are

grounded in social experience. This is largely true, though it is beginning to change. As I argued earlier, if the emphasis is on defending the one correct ethical theory, much energy is directed toward foundational epistemological issues. How do we know our theory is the correct one? How do we know which principles compose the theory? How should they be ordered? What is the principle of priority? Moral philosophers spend little time looking at common moral practice, and many would see such practices as irrelevant. I suspect they would say that common moral practice could be rehabilitated by studying their foundational debates. But the pressing epistemological issues that arise in everyday experience (What should I do *now*? *How* should I do it? How will it affect others? How can I tell?) are often ignored or handed off to others (social scientists, economists, novelists).

In the next chapter, I will deepen my critique of moral philosophy by looking at more foundational questions. Finally, I will sketch desiderata for an adequate (and feminist) ethic. In the rest of the book, I will discuss and defend my choice for such an ethic, an ethic of care.

NOTES

1. Alasdair MacIntyre, *After Virtue* (Notre Dame, Ind.: University of Notre Dame Press, 1981).

2. Ibid.

3. Steven Toulmin, in a paper given at the Conference on the Theory and Practice of Teaching Ethics, University of San Diego, February 1987.

4. Kai Nielsen, in a paper given at the Conference on the Theory and Practice of Teaching Ethics, University of San Diego, February 1987.

5. Bernard Williams, *Ethics and the Limits of Philosophy* (Cambridge, Mass.: Harvard University Press, 1985).

6. Carol Gilligan, *In a Different Voice* (Cambridge, Mass.: Harvard University Press, 1982).

7. Sandra Harding, *The Science Question in Feminism* (Ithaca, N.Y.: Cornell University Press, 1986).

8. Michael Sandel, *Liberalism and Its Critics* (New York: New York University Press, 1984), 6.

9. John Rawls, *A Theory of Justice* (Cambridge, Mass.: Harvard University Press, 1971), 27.

10. David M. Potter, "American Women and the American Character," *Steton University Bulletin*, LXII (January 1962): 1–22.

11. Sandel, *Liberalism and Its Critics*, 5–6.

12. Obviously, this is not the only model of moral reasoning. The Greeks, for example, were not terribly interested in distinct judgments but in larger questions about how to live one's life. Here the question of virtue becomes central. In an

ethic of care, no principles are appealed to, though the primary focus is on the immediate situation.

13. Gilligan, *In a Different Voice*, 25–28.

14. Nel Noddings, *Caring: A Feminine Approach to Ethics and Moral Education* (Berkeley: University of California Press, 1984).

15. Harding, *The Science Question in Feminism*.

16. For a detailed discussion of a feminist epistemology for moral philosophy, see Margaret Urban Walker, "Moral Understandings: Alternative 'Epistemology' for a Feminist Ethic," *Hypatia* 4 (Summer 1989): 15–28.

17. Harding, *The Science Question in Feminism*, 21.

18. Ibid.

19. Ibid., 22.

20. Ibid., 23.

21. Ibid., 24.

22. For examples of how a feminist understanding suggests new problematics in medical ethics, see the special issue of *Hypatia* devoted to medical ethics, Summer 1989.

23. Harding, *The Science Question in Feminism*, 23, 123–24.

24. For more detailed discussion of the relation between emotion and rationality in moral philosophy, see Lawrence Blum, *Friendship, Altruism and Morality* (London: Routledge and Kegan Paul, 1980); Lawrence Hinman, "Emotion, Morality, and Understanding," in Carol Gibb Harding, ed. *Moral Dilemmas* (Chicago: Precedent Publishing Co., 1985); and Meredith W. Michaels, "Morality Without Distinction," *The Philosophical Forum* 17 (Spring 1986): 175–87.

25. Harding, *The Science Question in Feminism*, 119.

26. Susan Griffin, *Women and Nature: The Roaring Inside Her* (New York: Harper and Row, 1979).

27. Harding, *The Science Question in Feminism*, chap. 5.

28. Nietzsche, "The Problem of Socrates,"*Twilight of the Idols*, 10, Walter Kaufmann, trans., *The Viking Portable Nietzsche* (New York: Viking Press, 1968).

29. Nietzsche, "Morality as Anti-Nature," *Twilight*, 4.

30. In citing Nietzsche, I do not mean to suggest that he identified women with nature, nor do I think he would approve of an ethic of care. On the contrary, I suspect that he would find it abhorrent. Still, I think he is right to reject a rigidly reason-based morality.

Chapter Two

Crumbling Foundations

There are two key issues that I will describe as foundational, for lack of a better term, that both motivated my search for a feminist ethic and convinced me that I was on the right track. In this chapter, I will discuss these foundational issues. The first is the anti-theory critique of ethical theory. The second is the nature of moral language and moral practice. Finally, I shall argue for a revised job description for moral philosophers in general, and feminist moral philosophers in particular.

I. THE THEORY/ANTI-THEORY DEBATE

At the outset, I should say that I am not convinced that a feminist cannot be an ethical theorist, though this might follow from what I have argued earlier. In this section, I will simply speak for myself.

There are different conceptions of ethical theory, from the deductive textbook model of moral reasoning to Aristotle's attempt to make our intuitions and current practices consistent and vaguely grounded. Anti-theory positions are developed in response to some particular conception of theory, so I will discuss anti-theory by focusing on the conceptions of moral theory that each position rejects. I will identify and discuss three conceptions of theory, all of which have been critiqued by anti-theorists, and will provide the corresponding anti-theory critiques. In much of what follows, I will be devising a schema to distinguish anti-theorists from theorists and other types of anti-theorists, as these distinctions are not clearly drawn in the literature.

The first conception is what I call the textbook model of moral reasoning. This model makes two assumptions: (1) that all moral "problems" have a definitive "solution" and (2) that solving these problems requires nothing more than the application of general principles which can themselves be justified and ordered.

The second conception, which I call the rules conception, is that we should appeal to rules when deliberating about what to do or when justifying moral decisions. This conception is typically neutral about the content of the rules.

The third conception, which I call the justification conception, is that moral action requires justification (as opposed to mere deliberation).

This tripartite distinction does not distinguish different ethical theories; it is possible to be a theorist of sorts while committed to any of these conceptions. For example, it is possible to be a Kantian of the first type. This Kantian would see the categorical imperative as licensing certain principles which would be universalizable and absolute. A Kantian of a looser stripe might embrace the third conception and see the categorical imperative as applying directly, allowing us to decide on a case-by-case basis what constitutes respect for persons. (I will not attempt to settle here the question of which is the best interpretation of Kant.)

A. Critique of the Textbook Conception

Each of these conceptions is susceptible to different critiques. I will begin with the first, which is the easiest to criticize. It seems to me that there are nine separate arguments that can be brought to bear against this first conception.

The first is offered by Martha Nussbaum.[1] She argues that a morally good person will not appeal to rules principally, but will use a rich moral imagination instead. She seems to allow for the use of something approximating rules, but her rules are merely rules of thumb, generalizations made on the basis of past experience. One still needs to know what is involved in using one's moral imagination. She describes this as analogous to the good novelist drawing upon a rich knowledge of human nature, an uncanny ability to understand how one's characters are feeling, and to imagine every possible scenario and its effects upon one's characters. The person with a rich moral imagination works very hard at developing such an imagination and never allows her rules to become inflexible. Instead, she is sensitive to the actual situation in which she finds herself.

I am sympathetic to this critique, though I think it is less effective against other conceptions of what an ethical theory is. I will return to a discussion of moral imagination in Chapter Four.

Annette Baier offers the second critique.[2] She argues that ethical theories are sought and embraced with the expectation that they will give us guidance in virtually every situation. Unhappily for the theorist, they fail because they lack the spiritual world view that is required for such guidance. To put the point another way, they assume a conception of the good life that cannot be defended within the theory. Again, I agree with Baier, but it is important to keep in mind that this criticism applies only to the textbook conception.

The third objection is also from Baier, and it is that teaching ethical theory creates moral skepticism.[3] Whether it does so or not is obviously an empirical question, though I share Baier's suspicion that teaching competing ethical theories while telling students that the textbook model is the right one is not the way to moral clarity.

The fourth is the Sartrean objection that the principles offered by competing ethical theories are too vague to yield decisions.[4] There are at least two ways in which the process can be vague, corresponding to the distinction between deontological and teleological ethical theories. Deontological principles, in virtue of their generality, are too vague to yield clear outcomes when applied to real cases. Teleological principles, while not necessarily suffering themselves from vagueness, result in vagueness when we try to measure whatever it is that we are supposed to create or maximize. This objection has real force against a conception of ethical theory that sees principles as tools in a calculus of moral decision making.

The next objection, also drawn from Sartre, is that appealing to principles blinds us to the fact that humans create moral values.[5] When we search for the kind of principles that could play a crucial role in a moral calculus, we often assume that the principles must have a necessary character. This is often seen as incompatible with our character as contingent and fallible beings. Again, I agree, though this criticism is much less compelling against a looser conception of ethical theory.

The sixth objection, argued for most eloquently by Alasdair MacIntyre in *After Virtue*[6] and Bernard Williams in *Ethics and the Limits of Philosophy*,[7] is that no ethical theory has yet won widespread acceptance. One wonders if this is due, in part, to the impossibly high standards for an ethical theory set by the textbook conception.

The seventh objection is from Cheryl Noble. She argues that there are no purely moral acts, just moral and immoral ways of doing everyday things; morality is not a "realm superimposed on other realms of life but a dimension or integral part of them."[8] The point here is that the textbook model, which assumes that appealing to moral principles is the only way to make moral decisions, must allow that there are other ways of making other decisions. Although I don't think that John Stuart Mill holds a text-book conception, he makes this explicit when he responds to the objection that being a utilitarian would be enormously difficult because it would require us to maximize utility in every situation by saying that few situations are distinctly moral, and that other decision-making procedures are perfectly appropriate in the other cases.[9] But, if we recognize that every situation is loaded with moral significance, then we will be required to apply the moral calculus continuously.

The other point Noble makes is that moral principles are not applied from some external realm, but arise from within institutions and practices. Hence, moral principles do not have a life of their own and cannot be justified independently of the institutions and practices in which they are embedded.

The next objection, offered by Steven Toulmin,[10] Baier, and Noble, is that focusing on ethical theory will inevitably lead us away from the study of concrete social institutions. Baier points out that moral philosophers seldom if ever feel the need or even the desire to "get out of their arm-chairs" and do or even look at any empirical research. This is an empirical point, not the theoretical one about the relationship between theory and praxis. Although it needs to be settled empirically, my hunch is that it might be even worse than Baier thought; not only might it lead us away from studying concrete social institutions, it might also lead us even farther away from concrete social action.

Finally, Cheryl Noble echoes Gilbert Harmon in pointing out that ethical theories are not theories in any sense recognized by science.[11] If someone who holds a textbook conception must be able to show that his/her theory is true, and truth can only be a property of a theory that is a theory in the same sense as a scientific theory, then this is a telling objection.

B. Critique of the Rules Conception

The second conception holds that an ethical theory is a set of rules to be appealed to when deliberating about what to do or when justifying one's moral decisions. This conception does not explicitly make the two assumptions made by the first conception, so one might accept this conception even while rejecting the first. Critics of this conception reject any appeal to moral rules, so the anti-theory position that is staked out by appeal to a rejection of this conception is more radical than the anti-theory position that merely rejects the textbook model.

The first criticism is that the moral reasoning involved in this conception must be one of two types: either legalistic (mechanical and foundational) or vague. In the first case, we are back with our textbook model and its attendant problems. In the second case, the reasoning will be too vague to be very useful. It is not clear which rule applies, which are the right rules or what the facts are.

I am not persuaded by the vagueness objection, in large part because I am not persuaded that vagueness in this case is a bad thing. Any moral conception that made moral life simple would be deeply suspect as far as I am concerned. I would be inclined to say that as long as our rules give us some guidance, they are a help and not a hindrance. However, if we are accepting such vagueness, why characterize our position as an ethical theory? It is not clear exactly where to draw the line, but I would be inclined to draw it this way: If the rules are mere rules of thumb, mere generalizations based upon our past experience, then describing them as making up an ethical theory seems a bit too grand. On the other hand, if the rules have a special force, perhaps because they are absolute or grounded in some unshakable fact, then this conception can legitimately be called an ethical theory. This is admittedly an arbitrary line, and I don't think it really matters how the line gets drawn. What does matter is that we understand each other when we refer to someone as a theorist or an anti-theorist.

The second objection is that persons who see morality as requiring rule following are deficient in some way. One diagnosis is that they are alienated from self or others. The second is that they are willing to put rules above friendship. I take it that this is the force of Bernard Williams's example about the moral agent who hesitated before rescuing his drowning wife rather than the stranger who was drowning with her.[12] The third objection, which runs throughout Nietzsche's moral writings, is that rule followers think that humans need rules to repress "bad" impulses. This assumes a picture of humans as basically bad, and natural impulses as selfish.[13]

These objections depend upon blurring distinctions between different kinds of rule following. At one extreme we have the rule fetishist, who cares for nothing but the rules, while at the other we have the person who cares for the rules out of a profound love for humanity and a belief that the rules reflect humankind's best understanding about how to express such a love. I agree that the rule fetishist is deficient in human kindness and related virtues, but I am not persuaded that the second rule follower is. At best, I would be inclined to describe the second rule follower as overly optimistic about the benefits of following rules.

The third objection is that rules must be applied impartially, but impartiality assumes that we need to repress our natural motives and requires that we ignore merit, loyalty, and affection. This is the point that Williams makes when he says that impartiality requires that we "treat friends as strangers."[14] At this point, we need to get clear about whether rules must be impartial and applied impartially.

Impartiality is a concept that is often invoked but seldom analyzed. An account of impartiality must refer to procedures for applying rules. An impartial judge does not let personal bias or preference interfere with the application of the rules. Rather, the impartial judge will always apply the same rule in the same way, regardless of who is before the bench, so to speak, and will act on the judgment in the same way. An impartial rule is one that is sufficiently general so as to apply to anyone. Laws on sleeping on public benches, for example, are insufficiently general because they apply differently to those who have no other place to lay their heads. But a merely formal characterization of impartiality is not enough. Rawls cautions us not to confuse impartiality with impersonality and goes on to define impartiality in terms of the original position. "An impartial judgment, we can say, is one rendered in accordance with the principles which would be chosen in the original position. An impartial person is one whose situation and character enable him to judge in accordance with these principles without bias or prejudice."[15]

I think he is right to distinguish impartiality from impersonality; it would be odd to describe someone who applied cruel principles to all without hint of bias or personal preference as impartial. This person would be better described as impersonal, unconcerned about anyone's welfare. So an analysis of impartiality must include reference to some standards for judging whether the rules to be applied are themselves appropriate.

But even on the best account of impartiality, we still have the result that Williams bemoans—that we ask one question too many. One can imagine the reaction of the drowning wife who, upon being rescued by her husband, asks, "What took you so long?" If he tells her, "I was trying to see if I could justify rescuing you rather than the stranger drowning with you. When I realized that I could apply an impartial rule impartially and still save you, I immediately proceeded to do so."

Finally, a virtue theorist might object that the virtuous person does not and should not appeal to rules, but should simply act from a settled disposition. This does not mean that a virtuous person can never reflect upon his/her actions, but that he/she fails to be virtuous unless action springs from character rather than deliberation.

C. Critique of the Justification Conception

The last conception is concerned with any practice of moral justification. This is by far the broadest conception, describing just about any ethical theory, and hence an anti-theory position that rejected this would be more radical than any anti-theory position we have yet discussed. I take it that Nietzsche is an anti-theorist of this type. He rejects any attempt at moral justification, first, because it assumes that our nature is evil and hence our actions need justifying, and second because this adds nothing to the decision. MacIntyre makes a similar point when he says, "behind the masks of morality [lie] what are in fact preferences of arbitrary will."[16] The third reason for rejecting this conception is that justification is usually self-serving, and the final reason is that we ought to live in such a way that it is unnecessary. This is the force of the myth of eternal recurrence.[17] Rather than look for justifications after the fact, we should ask ourselves how we would decide if we were condemned to relive this moment an infinite number of times.

We need to distinguish two theses here. The first is that we should reject moral justification after the fact, though not moral deliberation. The second is that we should reject both practices. If Nietzsche is saying the first, then I am in some sympathy with him. If he is committed to the second, then I am less sympathetic. Though I agree with his attempt to rehabilitate our conception of human nature, I am not convinced that my first impulse is always the right one. In any case, even if we are persuaded to give up both moral justification and moral deliberation, we will still have moral reflection. Presumably Nietzsche does not reject this practice, since he spends so much of his time engaging in it. As long as we are justified (morally?) in reflecting about morality, we will have gone a long way toward deliberating. One might argue that Nietzsche simply wants to get rid of normative ethics. His style of moral reflection is primarily focused on metaethics and moral psychology. If this is right, then I part company with him. I simply do not want to give up moral reflection rich enough to give me real insights about how to live.

D. Summary of Theory/Anti-Theory Debate

We can now summarize the objections to the project of developing ethical theories that compete for the title of "one right theory" and profess to end all our moral confusion. I shall divide the objections into the metaphysical, pragmatic, and political.

The metaphysical objections are that there are no ultimate foundations. Each depends upon a conception of the good life that is, in the final analysis, arbitrary.

The second set of concerns I describe as pragmatic. The conception of ethical theory as the search for the right theory assumes that good moral reasoning involves searching for and then applying the right theory, but this is not what people actually do when they reason, nor, in my view, is it what they ought to do. Hume was right to point out the importance of sentiment, while Aristotle correctly identified the role that settled dispositions played.

Next, I want to address the political issues. *If* there were a correct ethical theory and we could discover what it was and *if* we could persuade other people that it was the correct one and *if* it unambiguously endorsed a practice we wanted to encourage or condemned a practice we wanted to discourage, then it would be reasonable to search for this theory. But there are so many assumptions here. If our commitment to the search for the one correct ethical theory is motivated by our desire to effect social change, then we must ask ourselves if we are having any success. I am not at all persuaded that there is one correct ethical theory or that we can persuade anyone who holds a competing theory. I am not even sanguine about the possibility of convincing someone who holds the same theory but who interprets it differently on an issue to change his/her view.

And finally, my position on all of this is that the rejection of the textbook model is certainly justified. I agree that rule fetishism is not a good thing, though I think we can benefit from rules of thumb derived from both our own experience and the collective experience of our various communities. Finally, I am in considerable sympathy with Nietzsche's desire to rehabilitate our conception of human nature, though I certainly do not want to give up all moral reflection.

II. MORAL LANGUAGE

I am in substantial agreement with Gilbert Harmon that moral language most often functions as an appeal to shared moral conceptions.[18] This is not to say that it cannot function in any other way. For example, I might make a moral claim on someone who does not share my moral conception. I understand this claim as representing a conception that I want to share with this person, but if this person does not share my moral conception to some degree, my appeal will be unsuccessful. Worse, if our conceptions are sufficiently different, it will be gibberish. In situations like this, moral language must give way to more overt action. Typically, moral language functions as part of a moral practice (which includes critiquing, persuading, comforting, making explicit, and consciousness-raising) that involves an appeal to a shared moral conception. A moral conception is not a mere feeling, but includes beliefs about human nature, metaphysics, and the good life, in addition to feelings, values, virtues, and attitudes.

The strongest objection to this view is that there are no grounds, save another moral conception, to criticize actions and practices that strike us as morally repellent. I quite agree, but the proviso "save another moral conception" does not exactly leave us speechless. What I want to insist on here is that moral conversation across wildly disparate moral paradigms is pointless and does not succeed in being conversation at all. If we are truly repelled, we must express it some other way.

The underlying worry here is that we will lose something valuable when we give up on the idea that in addition to holding a moral conception we might be holding the correct one. But what follows from holding the correct one? I suppose we would take great comfort from knowing that our judgments, actions, practices, and attitudes were correctly grounded, but I am skeptical that holding the correct conception will make us winners when moral controversy erupts. Why isn't it sufficient to say, "This is the moral conception that I am passionately committed to, want others to accept, and will fight to defend if it comes to that."

It doesn't follow that the moral reformer is wrong. The moral reformer might well be appealing to a widely shared moral conception that is violated in practice. I take it that this was precisely what Martin Luther King Jr. was doing. On the other hand, a moral reformer might be trying to advance a radically new moral conception. In this case, it will be very difficult, if not impossible, to be heard. Moral conversation between the reformer and the unconvinced will not be possible except by appeal to some shared conceptions. In this case, the reformer must look to other strategies. Again, the worry here is that we won't be able to "tell" whether our moral reformer is a true reformer. How do we distinguish between Malcolm X and the former(?) Ku Klux Klan leader and Nazi David Duke? Unfortunately, my critics won't be satisfied by my answer that we appeal to a moral conception and that this conception must be defended by defending its components. The empirical components will be defended by one strategy, the metaphysical by another. The values and feelings can only be asserted. Ultimately, our moral conceptions will rest on value commitments that cannot be defended. In this sense, they are arbitrary. But they are not arbitrary in the sense that they do not matter to us, that they are interchangeable with other values. In this respect (and in this respect only) they are absolute.

The upshot of all this is that if we want to engage in moral conversation, we must do so by appeal to a shared moral conception. In most cases, we will share parts of a moral conception, and thus we may appeal to the shared components. If we do not share a moral conception and we want to change a practice or action, we must look beyond moral conversation to some other practice. I suspect, however, that negotiation across widely disparate moral conceptions happens very seldom, since negotiation rarely takes place where we share no common experience.

III. DESIDERATA FOR AN ADEQUATE ETHIC

Listed below are seven desiderata that correspond to the eight critiques outlined in this chapter and in Chapter One. I describe these as desiderata for an adequate ethic, but I want to make clear that I think an adequate ethic ought to be a feminist ethic. By this I do not mean an ethic that ought to be accepted by women only, or by feminists only, but an ethic that is the most adequate overall because it does not pose obstacles to the liberation of women and does not ignore the moral experience of women. I think an adequate and thus a feminist ethic should offer

1. a picture of the self that grants the connected nature of humans,
2. a model of reasoning that is contextual, with rules of thumb grounded in experience,
3. no sharp division between theory and practice,
4. an understanding of beliefs grounded in experience, and guidance about practical life,
5. no dichotomies between reason and emotion, mind/body, culture/ nature,
6. a concern with problematics from the private as well as public sphere,
7. an explicit discussion of the moral conceptions expressed by the ethic.

The first desiderata follows from my critique of the unencumbered self in Chapter One. A feminist ethic should not take competent, independent, adult humans as its paradigm, nor should it presuppose that humans are abstract individuals.[19] It must recognize that humans are connected by social relationships, that their self-identities are colored by these relation- ships, and that their welfare requires that at least some of these relation- ships be intimate and sustaining.

The second desiderata follows from my discussion of the theory–anti- theory debate in this chapter and my discussion of the textbook model of moral reasoning in Chapter One. A feminist ethic, as I conceive it, must adopt a model of moral reasoning that allows us to focus on the particu- larity of each situation. Rules that condition expectations, reflect past experience and the collective wisdom of our societies shall function as rules of thumb.

The third desiderata follows from my discussion of the applied-theo- retical moral philosophy distinction in Chapter One. A primary task will be to offer moral guidance, so no ethic that relies on a rigid split between application and theory will be satisfactory. The "theory" must be tested by experience and not by abstract theorizing alone.

The next three desiderata follow from my extrapolation to moral philosophy of Harding's critique of science. The ethic must be aware of moral psychology, and moral education must be sensitive to actual moral practice and diverse moral conceptions. This is not to suggest that it be mere moral anthropology, but that ignorance of these issues will make it hard, if not impossible, for it to offer moral guidance.

A concern with the issues that arise in private as well as public life must infuse this ethic. Accordingly, it will have something useful to say about caring for children as well as creating just states.

The last desiderata follows from my discussion of moral language; it will be concerned with making a moral conception explicit insofar that it can be made so. This involves spelling out its assumptions and offering some discussion of its organizing principles. This discussion must be grounded in a discussion of concrete moral experience. The ethic will, in this sense, take our moral intuitions seriously.

IV. THE TASK OF THE MORAL PHILOSOPHER

The task of the moral philosopher is spelled out to a large extent by the desiderata outlined above. Making moral conceptions explicit is the central task. Developing organizing principles is a secondary task. It is possible to take this too far and end up with a deductivist textbook model, but I think that we can go a long way before we slip into this error.

Philosophers have given over the task of sketching utopias to novelists, but I want to return to it. We can and should offer alternative moral visions. Perhaps fiction is the best way to motivate the acceptance of such visions, but philosophers can do much to fill in the details.

The task of the philosopher depends crucially on the audience. In what follows, I will focus on three audiences: the converted, the neutral, and the opposed. Even when we share a moral conception to a large extent, we often want to get clear about exactly what it entails and what it assumes. Next, we want to extend this conception and apply it to new territory. Finally, we need aid and comfort. These are the things that we can do with and for the converted.

When talking with students who are neutral or, more typically, confused about their moral commitments, I am inclined to want to persuade them. As a philosopher I understand the obligation to offer competing conceptions, but the desire to proselytize is very strong. When I write philosophy or talk with my peers, I freely give in to this desire. I think that consciousness-raising is the first step when dealing with a truly neutral party, because they must first come to understand what their moral conceptions are. Next on the agenda is sorting out the confusion, the inconsistency, and the bad faith. Finally, the neutral will either join the converted or the opposed.

In conversations with those who disagree with us, we can and should critique their conceptions. Next, we can and ought to make our conceptions explicit. We spend a great deal of time trying to persuade our worst critics, often at the expense of the converted and the neutral, and some of this effort is clearly wasted. If we want to influence social policy, for example, we, as academics, as philosophers, are quick to pick up the pen. I suspect that there is the hope here that matters can be settled rationally, and I think much of this work is useful and persuasive. Still, we should not let this work substitute for action.

Finally, our work in moral philosophy should be grounded in our moral experience and moral commitment. As Daniel Callahan puts it:

> For one reason or another—the desire to ape the sciences, peer pressure, a failure in self-examination, excessive specialization, shelter from the hurly-burly of the actual world in which we live—ethical theory has too often become the private language of a private world. Within that world, the prizes go to those who can speak most tellingly to those in that world; and that means by following the given rules of technical proficiency. But the point of ethical theory, or so I have long taken it, is to find a way to think through the living of a moral life, the devising of moral societies, and the making of moral judgments that can be grounded in some adequate theory. I fail to see how that kind of grounding can be sufficient, or ultimately satisfactory, if it does not spring from a private moral life that is itself rich and struggling, and if it cannot make sense in the actual world of human affairs, where it is most needed, and will have its only real meaning.[20]

To make my moral conception explicit, the following chapters draw heavily on my experiences and intuitions as well as on the very good work in feminist philosophy and moral psychology. Since I think that an ethic must be grounded in experience, I will also give a lot of attention to concrete moral cases; in other words, I will tell stories.

NOTES

1. Martha Nussbaum, "Finely Aware and Richly Responsible: Literature and the Moral Imagination," *The Journal of Philosophy* 82 (1985): 516–29.

2. Annette Baier, "Doing Without Moral Theory?" in Stanley Clarke and Evan Simpson, eds., *Anti-Theory in Ethics and Moral Conservatism* (Albany: State University of New York Press, 1989).

3. Baier, "Doing Without Moral Theory?"

4. Jean-Paul Sartre, "Existentialism is a Humanism," in Robert Solomon, ed., *Existentialism* (New York: The Modern Library, 1974).

5. Sartre, "Existentialism is a Humanism."

6. Alasdair MacIntyre, *After Virtue* (Notre Dame, Ind.: University of Notre Dame Press, 1981).

7. Bernard Williams, *Ethics and the Limits of Philosophy* (Cambridge, Mass.: Harvard University Press, 1985).

8. Cheryl Noble, "Normative Ethical Theories," in Clarke and Simpson, *Anti-Theory in Ethics and Moral Conservatism.*

9. John Stuart Mill, *Utilitarianism* (Indianapolis: Bobbs Merrill, 1977), 25.

10. Steven Toulmin, "How Medicine Saved the Life of Ethics," in Joseph DeMarco and Richard M. Fox, eds., *New Directions in Ethics: The Challenge of Applied Ethics* (New York: Routledge, Chapman and Hall, 1986).

11. Gilbert Harmon, "Ethics and Observation," in *The Nature of Morality: An Introduction to Ethics* (Oxford: Oxford University Press, 1977); and "Is There a Single True Morality?" in David Copp and David Zimmerman, eds., *Morality, Reason and Truth* (Totowa N.J.: Rowman and Allanheld, 1984), 27–48. Not everyone agrees with Harmon about this. See, for example, David O. Brink, *Moral Realism and the Foundations of Ethics* (Cambridge: Cambridge University Press, 1989); Sabina Lovibund, *Realism and Imagination in Ethics* (Minneapolis: University of Minnesota Press, 1983).

12. Bernard Williams, "Persons, Character and Morality," *Moral Luck* (Cambridge: Cambridge University Press, 1981).

13. Nietzsche's moral writings run throughout his work, but see especially *The Birth of Tragedy, Beyond Good and Evil*, and *Thus Spake Zarathustra*.

14. Williams, "Persons, Character and Morality."

15. John Rawls, *A Theory of Justice* (Cambridge, Mass.: Harvard University Press, 1971), 190.

16. MacIntyre, *After Virtue*, 69.

17. Though I am persuaded by the normative interpretation of the myth of eternal recurrence, there are other interpretations. Bernd Magnus, for example, sees it as descriptive of the attitude toward life taken by an Ubermensch. See *Nietzsche's Existentialist Imperative* (Indianapolis: Indiana University Press, 1978).

18. Harmon, "Ethics and Observation," and "Is There a Single True Morality?"

19. Alison Jaggar offers a compelling description and critique of abstract individualism in *Feminist Politics and Human Nature* (Totowa, N.J.: Rowman and Allanheld, 1983).

20. Daniel Callahan, "Moral Theory: Thinking, Doing, and Living," *Journal of Social Philosophy* 20 (1989): 18–24.

Chapter Three

A Moral Philosopher Leaps
from Her Armchair

Lawrence Kohlberg's early research on moral development suggested that women were deficient in moral reasoning.[1] This came as no surprise to many, since this conclusion already had a certain currency in the West. Arthur Schopenhauer, in commenting on the differences between the moral perspectives of men and women, wrote: "The weakness of their reasoning function also explains why women show more sympathy for the unfortunate than men."[2] Freud shared this part of Schopenhauer's views and offered an explanation in terms of women's weak superegos:

> I cannot evade the notion (though I hesitate to give it expression) that for women the level of what is ethically normal is different from what it is in men. Their superego is never so inexorable, so impersonal, so independent of its emotional origins as we require it to be in men. Character-traits which critics of every epoch have brought up against women—that they show less sense of justice than men, that they are less ready to submit it to the great exigencies of life, that they are more often influenced in their judgment by feelings of affection or hostility—all these would be amply accounted for by the modification in the formation of their superego which we have inferred.[3]

Carol Gilligan rightly complains about this view of women's moral reasoning: "herein lies a paradox, for the very traits that traditionally have defined the 'goodness' of women, their care for and sensitivity to the needs of others, are those that mark them as deficient in moral development."[4]

A feminist response here might be to insist that women are just as capable of modifying their behavior by appeal to a sense of justice as men are, that they are perfectly capable of ignoring feelings of affection and hostility

33

and ready and willing to do so. Indeed, much recent research on sex-related differences in moral reasoning seems to support this response.[5]

Other research has suggested that there is a gender-related difference.[6] But we needn't accept Kohlberg's conclusion that feminine reasoning is defective. Another option might be to agree that women and men have different moral perspectives but that the perspective of women is superior.[7] Finally, one might argue, as Gilligan does, that male and female reasoning is complementary. In this respect she echoes Kant, who argues in *Observations on the Feeling of the Beautiful and the Sublime* that the ideal moral agent is the married couple, with the husband contributing abstract principles and the wife sentiment.[8]

Some have pointed out that it is not surprising that males and females adopt a different moral perspective since the feminine gender role differs so markedly from the masculine gender role.[9] Those who adopt a feminine orientation see themselves as caring, understanding, and intimately connected to others. They feel most threatened by separation and abandonment.[10] They tend to see moral issues as concerned with connection and intimacy and requiring a response of understanding and care in order to preserve intimacy and connection. Those who adopt a masculine orientation see themselves as independent and forceful. Their greatest fear is of intimacy. Hence, they see moral issues as conflicts between separate individuals who wish to remain autonomous.

I find Carol Gilligan's *In a Different Voice*[11] frustrating because the data are not there. I am persuaded she is right that gender affects moral reasoning, but the evidence in the book is primarily anecdotal and impressionistic. I am also puzzled by Gilligan's care and responsibility model of moral reasoning. What precisely did the respondents say that justified this label? Is the characterization accurate? In general, I find some areas of social science frustrating for the same reasons; I long to have the raw data (what is actually observed—not mere statistical analysis) in my hands to answer the questions that arise as I read published studies. This is certainly not meant as a criticism of social science, but as a confession of my desire to take part in it. I have been greatly stirred by the postmodernist call for blurring disciplinary boundaries and by Annette Baier's cry for moral philosophers to get out of their armchairs.[12] In that spirit, I took the leap and designed a survey to gauge the influence of gender, class, age, and race on moral reasoning, and administered the survey to a large undergraduate class. In what follows, I will describe the survey and provide some of my results.[13]

I had many vague and other not so vague ideas about moral reasoning that I wanted to test. Rather than test each of them systematically, I designed a survey that would give me some general information about them all. In doing so, I designed a study that was testing for too many variables to test for any one of them reliably. But it was not my intention to settle these issues; very good social scientists are at work on the question of moral development. I see my project, as I see much of philosophy, as the vague stage of scientific discourse. If my study suggests guidelines for future research, I would be more than satisfied.

For the survey, I adapted one of Aesop's classic fables. Some have argued that the choice of dilemma affects the choice of moral voice. I chose a dilemma that I think is open to either moral voice.[14] I administered this survey in an undergraduate class, Professional and Business Ethics, on the first day of instruction. I described the survey as part of my research and something that was optional for them. I received 118 complete responses out of approximately 160 students. The class was ethnically mixed, and approximately half were men. I read the fable so that I did not slip anything in that would change the students' responses. Here is the fable as I read it:

> A group of moles spent the summer digging out a comfortable burrow for the winter. When winter came, a lazy porcupine who hadn't bothered to dig its own burrow begged the moles to be let into the moles' burrow. The moles let the porcupine in, but it soon became apparent that things weren't as comfortable as they had once been. The porcupine's sharp quills were jabbing the moles.

I then asked a series of questions and gave the students five minutes to reply to each question. The questions were:

1. What should the moles do and why?
2. Now, give an answer to this question from a different perspective.
3. Which answer do you like better?
4. Suppose that the porcupine had built a burrow but that it had been destroyed in a flood. What should the moles do and why?
5. Suppose that we add that the porcupine would die if forced outside the burrow. What should the moles do then and why?
6. Suppose that the moles were being seriously injured by the porcupine's quills. What should the moles do then and why?

I asked question one to elicit their initial, prereflective response to the fable. Question two is designed to give them another chance to think about the fable. I included question three to test the claim that people generally favor a "caring" response even if it is not their initial response. Question four allows me to see if the initial response is sensitive to moral fault on the porcupine's part. I included it to see if the gender differences in response might be explained by different background assumptions about circumstances unstated in the fable. For example, women might be more generous than men in their background assumptions about blame. This would provide an explanation of gender differences which would not require hypothesizing differences in moral reasoning. Question five allows me to see if gender differences might be based upon different assessments of outcomes of action. One explanation of gender differences might be that women have more faith in compromise than men, while men might be more willing to assume that the porcupine can make it on its own.[15] By phrasing the question this way, I hoped to screen out such differences. I was also interested to see if the seriousness of the threatened harm would cause anyone to choose a different outcome or change his/her justificatory strategy. I included question six for much the same reason. In addition, I was interested in seeing if the impossibility of compromise would occasion a change in choice of outcome or justification.

I distinguished between the two parts of question one. First, I asked for a decision. I call this an outcome (O). Second, I asked for a reason. I call this a justification (J). The answers to the call for outcomes fell into two categories: throw the porcupine out (O1) and accommodate the porcupine (O2). In the first section of what follows, I will discuss differences in outcome. The answers to the call for justification were more complicated, and I will discuss them in section II.

I. OUTCOMES

A. Gender Differences

There were fifty-six men and sixty-two women in my sample. Fifty-seven percent of the men gave O1 as their answer to question one, while forty-three percent gave O2. Forty-two percent of the women gave O1, while fifty-eight percent gave O2. (Percentages will not always equal 100 due to rounding.) (See Table 3-1.) This fits in with Gilligan's claims that men focus on locating the party with the right, while women strive for compromise for the sake of maintaining relationships. The investigation is not complete until we look at the justifications given by men and women, since it is not impossible that one could choose O1 out of concern for maintaining mole-to-mole relationships. I will return to this point in section II.

Another possible explanation is that men and women reason in roughly the same way but depend upon different background assumptions. Perhaps, for example, men are more willing in general than women to assume

Table 3-1.

Outcomes

O1 = Throw the porcupine out.
O2 = Accommodate the porcupine.
Percentage of respondents choosing O1 or O2

	Overall	
	O1	O2
	50	50
	Gender	
	O1	O2
Men	57	43
Women	42	58

---

that creatures are to blame for their own situation. Question four asks the respondent to assume that the porcupine is not at fault. When this assumption is made, eighty-nine percent of the men and ninety-two percent of the women chose O2.

Another explanation would be that men are more optimistic in general than women about the ability of others to survive without help. Question five asks the respondent to suppose that the porcupine would die if forced into the cold. When this assumption is made, the response of men and women is virtually identical. One man and one woman gave O1 as a response to this question; everyone else gave O2 as a response.

Another plausible explanation would be that women are more optimistic in general than men about the outcome of attempts to compromise. Question six was designed to test this explanation. Here, I am asking the respondent to assume that compromise is not possible. Still, there was a slight difference between male and female responses. Sixty-three percent of the men and fifty-eight percent of the women gave O1 as their answer to question six. I don't think this settles the issue since the gap between men and women on question six is much smaller than the gap in question one. The closing of the gap might be due to the new element introduced in question six—the concern about grievous bodily harm to the moles. Another question that rules out compromise without introducing new elements would better help us to assess the impact of different beliefs about the success of attempts at compromise.

All of this provides a real challenge to Gilligan's claim that women reason in a radically different way than men. The answers to questions four, five, and six suggest that the difference might simply be in background assumptions. It is entirely possible that the men and women were all appealing to similar general moral principles. The difference in background assumptions can be explained by the different experiences of men and women, boys and girls. Here, we need to look at the justifications offered by men and women. This is difficult to do with this survey as the only tool, since the respondents were not very articulate about their justifications. I will return to this in section II.

At this point, I don't think we can discard the hypothesis that the differences are primarily differences in background assumptions. Still, even if this were the only difference, it might have a profound effect on outcome. Of course, it would be far more interesting from the point of view of moral philosophy if we uncovered more profound differences. I am not convinced that there isn't a more profound difference, and the work in feminist moral philosophy has given us a fuller sense of what care and responsibility reasoning would look like. If all else fails, moral philosophers can still retreat to their jobs as gadflies and argue for the adoption of such a model.

B. Class Differences

On the back of my survey form I included a set of questions that I asked each respondent to answer. While there have been many studies investigating the role of gender, age, and culture, no one has, to my knowledge, investigated the effect of parenting or economic class. I wanted to see if class, age, ethnicity, and experience as a parent would be predictors. My initial supposition was that these might make a difference. The results were striking. I used four categories for economic class: (a) blue collar, (b) service, (c) professional, and (d) often unemployed or underemployed. I chose these categories because I was asking the respondents to identify themselves and I thought that these categories would be more descriptive and less loaded than other possible categories. I interpreted blue collar/clerical as roughly equivalent to working class. I left service as a separate category since there are many working-class jobs that are not blue collar or clerical. I identified respondents by economic class by using their answers about their jobs and the jobs of their families. Thirty-seven students were described as blue collar. Of these, forty-six percent gave O1 as the answer to question one, while fifty-four percent gave O2. Only twenty-four students described their parents as having service jobs. Of this group, twenty-nine percent gave O1, and seventy-one percent gave O2. Of the fifty-seven students who described themselves as professional class, sixty percent chose O1, while forty percent chose O2. (See Table 3-2.)

Table 3-2.

Percentage of respondents choosing O1 or O2

	Class	
	O1	O2
Blue collar	46	54
Service	29	71
Professional	60	40

Nel Noddings argues that enrichment of the capacity to care requires practice in caring.[16] This suggests one explanation for the differences here. Service workers must learn to care for others and continually practice this art. As they do so, they become more likely to transmit this caring orientation to their children. Blue-collar workers live in economically unsettled circumstances and must learn to care for others in order to have a network of care to depend on when they need it. On this explanation, members of professional classes (or the upper middle class) do not see the same need for developing their caring capacities and hence don't spend the same amount of time in caring activity. One might respond that mothers in these classes do engage in caring activity and transmit such skills and dedication to their daughters, hence we should see differences between men and women in this class. Indeed, we do see such differences. Professional men chose O1 over O2 by seventy-one percent to twenty-nine percent, while professional women chose O2 over O1 by fifty-two percent to forty-eight percent. In sharp contrast, blue-collar men chose O2 over O1 by fifty-eight perecnt to forty-two percent, while blue-collar women split fifty fifty. Service class men chose O2 over O1 by fifty-five percent to forty-five percent, while the women chose O2 over O1 by a lopsided eighty percent to twenty percent. (See Table 3-3.)

A related explanation might be that members of the professional classes are overly optimistic about the ability of creatures to survive without help. I designed question five to screen out such optimism. Unfortunately, I think I painted too stark a picture. Interestingly though, the only two people to pick O1 for question five were members of this class.

A crude way to sum up both these explanations is to describe members of the professional class as more selfish than members of the other classes. While I think this is a correct description, it does not explain anything,

Table 3-3.

Percentage of respondents choosing O1 or O2

	Class and Gender	
	Blue Collar	
	O1	O2
Men	42	58
Women	50	50
	Service	
Men	45	55
Women	20	80
	Professional	
Men	71	29
Women	48	52

it merely restates the data. In answer to question six, which invites the respondent to assume that the moles are being seriously injured by the porcupine's quills, fifty-seven percent of the blue-collar class, fifty percent of the service class, and sixty-seven percent of the professional class chose O1. The differences are especially interesting when we look at the responses of professional-class women: fifty percent of blue-collar class women, forty-seven percent of service-class women, and seventy-one percent of professional-class women chose O1 in answer to question six.

C. Age Differences

While there has been a great deal of research on child moral develop-ment, not much has been published on adult moral reasoning. If there are differences in adult responses that correspond to age, one must ask whether experience, rather than cognitive development, explains the variation. The only variable that has emerged as an explanation of adult moral development is education.[17] But this doesn't tell us what it is about education that influences moral development.[18] I looked at parenting as another possible variable. Those results will be discussed later in this chapter.

I divided my responses into three age groups: 18–22, 23–27, and over 27. I did not have any presuppositions about similarities within each category, but simply tried to break them into three roughly equal spans. Again, the differences were striking. In the 18–22 group, forty-eight percent chose O1 and fifty-two percent chose O2 as an answer to question one. Men in this age group split fifty/fifty, while women chose O2 over O1 by fifty-two percent to forty-eight percent. In the 23–27 group, fifty-four percent chose O1 while forty-six percent chose O2. Men chose O1 over O2 by fifty-nine percent to forty-one percent. Women chose O2 over O1 by fifty-three percent to forty-seven percent. In the over 27 group, thirty-three percent chose O1 while sixty-seven percent chose O2. Men chose O1 over O2 by sixty percent to forty percent. Fully 100 percent of the women chose O2. I think we can see the results of culture here. There are clearer differences in the responses of the men and women over 27. This might be seen as evidence of the stricter gender roles that prevailed when they were growing up. By the time we get to the 18–22 group, the differences between the men and women are very slight. Unfortunately, this happens at the expense of O2 responses. This suggests that while men and women are beginning to reason in a more similar fashion, the overall social commitment to compromise and accommodation has lessened (see Table 3–4).

Table 3-4.

Percentage of respondents choosing O1 or O2

	Age	
	O1	O2
18–22	48	52
23–27	54	46
Over 27	33	67

My results here might be read as undermining Kohlberg's claim that, all things being equal, as we get older we become more morally developed. Perhaps if we accepted Kohlberg's claim that moral development consisted in appealing more and more to general principles, we could interpret the results here as moral progress. I would rather see the willingness to take the porcupine in as evidence of moral development. Here, we see that the 18–22 group is more willing to make room for the porcupine than the 23–27 group. The over 27 group is the group most willing to take the porcupine in. This suggests that if moral progress is measured in terms of willingness to take in the porcupine, this progress is not linear.

D. Racial Differences

Although there are some studies on cross-cultural differences in moral development, this is an area that needs more work.[19] My sample was far from ideal since it did not distinguish between first-, second-, and perhaps third-or-more generation Americans, and it grouped together ethnic groups with different cultures. Still, I thought it would be interesting to see if there were some differences between racial groups of students in the United States. I should say at the outset that I understand racial classifications as primarily social constructs, but since these constructs do make a great deal of difference in one's life in a racist society, I appealed to standard racial divisions in this study. I discovered that some patterns did emerge. I asked the respondents to list their national origin and first language. Based upon this information and appealing to existing social constructions of race and ethnicity, I categorized them as either Anglo, Latino, African-American, Asian, or Other. I included all native English speakers with European origins as Anglos. I categorized all respondents with Latin American national origins as Latino whether or not they spoke Spanish as a first language. I included Pacific Islanders as Asians. Unfortunately, I had only two African-American students who returned the survey. Though I did not draw any inferences on the basis of this small sample, there are other surveys of African-American moral reasoning and discussions of world views which suggest that this group would be more likely to give O2 responses and justifications in terms of care.[20]

Here again, we find interesting differences. Anglos favor O2 over O1 by fifty-seven percent to forty-three percent. Anglo men favor O1 over O2 by fifty-one percent to forty-nine percent. Anglo women chose O2 over O1 by a striking margin: sixty-five percent to thirty-five percent. Latinos split fifty/fifty, and the responses of the men and women were identical. Asians chose O1 over O2 by sixty-three to thirty-seven percent. The differences between Asian men and women and men and women of the other ethnic groups I looked at were striking: fifty-four percent of Asian men chose O1 over O2, while seventy-three percent of Asian women chose O1 over O2. I don't have any specific explanations for the ethnic differences, but I think that it's reasonable to suppose that culture plays a role here as well. (See Tables 3-5 and 3-6.)

Table 3-5.

Percentage of respondents choosing O1 or O2

	Race	
	O1	O2
Anglo	43	57
Asian	63	37
Latino	50	50

Table 3-6.

Percentage of respondents choosing O1 or O2

	Race and Gender	
	Anglo	
	O1	O2
Men	51	49
Women	35	65
	Asian	
	O1	O2
Men	54	46
Women	73	27
	Latino	
	O1	O2
Men	50	50
Women	50	50

E. Parenting

The number of parents in the sample was too small (twenty) to make any reliable inferences, but I shall include them in the interest of completeness and as data for speculation. Nine parents chose O1 while eleven chose O2. This indicated a slight preference for O2. By comparison, the non-parents split approximately fifty/fifty.

II. JUSTIFICATIONS

Rather than come up with a set of possible justifications and then categorize the responses, I read through the responses and used them to come up with a list of justifications. Unfortunately, a very high percentage gave no response at all to the request for justification, in spite of my being very clear about wanting them to give a justification and giving them a full five minutes to do so. There were no obvious differences between the groups, so I have no explanation for this. I would like to have followed Kohlberg and Gilligan in using extensive questioning of individual respondents, though I think care must be exercised not to simply supply a justification in the questioning.

Sixty-three respondents gave justifications to questions one and at least two other questions. I did not use responses that gave no justifications to question one, but these responses gave no justifications to most of the other questions either. I offer all of the discussion of justifications with a grain of salt because the sample is so small.

Of the responses that gave justifications, I found that the justifications were divided between appeals to virtue, principles, self-interest, reciprocity, and compromise and accommodation. As mentioned above, in order to avoid prejudging responses, I used the responses themselves to generate categories, rather than deciding on categories first and then sorting answers. The justifications fell into the following categories:

Virtue: Laziness should be penalized, hard work rewarded.

Principles:

P1. You should alleviate suffering.
P2. You should honor your commitments.
P3. You should protect life.
P4. You should honor property rights.
P5. You should maximize utility.
P6. You should help one another.

Reciprocity: You should help those who will be in a position to do the same for you.

Self-interest: People should help themselves first. My group is more important than any other group.

Care: You should try to construct a compromise that will allow you to accommodate everyone.

A. Virtue

It was relatively easy to identify appeals to virtue. The only virtue that was discussed was thriftiness/hard work and its opposite vice, laziness. All of the eighteen virtue respondents (twenty-nine percent of the respondents) cited the porcupine's lack of hard work, and all chose O1. In fact, a virtue justification (VJ) was the most common justification for O1; fifty-three percent of those who chose O1 offered VJ. Men and women did not differ a great deal here. Thirty-one percent of the men and twenty-seven percent of the women gave virtue VJ. (Numbers do not always add up to 100 due to rounding and incomplete responses.)

There were some interesting variations among racial groups. Twenty-five percent of the Anglos and thirty-seven percent of the Asians chose VJ. It was the most common justification chosen by Asians. No Latinos chose VJ.

Class differences showed up here as well. Twenty-four percent of blue-collar respondents and thirteen percent of service respondents chose VJ. In sharp contrast, only eight percent of professionals chose VJ.

There were age differences, too. Thirty-three percent of the 18–22 group and twenty-nine percent of the 23–27 group chose VJ while none of the over 27 group did. Since there were only four over 27 respondents, I am not sure how seriously to take this result.

Finally, eleven percent of those with children chose VJ, while thirty-four percent without children chose VJ.

In spite of the fact that the sample is so small, these results are suggestive and I am going to go out on a limb and hazard a guess about these differences. It appears that younger, non-parent respondents are far more likely to offer VJ than older respondents with children. One explanation might be that the latter group has had sufficient experience to know that hard work does not guarantee success. One now needs to show why blue-collar and service workers were so much more likely to offer VJ than professionals. One might point to the widespread myth that anyone can make it if only they work hard. Perhaps the need to believe this myth is greater among struggling groups. But we need to be very cautious here not to attribute this explanation to blue-collar and service workers as a whole, because most of them chose O2 and some justification other than VJ. All of the VJs chose O1. Finally, our Asian response, which can be explained by culture, suggests that we be open to complicated and varied explanations. Indeed, it would be extremely odd to expect one explanation to explain all the differences we see here.

B. Principle

Twenty respondents (thirty-two percent of the sample) chose what I describe as a principle justification (PJ). Of these, eight chose O1 and twelve chose O2. Virtually all of them made an explicit appeal to a general principle that could be used in similar cases. The six different principles suggested are listed above.

PJ was more often used to defend O2; Forty-one percent of the O2s used PJ, while twenty-four percent of the O1s used PJ.

Despite what Gilligan says about the reluctance of women to speak in a justice voice, I found that thirty-eight percent of the women and twenty-three percent of the men used PJ. In fact, PJ was the most common justification used by women.

It was also the most common justification used by Anglos. Thirty-four percent of Anglos, twenty-one percent of Asians, and twenty percent of Latinos used PJ.

The differences among classes were quite striking. Thirty-three percent of blue-collar, no service workers, and fifty-four percent of professionals used PJ. The next most common justification was chosen by only twenty-one percent of professionals.

Kohlberg's thesis that moral development is toward moral principles was not supported by my results. Forty-two percent of the 18–22 group, twenty-nine percent of the 23–27 group, and twenty-five percent of the over 27 group chose PJ.

Finally, among those with children, thirty-three percent chose PJ, and it was ranked with CJ as the most common justification among this group. Thirty-four percent of the non-parents chose PJ.

I will confine my speculation here to the results about class and gender. I have long suspected that appeals to principle are liable to benefit the ruling class. This ought to come as no surprise to anyone who believes that this is because they invented the rules. What is puzzling here is why so many more women than men chose PJ. I have a fairly lengthy diagnosis, but here I will just suggest that women have learned to play the justification game by appeal to principles and, as liberal feminists would be quick to respond, have achieved some success by doing so. I am not unaware of the efficacy of appeals to principles in many cases, but I wonder if it hasn't gotten us into many quandaries. Finally, I wonder if it hasn't wasted our energy, energy that might be better spent in political action.

C. Reciprocity

Four respondents, less than six percent of the total sample, appealed to a notion of reciprocity. They made it clear that there would be an obligation to help the porcupine if the porcupine could stand in a reciprocal relation to the moles in the future. Since the sample was so small and I am not sure that this is a distinctly moral justification, I will not discuss it further.

D. Self-Interest

Six students, ten percent of the respondents, made a straightforward appeal to self-interest (SJ). I am not impressed with ethical egoism, so I do not see this as a moral justification. Still, there were some interesting responses that I wanted to discuss.

Men were slightly more likely than women to chose SJ. Twelve percent of the men and eight percent of the women chose SJ.

Only three percent of the Anglos and none of the Latinos chose SJ, while twenty-six percent of the Asians chose SJ.

Five percent of blue-collar workers, thirteen percent of service workers, and sixteen percent of professionals chose SJ.

Sixteen percent of the 18–22 group, sixteen percent of the 23–27 group, and none of the over 27 group chose SJ. Eleven percent of the respondents with children chose SJ, while twelve percent of the non-parents chose SJ.

So the young are more likely to chose SJ than their elders, professionals are more likely than blue-collar or service workers, and those without children more likely than parents. A facile explanation might be that these groups are more selfish than the others. A more charitable explanation would be that the groups more likely to chose SJ have not had as many of the experiences that convince us of the need to look beyond self-interest as have the groups who are less likely to chose SJ.

But this explanation should not be invoked to explain the relatively high percentage of Asians who chose SJ. SJ was the second most popular justification for Asians, followed by PJ, which was chosen by twenty-one percent of Asians. It is entirely possible that this was a statistical anomaly caused by the size of the sample. One other possiblity might be that being Asian was merely an accidental factor, the determining factor might have been age or class. Indeed, all of the Asians who chose SJ were professionals, and all were 18–22. Still, I am not convinced that there isn't some other cultural factor at work here. One possibility is that the analysis in terms of self-interest is incorrect. The Asian respondents who chose SJ seemed to take it for granted that the situation should be decided in terms of what would be good for the moles. Perhaps a better description might be that they were not being self-interested here, but interested in the group that they identified with. This is not surprising in light of the Confucian prescription to value community over individual rights.

I suspect that many would be inclined to see the special valuing of one's group (whether family, neighborhood, state, etc.) as a special case of self-interest, but I am persuaded that we ought to take a second look at this.

My results with respect to ethnicity differed from the results of studies done in China and Korean.[21] Neither of these studies found any significant differences between their samples and subjects in the United States. Obviously, this is an area that needs further work.

E. Care

A new voice emerged as I read the responses. At first, I didn't hear it and categorized those who spoke in this voice as non-respondents. It sounded like they were saying that we should accommodate the porcupine because we should accommodate the porcupine. If so, they were just repeating themselves. But then I listened more carefully and began to hear a voice arguing for the value of compromise and accommodation, in this and in every similar case. I have identified this as the voice of care. I have since given this voice a great deal of thought and spelled out what might be involved in this call for compromise and accommodation. I won't discuss all that here, in part because I am not sure how much of it I got from the survey responses and how much I got from introspection. Here, I will just briefly describe the voice of care (CJ).

Those who chose CJ seemed to think it obvious that compromise and accommodation were good things, at least in cases of conflict. Since they were valuable, they should be appealed to in this case. These were the voices who were most creative about how to accommodate the porcupine, and most unwilling to believe that accommodation was impossible. Compromise and accommodation is not the same as appealing to utility. In the care view, no one is expendable and no one is a mere receptacle for utility. What this voice suggests is that if we are creative and committed to accommodating everyone, we can often discover a solution. The solution will often require sacrifice, but not necessarily. In many instances, the solution will result in everyone becoming more comfortable. If we look instead for the principle that tells us which one is right, we will not even see the creative solutions. The importance of intimacy and connection to others is assumed in this voice. We compromise and accommodate in order to preserve relationships. But this voice needn't be seen as the voice of self-sacrifice. Rather, we can see it as motivated by a desire to remain connected, where being connected is seen as a good thing.

The voice of care resembles the concept of *marawa wawe* of the Maisin people of New Guinea. Anne Marie Tietjen describes this concept in her study of moral reasoning among the Maisin:

> The term implies a shared emotional sense of trust and harmony in relations among community members, which arises when reciprocal obligations are in balance and the moral imperative equivalence is being upheld. . . . It also implies the norm of reciprocity in the sense of an expectation that the other will at some unspecified time repay a prosocial act, although not necessarily in kind.[22]

Fifteen respondents (twenty-four percent) chose CJ. Of the fifteen, thirteen chose O2 and two chose O1. There was no real difference between men and women here: twenty-three percent of the men and twenty-four percent of the women chose CJ.

There was a clear difference when we look at race: twenty-eight percent of Anglos, eleven percent of Asians, and eighty percent of Latinos chose CJ.

The differences among class were also clear: twenty-nine percent of blue-collar workers, fifty percent of service workers, and twenty-one percent of professionals chose CJ.

Age differences were striking: sixteen percent of the 18–22 group, twenty-nine percent of the 23–27 group, and seventy-five percent of the over 27 group chose CJ.

Among those with children, thirty-three percent chose CJ, while only fourteen percent of those without children chose CJ.

Again, the small sample undermines the results. Still, there is much here to speculate about. It seems that those who are more likely to need compromise and accommodation are more willing to compromise in order to accommodate others. I take it that this is the voice Gilligan speaks about and I am not surprised that she describes it as a female voice. Women in our society are socialized to be the ones to do the compromising and accommodating. One of the intriguing things about my results are that men are as likely to hear the voice of compromise and accommodation as women are. The results concerning parents are not surprising either. Parents have daily opportunities to care for their children. The effect of parenting on choice of moral voice might explain the results of Boldizar, Wilson, and Deemer that marriage causes a regression of women on the Kohlberg scale.[23] Perhaps the experience of caring for children, which presumably is more likely to occur among married women than among unmarried women (though this differs greatly by culture and class), causes married women to begin to see things in terms of care rather than justice. (See Tables 3-7 through 3-13.)

Table 3-7.
Percentage of subjects choosing each justificatory strategy

	C	V	P	R	S
Total	24	29	32	6	10

C = care; V = virture; P = principle; R = reciprocity; S = self-interest. Numbers do not add to 100 due to rounding and incomplete responses.

Table 3-8.
Percentage of subjects choosing each justificatory strategy

Gender				
	C	V	P	R	S
Men	23	31	23	11.5	11.5
Women	24	27	38	2	8

Table 3-9.
Percentage of subjects choosing each justificatory strategy

Race				
	C	V	P	R	S
Anglo	28	25	34	9	3
Asian	10.5	37	21	5	26
Latino	80	0	20	0	0

Table 3-10.
Percentage of subjects choosing each justificatory strategy

	C	V	P	R	S
			Class		
Blue collar	28.5	24	33	9.5	5
Service	50	12.5	0	25	12.5
Professional	21	8	54	0	16

Table 3-11.
Percentage of subjects choosing each justificatory strategy

	C	V	P	R	S
			Age		
18–22	16	32.5	42	2.6	16
23–27	28.5	28.5	28.5	0	16
Over 27	75	0	25	0	0

Table 3-12.
Percentage of subjects choosing each justificatory strategy

	C	V	P	R	S
			Parents		
Yes	33	11	33	11	11
No	14	34	34	6	12

Table 3-13.
Percentage of choosers of outcomes O1 and O2
choosing justifications

	C	V	P	R	S
O1	6	53	24	3	15
O2	45	0	41	10	3

F. Changing Justifications

I was curious to see if justifications would change as the circumstances changed. In question four, I made it clear that the porcupine's reduced circumstances were not caused by the porcupine, but by a flood. In question five, I stipulated that the porcupine would die if forced outside the burrow. In question six, I stipulated that the moles were being seriously injured by the porcupine's quills. Part of my strategy was to see how decisions about outcome and justification were affected by different background assumptions.

Question four rules out the background assumption that the porcupine was the cause of its own distress. Of the eighteen VJs who chose O1 for question one, sixteen changed to O2 in response to question four. Eight of them offered a VJ, and eight offered no justification. I suspect that offering no new justification means that they did not change their justification strategy. It is clear, however, that there is no reason to expect VJs to change their strategy in response to question four; a switch to O2 is easily justified by VJ.

There were eight PJs who initially chose O1. Only five of the eight switched to O2 in response to question four. Of the three who kept O1, none offered a justification for their decision in question four. Of the five who switched to O2, four offered no justification and one gave VJ. Of the five who switched, three had initially offered P4 (a property rights justification), one offered P1 (alleviate suffering), and one offered P5 (principle of utility). In the absence of any further data, I can only guess that the four who offered no justification either saw the new circumstances as changing the outcome, even when the same principle was applied, or applied a new principle.

Two CJs initially chose O1 and neither changed. My guess here is that they were initially unconvinced that an accommodation could be reached that would be satisfactory for all. Changing the description of the porcupine's character and fault did not change that judgment. (See Table 3-14.)

Question five provided a severe challenge to VJs. When I suggested that the porcupine would die if left outside the burrow, all eighteen of the Vjs changed from O1 to O2. Three kept VJ, seven offered no justification, and eight switched to PJ. Of these eight, seven offered P3 (protect life) and one offered P1 (alleviate suffering). This suggests that they were willing to give up their commitments to VJ in a life or death situation. This impression was strengthened when I noted that thirteen of the eighteen VJs changed to PJ either in five or six.

Eight of the PJs initially chose O1. On question five, seven switched to O2. Of the seven, three offered a PJ. One changed from P4 to P5, one from P5 to P3, and one from P1 to P3. Four offered no justification.

There were two CJs who initially chose O1 and neither of them switched. There was one RJ who chose O1 on one and this RJ switched to O2 but offered no justification. Four of the five SJs who chose O1 initially switched to O2 on question five. (See Table 3-15).

Table 3-14.
Changing justifications: Responses of O1s on question 1 to question 4

VJs:
16 out of 18 changed to O2,
8 kept VJ,
8 offered no justification.

PJs:
5 out of 8 changed to O2,
4 offered no justification,
1 gave VJ.

CJs:
2 out of 2 stayed O1.

Table 3-15.
Changing justifications: Responses of O1s on question 1 to question 5

VJs:
18 of 18 switched to O2,
3 kept VJ,
7 offered no justification,
8 switched to PJ.

PJs:
7 out of 8 switched to O2,
3 offered PJ.

CJs:
2 out of 2 stayed O1.

Question six posed a problem for O2s, by stipulating that the moles were being seriously injured by the porcupine. This creates a conflict for those who depend on principles or rights, and a quandary for those who want to accommodate everyone.

None of the VJs initially chose O2, so there was no switching on question six. As I expected, there were some changes among the PJs and the CJs. Eight of the PJs initially chose O2. Four of them switched to O1 on question six. None of them offered a justification.

Thirteen CJs initially chose O2. Nine of them switched to O1 in question six, and seven of these offered a PJ. (See Table 3-16.)

Overall, there were twenty PJ, fifteen CJ, eighteen VJ, six SJ, and four RJ responses to question one. On question four, there were four PJs, no CJs, twelve VJs, no SJs, and two RJs. On question five, there were thirty-three PJs, one CJ, four VJs, two SJs, and two RJs. On question six, there were sixty PJs, one CJ, no VJs, four SJs, and two RJs. (See Table 3-17.) While we must be cautious here because many respondents did not give justifications to every question, it seems reasonable to suppose that when the harm becomes more serious and the possibility of accommodation more remote, common moral sentiment moves toward justification in terms of principles.

G. Multiple Justifications

I had little difficulty categorizing responses on individual questions because respondents almost always chose one justificatory strategy per question.

Table 3-16.
Responses of O2s on question 1 to question 6

VJs:
No O2s on 1.

PJs:
4 out of 12 switched to O1,
none offered a justification.

CJs:
9 out of 13 switched,
7 offered PJ.

Table 3-17.

Effect of setting on choice of justification

Question 1		Question 4	
PJs:	20	PJs:	4
CJs:	15	CJs:	0
VJs:	18	VJs:	12
SJs:	6	SJs:	0
RJs:	4	RJs:	2
Question 5		Question 6	
PJs:	33	PJs:	60
CJs:	1	CJs:	1
VJs:	4	VJs:	0
SJs:	2	SJs:	4
RJs:	2	RJs:	2

There were changes, however, as I've outlined above, from question to question. Gilligan suggests that the most morally well-developed person will hear a multitude of moral voices and I am inclined to agree that this is a sign of moral maturity rather than conceptual confusion. I was curious to see if there was a pattern in the number of justifications used, and indeed there was.

I looked to each category of justification, as identified by initial responses, to see how many respondents listed three or more justifications in their responses to questions one through six. Only one of eighteen VJs, three of the twenty PJs, one of the four RJs, and one of the six SJs used three or more justifications, while nine of the fifteen CJs used three or more justifications.

This final result was striking. If the mark of moral maturity is the willingness to compromise and accommodate and the ability to hear diverse moral voices, as Gilligan suggests, then our CJs are clearly the most morally mature. There is no question that there is a correlation between choosing CJ and hearing diverse moral voices. Whether we couch this in terms of moral maturity or goodness, I am inclined to agree with Gilligan that it is something we want to see in moral agents.

III. CONCLUSION

I now want to make some conclusions based upon sections I and II. My first conclusion is that all the factors I looked at affected moral reasoning. This does not undermine Gilligan's claim that gender affects moral reasoning, since her assumption is that it does so through social conditioning via gender roles. My hunch here is that gender may be less of a determinant that Gilligan assumes. Obviously, more work on class, age, and ethnic differences is called for.

My second conclusion is that it is possible that differences in male and female moral reasoning might be due to differences in background assumptions rather than differences in reasoning style.

My third conclusion is that moral philosophy cannot be done in ignorance of moral psychology and common moral practice. Listening to the voices of real moral agents has much to teach us.

My fourth conclusion is that as harm becomes more grievous or accommodation less possible, common morality moves toward a justification in terms of principle. This has real consequences for the debates about ethical theory and moral pluralism.

My fifth conclusion is that the ability to hear diverse moral voices seems to be correlated to the willingness to compromise with an eye to accommodation. I would add that this is something we should want to see in our moral communities.

My final conclusion is that there *is* a different voice, one I describe as the voice of compromise and accommodation. Though I am not sure that I would describe it as a female voice, it is this voice that I have recognized as my private voice and the one that I hope to begin to speak with in public. I think that there is much that needs to be said about this voice. In the rest of this book, I will try to add to the conversation both in and about this voice.

NOTES

1. Lawrence Kohlberg, "Stage and Sequence: The Cognitive-Developmental Approach to Socialization," in D. A. Goslin, ed., *Handbook of Socialization Theory and Research* (Chicago: Rand McNally, 1969).

2. Arthur Schopenhauer, "The Weakness of Women," *Studies in Pessimism* (1851), reprinted in Rosemary Agonito, ed., *History of Ideas on Women* (New York: Perigee Books, 1977).

3. Sigmund Freud, "Some Psychical Consequences of the Anatomical Distinction

Between the Sexes" (1925), James Strachey, trans. and ed., *The Standard Edition XIX* (London: Hogarth, 1961), 257–58.

4. Carol Gilligan, *In a Different Voice: Psychological Theory and Women's Development* (Cambridge, Mass.: Harvard University Press, 1982), 19.

5. L. J. Walker reviewed hundreds of studies on moral reasoning and concluded that there were no significant differences between men and women with respect to moral reasoning. See "Sex Differences in the Development of Moral Reasoning: A Critical Review," *Child Development*, 55 (1984): 677–91.

6. Defenders of Gilligan have argued that Kohlberg selected dilemmas that would naturally call up a justice voice. These critics organized studies to test the results of using dilemmas that would either naturally suggest a caring voice or give respondents an opportunity to describe their own dilemmas and their own responses. Their results supported Gilligan. See, for example, Nona Lyons, "Two Perspectives: On Self, Relationships, and Morality," *Harvard Educational Review* 53 (1983): 125–45; Mary K. Rothbart, Dean Hanley, and Marc Albert, "Gender Differences in Moral Reasoning," *Sex Roles* 15 (1986): 645–53; Geri R. Donenberg and Lois W. Hoffman, "Gender Differences in Moral Development," *Sex Roles* 18 (1988): 701–17; Edward Lonky, Paul A. Roodin, and John M. Rybash, "Moral Judgment and Sex Role Orientation as a Function of Self and Other Presentation Mode," *Journal of Youth and Adolescence*, 17 (1988): 189–95.

7. An interesting challenge to Kohlberg's assertion that what Gilligan describes as the justice voice is morally more developed than what she describes as the voice of care is DeWolfe et al.'s study of convicted felons. In this study male felons scored higher on Kohlberg's scale than female felons, in spite of the fact that eighty-six percent of the male felons were incarcerated for crimes involving violence while only twenty-eight percent of the women were incarcerated for crimes involving violence. See Thomas E. DeWolfe, Lee Jackson, and Patricia Wintergerger, "A Comparison of Moral Reasoning and Moral Character in Male and Female Incarcerated Felons," *Sex Roles* 18 (1988): 583–93.

8. Immanuel Kant, *Observations on the Feeling of the Beautiful and the Sublime*, John T. Goldthwait, trans., (Berkeley: University of California Press, 1960), sec. 3.

9. McGraw and Bloomfield focus on gender rather than biological sex in mapping differences in moral reasoning. Kathleen M. McGraw and Jeremy Bloomfield, "Social Influence on Group Moral Decisions: The Interactive Effects of Moral Reasoning and Sex Role Orientation," *Journal of Personality and Social Psychology* 53 (1987): 1080–87.

10. S. Pollak and Carol Gilligan, "Images of Violence in Thematic Apperception Test Stories," *Journal of Personality and Social Psychology* 42 (1982): 159–67. In this study, Pollak and Gilligan gave subjects stories to finish. Male subjects were far more likely than women to end stories about intimacy unhappily, often violently. Women subjects responded negatively to stories that hinted at separation and abandonment. From this they inferred that males feared intimacy while women feared abandonment.

11. Gilligan, *In a Different Voice*.

12. Annette Baier, "Doing Without Moral Theory?" in Stanley Clarke and

Evan Simpson, eds., *Anti-Theory in Ethics and Moral Conservatism* (Albany: State University of New York Press, 1989).

13.   Lyons, Rothbart et al., and Donenberg and Hoffman (cited in n.6) all designed studies that included dilemmas which did not force subjects to see the moral issue along justice lines. Their research supported Gilligan's contention about sex-based moral reasoning.

14.   There are several tests used to measure moral development. Some of them presuppose Kohlberg's theory of moral development:

A. Colby, L. Kohlberg, J. Gibbs, D. Candee, B. Speicher-Dubin, K. Kauffman, A. Hewer, and C. Power, *The Measurement of Moral Judgment: A Manual and its Development* (Cambridge: Cambridge University Press, 1986).

J. C. Gibbs and K. F. Widaman, *Social Intelligence: Measuring the Development of Sociomoral Reflection* (New York: Prentice Hall, 1982).

Perhaps the most widely used test in the Kohlberg tradition is the Defining Issues Test (DIT) developed by James Rest, *Development in Judging Moral Issues* (Minneapolis: University of Minnesota Press, 1979).

Texts in the Gilligan tradition include:

Nancy Eisengerg-Berg, "Development of Children's Prosocial Moral Judgment," *Developmental Psychology* 15 (1979): 128–37.

Nona Lyons, "Two Perspectives on Self, Relationships, and Morality," *Harvard Educational Review* 53 (1983): 125–45.

I agree with the defenders of Gilligan that dilemmas used on tests must allow for responses of both care and justice. I designed my own test to allow for this. I did not use either of the Gilligan-type tests because there were certain hypotheses that I wanted to investigate that were not tested by any available test.

15.   This was pointed out to me by Thomas Leddy.

16.   Nel Noddings, *Caring: A Feminine Approach to Ethics and Moral Development* (Berkeley: University of California Press, 1984).

17.   Charles B. White, "Age, Education, and Sex Effects on Adult Moral Reasoning," *International Journal on Aging and Human Development* 27 (1988): 271–81.

18.   See Chapter Two, James Rest, *Moral Development: Advances in Research and Theory* (New York: Praeger, 1986) for a discussion of the effects of education on adult moral reasoning.

19.   For a discussion of another cross-cultural study, see Mordecai Nisan, "Moral Norms and Social Conventions: A Cross-Cultural Comparison," *Developmental Psychology* 23 (1987): 719–25; Elliot Turiel, Judith G. Smetana, and Larry P. Nucci, "A Cross-Cultural Comparison About What? A Critique of Nisan's (1987) Study of Morality and Convention," *Developmental Psychology* 24 (1988): 140–43; Mordecaui Nisan, "A Story of a Pot, Or a Cross-Cultural Comparison of Basic Moral Evaluations: A Response to the Critique by Turiel, Nucci and Smetana (1988)," *Developmental Psychology* 24 (1988): 144–46.

20.   Sandra Harding argues that the African world view on caring is very similar to the view of women in the United States. See "The Curious Coincidence of Feminine and African Moralities," in *Women and Moral Theory*, Eva Kittay and Diana Meyers, eds., (Totowa, N.J: Rowman and Littlefield, 1987). See also Vernon

Dixon, "World Views and Research Methodologies," in L. M. King, V. Dixon, and W. W. Nobles, eds., *African Philosophy: Assumptions and Paradigms for Research on Black Persons* (Los Angeles: Fanon Center Publications, Charles R. Drew Postgraduate Medical School, 1976).

21. Two studies on cross-cultural moral development which used Asian samples supported Kohlberg's theory of moral development: Myung-Ja Song, Judith G. Smetana, and Sang Yoon Kim, "Korean Children's Conceptions of Moral and Conventional Transgressions," *Developmental Psychology* 23 (1987): 577–82; Hing-Keung Ma and Wing-Shing Chan, "The Moral Judgments of Chinese Students," *The Journal of Social Psychology* 127 (1987): 491–97.

However, D. S. Dien, in a study using a Chinese sample, concluded that mature moral reasoning for the Chinese is toward a recognition of the importance of community rather than individual autonomy. This suggests a parallel with Gilligan. See D. S. Dien, "A Chinese Perspective on Kohlberg's Theory of Moral Development," *Developmental Review* 2 (1982): 331–41.

22. Anne Marie Tietjen, "Prosocial Reasoning Among Children and Adults in a Papua New Guinea Society," *Developmental Psychology* 22 (1986): 861–68.

23. Janet P. Boldizar, Kenneth L. Wilson, and Deborah Kay Deemer, "Gender, Life Experiences, and Moral Judgment: A Process-Oriented Approach," *Journal of Personality and Social Psychology* 57 (1989): 229–38.

Chapter Four

Just Caring

In this chapter, I shall sketch a model of ethical considerations which I shall call, following Nel Noddings, an ethic of caring.[1] In the next two chapters, I shall flesh out this discussion: Chapter Five will focus on caring for persons, and Chapter Six will address caring for animals.

I must confess at the outset that this model owes more to my experience as a woman, a teacher, and a mother than it does to my training and experience in moral philosophy. Over the years, my students have convinced me of the barrenness of standard ethical theories. It has occurred to me only very recently that, in sketching a more adequate model, I might appeal to my own experience as a moral person. I credit Hume,[2] Annette Baier,[3] and Carol Gilligan[4] with waking me from my dogmatic slumber and Nel Noddings with allowing me to take caring, which is central to my moral experience, seriously.

An ethic of caring, as I shall defend it, includes two elements. First is a disposition to care. This is a willingness to receive others, a willingness to give the lucid attention required to appropriately fill the needs of others. In this sense, an ethic of care is contextual; my actions must be guided by this lucid attention.[5] I see this disposition to care as nourished by a spiritual awareness similar to the awareness argued for by proponents of the women's spirituality movement. As Starhawk describes this awareness: "Immanent justice rests on the first principle of magic: all things are interconnected. All is relationship. Perhaps the ultimate ethic of immanence is to choose to make that relationship one of love . . . love for all the eternally self-creating world, love of the light and the mysterious darkness, and raging love against all that would diminish the unspeakable beauty of the world."[6]

This disposition to care assumes a commitment to an ideal of caring; the ethically preferred world is one in which creatures are caring and cared for. Its institutions support and sustain caring while simultaneously reducing the need for care by eliminating the poverty, despair, and indifference that create a need for care.

Second, in addition to being sensitive to one's place in the world and to one's general obligation to be a caring person, one is also obligated to care for. (I am following Noddings in using "care for" to indicate caring as expressed in action.) In the paradigm case, caring for involves acting in some appropriate way to respond to the needs of persons and animals, but can also be extended to responding to the needs of communities, values, or objects.

We are obligated to adopt this model of caring, insofar as we can, in our moral deliberations. This qualification refers not only to physical, emotional, and psychological incapacity, but to the larger inability to simply adopt a moral life, which is radically different from the way of life we have participated in all our lives. This is a kind of incapacity that we all share. We simply cannot choose to have another's moral sensibilities, even if we are convinced that they are finer in some sense than our own. It doesn't follow that we have no obligations to become more morally sensitive; the point here is that we cannot simply will ourselves to begin to see the moral universe in some radically new way. But even where we can adopt a model of caring, we are morally permitted and sometimes morally obliged to appeal to rules and rights. In Gilligan's idiom, we are required to listen to the voices of both care and justice.

In what follows, I shall first fill in some of the details of this model. Specifically, I shall discuss what it is to care for someone or something and when we are obligated to care for. Next, I shall say something about the role of rules and rights in this model. Chapters Five and Six return to a discussion of many of the issues raised in this chapter, and in Chapter Seven I respond to objections.

I. CARING

I have often wondered if taking a class in moral philosophy was the best way for students to become sensitive to moral concerns. It seemed to me that a better way would be to have students work in soup kitchens or shelters for the homeless.[7] Taking care of my children has made me more open to moral concerns. In taking care of the hungry, homeless, and helpless, we are engaged in caring for. In the standard case, caring for is immediate; it admits of no surrogates. When we directly care for some creature, we are in physical contact. Our eyes meet, our hands touch. However, not every need can be met in this immediate way, and sometimes we must accept surrogates. Not every need can be met by individual action; in such cases, we must seek collective action.[8] But when we can do the caring for directly, we ought to do so, at least some of the time. The need of the other may sometimes require that a particular person do the caring for. If my child needs my attention, I cannot meet this need by sending her to a therapist. Even when the needs of the other do not require our personal attention, we must provide some of the caring for directly in order to develop and sustain our ability to care.

Day-to-day interactions with other persons create a web of reciprocal caring. In these interactions, one is obliged to be a caring person. One is free, to a certain extent, to choose when and how to care for these others. One's choice is limited by one's relationships with these others and by their needs. A pressing need calls up an immediate obligation to care for; roles and responsibilities call up an obligation to respond in a caring manner. In the first case, one is obligated (though this obligation can be limited by a principle of supererogation) to respond; in the second, one can choose, within limits, when and how to care.

A creature in need who is unable to meet this need without help calls for a caring response on my part. This response need not always be direct. Sometimes it is better to organize a political response. (Many, for example, who are confronted on the street by homeless people are unsure about how to respond, convinced that their immediate response will not be enough, and might even be counterproductive.) Certain relationships obligate us to provide direct caring for. When my daughter falls and asks me to "kiss it and make it better" I can't send her to my neighbor for the kiss.

Our roles (e.g., as mother, as teacher, as volunteer) put us in particular relationships to others.[9] These roles require and sustain caring. Obligations to infant children and animals involve meeting their basic needs for physical sustenance (food, shelter, clothing, health care) and for companionship and love. Obligations to students are grounded upon roles of teacher and philosopher and the students' psychological needs to discover who they are and how they can live with integrity. Here, one ought to feel a connection with the students but also with teaching and philosophy. But if a student needs another kind of care, we may be obligated to provide it, though not single-handedly. The response depends upon one's ability to care for, one's obligation to care for oneself, and one's sense of the appropriateness of the need and the best way to meet it.

In discharging obligations to care for, which are based on role responsibility, one should be conscious of the need to fill those roles conscientiously. The role of teacher, for example, requires a certain impartiality; the role of mother requires a fierce devotion to each particular child. But one is free, to a certain extent, to choose roles. In adopting or reshaping roles, one should be sensitive to the need to be cared for as well as the capacity to care. In critiquing socially designed and assigned roles, we should aim for roles and divisions of roles that make caring more likely to occur.

Caring for can involve a measure of self-sacrifice. The rescuers of Jessica McLure, the little girl who fell into a well, who went without sleep for days, the parents of an infant who go without uninterrupted sleep for months, are involved in caring for.

Caring for involves an openness to the one cared for; it requires seeing the real need and satisfying it insofar as we are able. In satisfying it, we should be sensitive not just to the need but to the feelings of those in need.

Caring for does not require feeling any particular emotion toward the one cared for, but an openness to the possibility that some emotional attachment may form in the process of caring for. Nor does it require an ongoing relationship with the one cared for.[10] One may meet the one cared for as stranger, though the caring for will change that.

Obviously, a model of caring along the lines I am defending must include an account of needs. An account of needs must recognize that needs are in some sense social, so identifying needs requires an understanding of biology, psychology, and other relevant social sciences.

Such an account would draw a distinction between subsistence needs and psychological needs. Subsistence needs will usually be needs that must be filled if physical existence is to continue, while psychological needs are needs that must be filled if human flourishing is to occur. Filling subsistence needs does not automatically benefit both the carer and the cared for. Rather, the carer is likely to feel burdened by filling such needs, though the recognition that one has filled such needs often creates a sense of virtue in the carer. Filling psychological needs can often be more fulfilling. It is more likely to be done in a reciprocal relationship, and in such a relationship filling psychological needs requires that both parties share the roles of carer and cared for.

Finally, one need not respond to every need. In choosing how and when to respond, one should consider the seriousness of the need, the benefit to the one needing care of filling this particular need, one's own capacity to fill the need, and the competing needs of others, including oneself, that will be affected by filling this particular need.

II. OBJECTS OF CARE

One can care for persons, animals, ideas, values, institutions, and objects. Later, I will discuss caring for persons and animals in some detail, but here I want to make some brief remarks about caring for ideas, values, institutions, and objects. In caring for ideas, values, and institutions, one devotes oneself to their survival, growth, and flourishing in much the same way as we devote ourselves to the growth and flourishing of a child. In doing so, we are caring for ourselves (insofar as these are our ideas and values) and persons and animals (insofar as these ideas and values support a network of care that embraces persons and animals). In caring for objects, one is devoted primarily to their survival (although some objects, trees, for example, can be said to grow and flourish). The choice of objects of care should reflect our own need to be cared for and our capacity to care. But decisions about what to care for should not depend exclusively upon our own needs and capacities. We should also be sensitive to the needs that summon the obligation to care for. If we understand our obligation to care for as following from the existence of need and helplessness, we should care for ideas, institutions, values, objects, and practices that would diminish such needs. One might argue that we could virtually eliminate the need to care for by creating appropriate institutions, values, and practices and hence undermine our capacity to care. But even in a perfectly just world, children would need care, and people and animals would get sick. Furthermore, human needs include more than needs for physical sustenance. Human needs for companionship and intimacy would exist even in a world free from the horrors of war, homelessness, sickness, and disease.

III. CARING AND HUMAN NATURE

Alasdair MacIntyre argues that morality has historically been defended by appeal either to "the ghost of conceptions of divine law" or "the ghost of conceptions of human nature and activity." Since neither conception is "at home in the modern world",[11] morality lacks a foundation. Since morality lacks a foundation, relativism and emotivism have gained a secure foothold, at least in the popular culture.[12]

Though I sympathize with the postmodern rejection of essentialist theories of human nature, I do not agree that there is nothing beyond mere historically conditioned, relatively pervasive human traits. The truth lies somewhere in between. While conceptions of human nature are too often overgeneralizations made on the basis of one's situated experience, one needn't reject the very possibility of finding sufficiently general human characteristics and experiences. Since there are such sufficiently general characteristics and experiences, we need not reject conceptions of human nature as providing a foundation for morality, though we do need to examine such conceptions. Conceptions of human nature generate a picture of the good life. The good life involves overcoming human nature, liberating human nature, or a combination of both: overcoming what is base and liberating what is pure. In this way, conceptions of human nature inform morality.

Many have argued that liberal ethical theories and political philosophies have assumed an unflattering and inaccurate picture of human nature. Marx, for example, criticizes the "individualistic monad"[13] lurking behind defenses of rights. A similar criticism has recently been made by Elizabeth Wolgast in her attacks on "social atomism"[14] and Alison Jaggar in her criticism of "abstract individualism."[15]

Jaggar identifies abstract individualism as the theory of human nature which underlies liberal political philosophy. I think we can assume that this theory provides a foundation for ethical theory as well. Abstract individualism is the view that essential human characteristics are properties of individuals and are given independently of the social context. This theory, as Jaggar describes it, is committed to the following claims.

1. Rationality is a mental capacity of individuals rather than groups and is possessed in approximately equal measure by all humans, though this capacity can be more or less developed.

2. Rationality is our most valuable capacity.

3. Each individual is intrinsically valuable because of this ability to reason.

4. Each human's desires can in principle be fulfilled separately from the desires of other humans.

5. People typically seek to maximize their individual self-interest.

6. Resources for fulfilling desires are limited.

7. Because of the value of rationality and the existence of scarcity and desires to possess certain goods, autonomy is protected by the good society.[16]

One can argue about whether Jaggar has accurately described liberal political and moral philosophy here, but even if we grant that the picture is overdrawn, a version of it undergirds Kantian and utilitarian moral theories. We can see how this conception supports Kantian ethics with its emphasis on duty. If one is unconnected to others, and basically self-interested, no other motivation to be moral could exist.

Utilitarianism is also a rational alternative if abstract individualism is true. An unconnected, basically self-interested individual would admit that social life is not worth living without some constraints on the self-interest of others. It is then rational to adopt a system of mutual restraint, as long as one's own interests will count. In this way, the rational person can protect his interests.

An ethic of care rejects the abstract individualism criticized by Jaggar. On this view, we are all connected, and, as Noddings puts it, "the primary aim is caring and being cared for . . . ."[17] This caring can take place only in potentially reciprocal relationships between human beings. The good society protects this aim and allows for the full development of our best selves, which are those selves represented by "our most caring and tender moments."[18] Since caring is not a totally rational process, although it is partly this, an ethic of care would reject claims number two and three. Rationality is not our most valuable capacity; the capacity for caring represents our "best selves." It would also reject claim four. If our primary desires are to care and be cared for in relationships with other humans, then we cannot fulfill our desires independently of other other humans. We should not be seen as seeking to maximize self-interest either, because caring involves the suspension of self-interest in many cases, so she would reject claim number five as well. Claim number six is noncontroversial, but claim number seven would also be rejected because it follows from number three.

We can see that an ethic of care requires a new conception of human nature, and such an account would involve a picture of humans as essentially involved in relationships with other humans.

IV. KNOWING HOW AND WHEN TO CARE

It is not unreasonable to expect an ethic to give us some guidance about how to act, though as I have argued in Chapters One and Two it is unreasonable to expect a calculus. An ethic of care, then, ought to give us some guidance about how and when to care.

Noddings explicitly acknowledges her great debt to Hume, as do I. It seems reasonable then to begin by looking at Hume's answer to this question. Hume saw morality as resting upon a human capacity for sympathetic identification with others.[19] When we see someone suffering, for example, we feel the suffering almost as if it were our own. Our desire to do something to relieve the suffering springs naturally from this empathic response. This natural sentiment is supplanted by an appeal to justice when the sentiment is lacking. Suppose, for example, that the suffering is taking place in a distant place and we are merely aware of it. Our awareness does not excite in us the same empathic response that the immediate perception of the suffering would. What we must do in this case is remind ourselves that although we do not know the sufferer, we can assume that the sufferer shares essential characteristics with someone who is close to us. Since we cannot find any reason to reject the appeal of the one while desiring to respond to the other, we recognize the demands made on us by the absent sufferer. Here what we see is sentiment, colored by reflection. This reflection results in rather general principles, though the principles are seen as derivative of our experience and our sentiments.

Noddings makes a similar move when she distinguishes natural from ethical caring.[20] Natural caring is the caring that one is inclined to do, that springs from ties of affection to others. In the absence of such inclination, one must summon up ethical caring. Both Hume and Noddings are vague about precisely what caring demands in any particular situation. Hume suggests that, at least with respect to general principles, we let experience be our guide; we look for those principles that will make the world more comfortable for the social creatures we are. Noddings rejects an appeal to general principles, but offers instead a strategy for deciding what to do. When natural caring is absent, one should ask oneself what the ideal caring self would do in this situation. She is not suggesting that we appeal to an impartial observer here. Instead, she asks us to remember a situation in which we were ideally caring; we appeal here to our own ideal of caring.

What is implied in both Hume and Noddings is that when sentiment and natural caring do motivate us, we freely follow their dictates. Both of them admit that this capacity can stagnate and die or it can flourish, and, accordingly, we have an obligation to support this capacity in ourselves. Noddings argues that we can only learn to care if we have been cared for as children, and if we have been given opportunities to care. If we have been, then, as adults, we sustain and enrich this capacity by continuing to seek opportunities to care actively for others.

Assuming we are caring persons, both Hume and Noddings suggest that we can trust our impulses; our instincts will guide us toward proper caring, at least when we are caring in the context of a fully present other. There is, of course, an additional requirement that Noddings in particular pays attention to: that we know how the other feels and what the other wants and how the other is likely to be affected by our actions.

Martha Nussbaum combines both sentiment and awareness in her notion of moral imagination. She describes moral imagination as the ability to see "a complex, concrete reality in a highly lucid and richly responsive way . . . taking in what is there, with imagination and feeling."[21]

I agree with Hume, Noddings, and Nussbaum that our interactions with others can and should be guided by our moral imaginations, by our sentiments balanced by our rich understanding of the context. Obviously our responses to strangers will not be guided by the same degree of understanding and sentiment as our responses to those close to us. However, Hume and Noddings are right to suggest that we imagine ourselves in contact with them, that we try to become as aware as we can be of their situations, that we allow this awareness to occasion an emotional response, and that we act, in the full knowledge that our actions, based as they are on insufficient understanding and often less than vibrant sentiment, might not be the right ones. I also agree with Nussbaum and Hume that general principles have a role to play. We appeal to our experiences with intimate others to generate a set of general principles, though we keep in mind that these are merely rules of thumb, based on past experience. But in the absence of understanding and rich emotional response, this might be the only way to guide our actions toward strangers.

V. DEFENSE OF A GENERAL OBLIGATION TO CARE

I am inclined to see the obligation to care as moral bedrock. If it can be said to rest on anything, it rests on our human capacity for caring interaction. Rather than offer a defense of care in terms of appeals to general principles, I would offer a defense of something like general principles in terms of care. Still, for those who find the appeal to general principles more compelling than the obligation to care, I offer a defense of care in terms of such suitably general principles.

The obligation to respond as carer when appropriate can be defended on three grounds. The first is the need. Here one might appeal to Peter Singer's principle, "If it is in our power to prevent something very bad happening without thereby sacrificing anything of comparable moral significance, we ought to do it."[22]

The second is the recognition that human relationships require a continuous kind of caring. This caring involves three components: being receptive to the other, being accepting of the other, and being on call for the other when he/she is in need.[23] Unless we want to do away with human relationships, we must be open to the demands of caring that such relationships require. But caring in human relationships is, as human relationships are, reciprocal.

The third defense is that we cannot develop and sustain the ability to care unless we do some active caring. This is an empirical claim, and we must look both to social science and to our own experience in evaluating it, but there is an obvious way in which caring for enhances our ability to care. When we make the real attempt to care for, we must understand the needs of the one cared for. We must also see how that one wants the needs to be addressed. This ability to notice needs and wants and to empathize as well as sympathize is developed through caring. Of course, one might ask here why one should want to develop this capacity to care. It seems to me that the right response is to point out that human lives devoid of caring impulses and responses would be nasty, brutish, short, and lonely.

Nel Noddings offers a different defense of the general obligation to care, one which seems to offer some problematic consequences. Noddings's theory is that morality essentially involves one obligation: the obligation to care. Caring involves two elements: natural caring and ethical caring. Natural caring requires engrossment in the other, "seeing the other's reality as possible for me,"[24] and the motivation to act "based on recognition of the other's wants and desires and . . . the objective elements of his problematic situation."[25] Ethical caring involves summoning natural caring by remembering "our most caring and tender moments"[26] and recognizing that these moments represent our best self. Ethical caring can only be achieved in situations where dynamic, mutual relationships are possible.

This analysis provides, according to Noddings, an analysis of obligation.

I can be obligated to P if: (1) There exists or is potential a relation between P and me; (2) There exists the dynamic potential for growth in relation, including the potential for increased reciprocity and mutuality.

We are only obligated when these conditions obtain because, in her view, it is only under these conditions that caring can occur. Noddings denies that "universal caring" is a possibility[27] and admits to the following three consequences of her analysis. First, "I am not obligated to starving children in Africa."[28] Her argument for this is not exactly clear, but it appears that she would want to say that my ongoing relationships confer obligations that are primary. She says that fulfilling obligations to the starving children in Africa would require me to "abandon my obligations"[29] to those to whom I am already related. Second, we have no obligations to animals because there is no possibility for genuine mutuality from animals.[30] Third, the life of one caring (the ethically preferred life for all according to Noddings) must, in some sense, be a private life. "Her public life is limited by her insistence upon meeting the other as one caring . . . when reaching out destroys or drastically reduces her actual caring, she retreats and renews her contact with those who address her."[31]

I want to take issue with each of these consequences, but I don't think that by doing so I am rejecting Noddings's account. Indeed, I am puzzled about why Noddings thought she was committed to them. It seems to be that a sympathetic reading of her could justify the exactly opposite conclusions.[32]

Noddings needn't grant that helping the starving in Africa requires abandoning obligations to those to whom one is related. However, I suspect that she would still want to insist that I am not obligated to the starving in Africa. There is no present relationship between me and the starving children in Africa, nor is it likely that such a relationship will begin in the future. She gives us the example of a missionary who decides to go to Africa to help the starving. She says that this person might well have such obligations because this person will begin to have such relationships.[33]

I don't agree that we have no obligations to the starving in Africa, in part because I don't accept Noddings's assumption about the primacy of current obligations. It seems to me that we have self-interested reasons for wanting to meet the obligations to those with whom we share a relationship. First, the possibility and hence the expectation of reciprocity gives us a self-interested reason for meeting these obligations first. Second, if we are truly "engrossed" by the persons for whom we care, we will receive some pleasure in meeting these obligations. I don't want to argue that no moral reasons can be offered where reasons of self-interest naturally obtain, but I do think that we should be suspicious of ethical theories that restrict our obligations to those duties that we have a self-interested reason to perform.

Noddings might have argued that we can have mutually reciprocal relationships with animals, or she might have taken the same stance with regard to animals that she takes with regard to abortion. In the latter case, she argues that the prospective mother can grant "sanctity" to the first-trimester fetus by viewing it as a "product of love between a man deeply cared-for and me,"[34] and, as such, "joined to others through formal chains of caring."[35] Because the caring exists for this mother, abortion would be immoral. If the mother chooses not to sanctify the fetus, no such relationship exists in the first trimester, and hence abortion would not be immoral. As the fetus begins to develop, it becomes "more nearly capable of response as cared-for."[36] At this point the relationship begins to exist and grow, and abortion is again immoral. It sounds like she is saying that if I choose to view myself as involved in a relationship with a fetus, then I have obligations toward it, even if it is not now capable of having a mutually reciprocal relationship with me.[37] Why can't I then choose to see myself as involved in a relationship with animals, or at least with some animals? If I choose to see the animal this way, then I do have an obligation toward the animal. But this is not a very satisfactory consequence for a defender of animal rights; according to this view, if I don't choose to view myself as in a relationship with animals, I am free to treat them any way I want.

I would be inclined to say that if we do have obligations toward animals, and I think we do, it is in virtue of qualities that the animals possess, for example the ability to suffer, and not in virtue of our willingness to recognize such qualities.

The claim that one must withdraw from the public sphere and retreat to the private when neglecting those to whom one is already related strikes me as a classic defense of the stereotypical role of the housewife. It tends to reinforce both self-interest and moral cowardice in the face of injustice, inequality, and suffering outside our own little worlds.

What is objectionable about all these consequences is the implication that one can choose all one's obligations. While obligations are created through voluntary commitments, this does not exhaust the possibilities. Further, Noddings's desire to thus limit our obligations is incompatible with the distinction she makes between natural and ethical caring. If one is obligated to do some ethical caring, and this involves calling upon one's ideal caring self, won't this ideal caring self feel some obligation toward animals and starving children in Africa? I'm convinced that it would, for much the same reasons that Hume thinks that the demands of justice will assert themselves after some reflection. We can come to recognize that the starving children in Africa share crucial characteristics with the children we know and love; we can see that animals share important characteristics as well. Surely, our ideal caring selves will not ignore this.

VI. LIMITATIONS ON OBLIGATIONS TO CARE

I don't think that we are obligated to be like Mother Teresa, who cares for continuously.[38] But how are we to limit our obligation to care? One strategy for limiting our obligation to care for focuses on the defenses of this obligation. First, we have a *prima facie* obligation to care for when we come across a creature in need who is unable to meet that need without help, when our caring is called upon as a part of a reciprocal relationship, or when caring is indicated as part of our role responsibility. Actual obligations rest upon the seriousness of the need, the assessment of the appropriateness of filling the need, and the ability to do something about filling it. But we must also recognize that we are persons who must be cared for and who deserve such care. The continuous caring for required to respond to needs for physical sustenance is, for most of us, incompatible with caring for ourselves. But not all caring for involves responding to physical needs. The caring for required to sustain relationships, which is usually reciprocal, can be a source of great strength to the person doing the caring for. And finally, allowing ourselves to suffer caring burnout also diminishes our ability to care for others in the future. I don't mean to argue that caring for requires no sacrifice. Indeed, where the need is great and the ability to meet it sufficient, we are required to sacrifice. But one is not required to adopt this as a form of life.

The obligation to care for is not an all-or-nothing thing. Being unable to care for now does not eliminate the possibility that one may be obligated to meet this need later. This is a general point about obligations. I might owe someone money and be unable to pay it back now, through no fault of my own. If I later come into a windfall, I am obligated to pay the money back then. In addition, there is no one right way to care for. Our assessment of the appropriateness of the need, our ability to meet the need, and our sense of the most successful way of doing so provide some guidance here. Perhaps immediate caring for is the best way to meet a need in one case, and cooperative political activity the most successful way of meeting other needs. I would want to leave these kinds of choices up to the agent.

VII. RULES AND RIGHTS

Larry Blum offers a useful taxonomy of the relation between what he calls impartialist positions and an ethic of care. He defines an impartialist position as one based on "impartiality, impersonality, justice, formal rationality, and universal principle."[39] He discusses seven different impartialist responses to an ethic of care, ranging from absolute dismissal to acceptance of an ethic of care as a subsidiary of an impartialist ethic. I want to turn the tables here and offer a defense of rules and rights in terms of care.

In my model, rules and rights serve three purposes. They can be used to persuade, to sketch a moral minimum below which no one should fall and beyond which behavior is condemned, and they can be used to deliberate in some cases.

The attention to rules and rights here does not reflect an unwillingness to make appeals to virtues and practices. I do include virtues and practices as fulfilling each of the three functions that rules and rights play in my model. We certainly can and do persuade by reminding others of virtues: "Would an honest man do that?" We likewise persuade by pointing to practices: "Native Americans don't have that kind of an attitude about the earth." Virtues and practices can serve as minimums: "I can see that you won't be doing me any favors, but at least give me the courtesy of a honest reply."

We don't live in a caring world. By that I mean that not everyone recognizes his or her obligation to care. Our society does not encourage the flourishing of this capacity, but undermines it in various ways. In a world notable for its lack of caring, we need tools of persuasion to protect the helpless. This is one of the roles that rules and rights fill. We can reason in the language of rules with those who lack a sufficient degree of caring. If their natural sympathies are not engaged by the presence of suffering, we can attempt to appeal to reason: How would you want to be treated if you were in their place? What would be the consequences of such behavior on a large scale? I am not convinced of the effect of such persuasion, and it is, I think, an empirical question whether such appeals would persuade where caring did not, but I suspect that such socially agreed upon minimums could serve as persuasive appeals.

Rules and rights provide a minimum below which no one should fall and beyond which behavior is morally condemned. Rules provide a minimum standard for morality. Rights provide a measure of protection for the helpless. But, on this level of moral discourse, morality is, like politics, the art of the possible. In the face of large-scale selfishness and inattention, perhaps the best we can hope for is a minimum below which no one should fall and beyond which behavior is roundly condemned. But we should not fool ourselves into thinking that staying above this minimum is a sufficient condition for being a morally decent person. I don't want to deny the importance of these socially agreed upon minimums; in a less than perfect world, they provide some real protection. They are not, in principle, incompatible with caring, but can, I think, encourage caring. Much caring requires collective action, and without a shared sense of moral minimums it will be difficult to organize such collective action.

Elizabeth Wolgast, in *The Grammar of Justice*, argues against the view that treating patients in a moral fashion is entirely a matter of respecting their rights.[40] She points out that patients are often sick and in need of care. In this situation, she argues, we want doctors and other health care workers to care for the patient. This involves far more than respecting rights. One could talk, I suppose, about a patient's right to be cared for, but, as Wolgast points out, rights talk suggests a minimum below which the doctor should not fall, and in this case, we are less interested in the minimum than in the maximum. We want all our moral citizens to be open to the obligation to care for.

Rules and rights can also be used to deliberate under some conditions. Often we don't need to appeal to rules in deciding whom to care for and how to care for them. A creature's need and our ability to meet it identifies it as a candidate for caring for. We decide how to care for by appeal to the need, the strategies for meeting it, and the desires of the one in need about how best to meet the need. But when we are not in direct contact with the objects of care, our actions cannot be guided by the expressed and observed desires of those cared for, and hence we might want to appeal to rules. In these cases, we must make assumptions about their desires, and we can assume that they do not wish to fall below some minimum. Rules that provide a minimum standard for acceptable behavior ought to be sensitive to the general desires and aims of creatures, so we may take these into consideration.

In some cases, we might be justified in appealing to our needs for care and on that basis decide that we do not wish to violate some socially approved minimum standard of behavior. Suppose, for example, that I think that you want me to lie to you and I also think that it would be better for you if I did lie. But we have an audience, and I know that our audience would disapprove of my lying. Am I justified in telling the truth? (One of the virtues of an ethic of care is that it allows us to frame this question.) It seems to me that it depends on how you and I will be affected by the lie, but the existence of a social rule about honesty can be taken into consideration.

We might also appeal to rules and rights when care must be allocated. For example, in a hospital emergency room we must make sure that the needs of the first accident victim of the night do not cause us to ignore the later victims. I will return to this example in Chapter Five.

Finally, since rules and rights can express a consensus about morally acceptable behavior, we should be sensitive to the expectations generated in the one cared for by the public recognition of such rules and rights. For example, suppose I want to make sure that my family and friends are happy and involved in the wedding of my son. I might be tempted to ignore the rules of etiquette in making sure that my guests are uniquely provided for. But if the mother of the bride feels slighted because I didn't treat her the way she expected to be treated (i.e., as the etiquette rules say you should treat the mother of the bride), then I haven't really responded to her in a caring manner.

One might argue here that meeting some expressed needs might violate the moral minimums in our society. I am willing to grant that this can happen. If it does, we must remember that the rules do not have a life of their own, but are guides. They help us to formulate a caring response because they speak to us of what most of us would want as a caring response in a similar situation. If the one needing care does not want the response suggested by the appropriate rule, we should listen to them very carefully and be willing to ignore the rule. For example, suppose someone wanted us to help him/her commit suicide. I suspect that ideally we could and should settle this kind of a case without appealing to rules. Instead, we should appeal to the facts of the case. Is the person terminally ill or merely depressed? These conditions require different remedies. In the first case, one might be doing the right thing by aiding in the suicide. Here one must count the cost to oneself, as well as the needs and desires of the one cared for. In the second case, we appeal beyond the expressed needs to the unexpressed needs. This person probably needs some other care. Here we make every attempt to listen to this person, to understand his or her pain, but we also remind ourselves that suicide is the final option for dealing with pain. We make this decision, not by appeal to a rule, but by reminding ourselves of the times when we or someone we know came close to suicide. We remember how it felt and how it was resolved.

In some cases, though, we cannot respond as one caring. As we approach caring burnout, we appeal to rules and rights. We do not want our behavior to fall below some minimum standard, nor do we want the one in need of care to fall below some moral minimum.

In the ideal caring society with sufficient resources to meet needs and to provide for some sort of flourishing, each of us would spend roughly the same amount of time being cared for. We would experience this as children and as adults. Hence, we would be surrounded by a nexus of caring. We would be persons who cared for and were supported by a history of being cared for. We would be free, to some extent, to choose whom to care for because there would be others to provide for needs and for flourishing. We would not be totally free, because social roles would commit us to some responsibilities to care. It is not clear that rules and rights would play a very big part in this world, but this is certainly not the world in which we live.

The people in our world differ in their ability and their willingness to care for others. Since I am both a creature who can care and who needs care, I would, if I were committed to caring, be faced with enormous needs for care while sometimes suffering from a lack of caring for myself. This is true even if we grant that the kind of caring (in particular, psychological caring) involved in reciprocal relationships sustains all parties in the relationship. But since such relationships don't come easily and naturally, I would have to spend some time and energy establishing a nexus of care to support myself. In creating and maintaining this nexus of care, I would be developing bonds and responsibilities of care.

But spending much of one's time getting one's own needs for care satisfied leaves little time for caring for others. At the same time, everyone else is in much the same boat, and the gross inequality in the distribution of resources means that many slip between the caring cracks and into dire need. This puts the caring person in a bind. Real need presents itself to a person who is often running a caring deficit of his or her own. Caring burnout results. The only way to effectively reduce caring burnout is to change cultural and social institutions toward a model of caring. This is not the path that our culture has taken. Instead we careen from me-first philosophies to paroxysms of guilt about the tremendous needs that have resulted. We make renewed commitments to care which are rejected as soft-headed a generation later.

What are caring persons to do? Caring persons should try to respond to need by caring for, but they must pay attention to their own needs for care. They must navigate through an uncaring world without falling into total caring burnout. They should work for institutions, cultures, and practices that would reduce subsistence needs by redistributing resources and increasing the supply of caretakers, and they should encourage social change toward a culture of reciprocity in meeting psychological needs. But while struggling in our pre-caring world, caring persons are not obligated to continue caring until they slip into caring burnout. This denies their own status as persons who deserve care and is counterproductive, and it diminishes, in the long run, the amount of care they can provide. As they approach caring burnout, they should refill their care tanks by taking care of their own needs. During this period of renewal, they are still required to respect the moral minimums represented by rules and rights.

I want to look now at Nel Noddings's claim that an ethic of care cannot make any appeal to rules. Clearly, she does not want to enrich traditional ethical theory with an account of caring; she wants to supplant it and thus argues that we must reject all rule-based ethical theories. Noddings offers three separate arguments, which I will examine in turn. The first argument looks like this:

1. Rule-based ethical theories require moral rules that are universalizable.
2. In order to accept the principle of universalizability, we must establish that human predicaments exhibit sufficient sameness.
3. We can only establish that human predicaments exhibit sufficient sameness by abstracting away those qualities that reveal the sameness.
4. If we abstract away the qualities that reveal the sameness, the situation no longer seems to reveal a moral question.[41]

I have filled in the gaps in this argument by adding the following claims:

5. Therefore, moral rules cannot be universalizable.
6. Therefore, rule-based ethical theories must either reject universalizability or be rejected.
7. But universalizability is the only criterion that distinguishes moral rules from nonmoral rules.

8. Therefore, without universalizability, rule-based moral theories are not moral theories at all.

9. Therefore, we must reject rule-based moral theories.

This argument depends upon premise three. Seyla Benhabib makes an even stronger claim, that, in the absence of the particularity of the moral situation, no rule could ever be applied since we wouldn't know what kind of a situation we are dealing with.[42] I'm not convinced that premise three is right. Consider the following two examples. Mary is told a malicious lie on Friday. "The company is going out of business. You're out of a job." Mary has worked hard for this job, very much wants to keep it, and there are no companies in the area that do similar work. Mary is committed to the area, loves her job, and needs the money. On Monday, Mary finds out that it was a lie. John is told on Friday by a malicious technician that the results of his wife's amniocentesis are that the baby has a neural tube defect. This is their first baby, and they both want the baby. They are in their mid-forties and fear that it would be extremely hard to have another one. On Monday, John finds out that it was a malicious lie.

What do we abstract away to uncover the similarities between these cases? Specifics such as who told the lie and the precise consequences of the lie, etc., would be abstracted away. What's left is that it was a deliberate lie and that suffering was caused by the belief that a heartfelt desire was to be thwarted. But these are just the qualities that make these moral situations.

Her second argument is the following:

1. To care is to act out of affection and regard.

2. If I am acting out of affection and regard, my actions will be unpredictable because they will spring from engrossment in a particular person, in a particular situation.

3. If I am acting by appeal to rules, my behavior would be predictable.

4. Therefore, to care is to reject an appeal to rules.[43]

What could premise two mean? The following interpretations suggest themselves: (a) an outsider wouldn't be able to predict my actions because she would lack knowledge of the individual and the situation; (b) I would be unable to predict my future actions because I do not now have knowledge of the situation.

But both of these claims are true about rule-based action as well. How can I or an observer know what rule I will apply if I don't yet know the situation?

The last argument is:

1. Caring requires an engrossment in the one cared for and a desire to help the one cared for.

2. Rule-based moral reasoning shifts our focus away from the particular individual and toward an abstract problem.

3. When we turn our attention away from a particular individual, self-interest may tempt us to rationalize the situation in a way that ignores the needs of the particular individual.[44]

This argument turns upon claim three, but three says only that self-interest may allow us to misapply the rules. This is not necessarily a criticism of rule-based ethical theories unless the temptation exists only for rule-based ethical theories. But self-interest may tempt us to do what is in the interest of the one most cared for when there is a conflict, so the care model can also be subverted by self-interest.

I have other reservations about rule-based moral reasoning that I discussed in Chapters One and Two, but here I would support a version of this argument with an amended third premise:

3. When we focus our attention primarily on rules, we fail to see the complexity of the moral situation. This can result in our doing harm to others involved in the situation.

There are two worries here. One is that the commitment to the impartialist position is incompatible with a strong degree of empathy. This is, in part, an empirical claim, which Alfred Bloom shed some light on in a study of the inclination to adopt impartialist or empathic responses. He concluded that "there was a very weak correlation between inclination to assume an autonomous stance and level of empathic response."[45] Empathy was most closely associated with a strongly supportive emotional environment in childhood. Obviously, this does not show that it is impossible to be both empathic and impartialist, but it does show that the commitment to the impartialist position does not guarantee empathy. The second worry is that even if one is both empathic and committed to the impartialist position, the commitment to principle undermines the motivation to take a close look at the situation. This is so because it doesn't really matter what the details are if you have already decided to follow your principles no matter what. You only need enough detail to tell which principle obtains. At this point, both Noddings and Benhabib would respond that it is impossible to tell which principle obtains unless we already take a very detailed look at the situation, but as I argued earlier, I think they are wrong about this.

I think that we can construct a sympathetic account of Noddings's theory

which will allow us to avoid this last criticism as well as the three consequences mentioned earlier (that if we adopt her caring perspective we
cannot care about strangers or animals). Her theory can be seen as an
attempt to describe the moral perspective. A rule-based moral theory
would tell us to make moral decisions by seeing which rule applies and
applying it. A perspectivist theory would say that we should instead adopt
a particular perspective and see what kind of a decision would emerge
from that perspective. Noddings suggests that we adopt the perspective
of the ideal caring self. When we are confronted with a moral decision,
we recall that self and ask ourselves what that self would do in this situation. Notice that we ought to be able to adopt this perspective even if
we are dealing with strangers or animals. We simply remind ourselves
how we would act if we were our ideal caring selves dealing with a cared
for one. Hence, this theory does not require, as Noddings thinks it does,
that we are in an ongoing caring relationship with the object of our moral
deliberation. Adopting this perspective in all cases, whether they involve
friends or strangers, would make this perspective less likely to lead to self-
interested decisions.

This strategy, interestingly enough, resembles the position taken by neo-
Kantians such as Barbara Herman and Marcia Baron who see the categorical imperative as a test for maxims rather than a strategy for developing
maxims which are then to be applied without exception.[46] I agree that this
is a more sympathetic rendering of Kant, though I doubt that he would
have much sympathy for it. In any case, it is not clear to me how testing
the maxim of my action at the moment of deliberation is very different
from stopping and adopting a particular perspective, since it is not clear
to me what role the maxim is serving here.

I think that we could simply conceive our maxims as rules of thumb
which are based on sentiment and past experience and which require constant
reevaluation. I agree with Noddings that we should not allow our attention to maxims to become rule fetishism, but should appeal to them only
when our moral imagination flags.

Some have argued that unless rules have some priority over care, we
won't know what kind of caring is appropriate. As Barbara Houston puts
it:

> The philosophical point here is simply that if we stick to a formal account of
> caring, then we have no way to rule out undesirable caring relations. We must
> appeal to other values to keep caring morally decent. Caring is not an ethic that
> can stand alone.[47]

Onora O'Neill makes a similar point:

> To show love or concern to others, or to maintain loyalty and fidelity is not just
> a matter of responding to the particularities of situations in some way or another

(villains may do that!), but of responding to those particularities in a principled way.[48]

I agree with Houston and O'Neill that defective caring can occur. I do not think, though, that we need to appeal to rules to tell us which is the appropriate care. In the first place, we would have the same problem with the rules: How do we tell which are the right rules? I think we can judge an instance of care by appeal to our ideal of caring. Here, we can look to Noddings's ideal caring self and to my ideal of a caring world.

Owen Flanagan and Kathryn Jackson offer a different criticism of the priority of care over rules.

Imagine someone who sees the problem of repaying foreign loans as an issue of love between nations; or a mother who construes all positive interactions with her children as something they are owed.[49]

Virginia Held makes a similar point.[50] The point here is that there are some settings in which care is appropriate and other settings in which rules should prevail. Although I agree about the example of the mother, I disagree about the example of nations. We should see the problem of repaying foreign loans as an issue of love, though not between nations. Thinking of it as an issue between nations blinds us to the reality that real persons are affected. Instead, we should understand the consequences of repaying or not repaying foreign loans on real persons. Consider the budget deficit of the United States, for example. If we think of it abstractly, merely in terms of obeying the appropriate rules, we wouldn't hesitate to say that we should pay the debts of the United States, especially if we conflate foreign banks with foreign nations. But let us reconceive this in terms of the people who would be getting the payment and the people who would be making the payments. The debtors in this case are the taxpayers. Since the bulk of taxes are paid by poor and middle-class taxpayers, the debtors are mostly poor or middle class. The holders of the bonds, on the other hand, are most often wealthy (those who would benefit from tax-exempt returns) and often wealthy foreign nationals. If the United States slides into a serious recession, the idea of writing off some of our government obligations doesn't sound so bad. The alternative would be to increase the disparity between rich and poor at a time when being poor has disastrous consequences. Imagine now the situation for some desperate debtor countries, tempted to borrow cheap dollars and forced to repay with expensive dollars.

Notice how differently we think about this case when we reconceive it in terms of an ethic of care. I think this example supports Noddings's claim that conceiving situations in terms of abstract principles blinds us to morally relevant facts.

My conclusion about rules is that appealing to moral rules, where moral rules are seen as rules of thumb, is morally acceptable in the following cases: to create socially recognized moral minimums, to respond to the expectations of others where such expectations are colored by moral rules, and where moral attention flags, for reasons which are beyond our control.

I have not yet talked about what the rules and rights should be. In drafting a set of rules and rights, I should be sensitive to two considerations. The first is that rules and rights provide a moral minimum. The second is that rules and rights reflect a consensus about moral minimums. In this sense, morality is the art of the possible.

The morally preferred way to live is to appeal to caring. This suggests that rules and rights should reflect a sense of what counts as need, a conception of flourishing, and a recognition of what would usually be accepted, by the ones cared for, as appropriate ways of responding to need and providing for flourishing. Notions of need and flourishing ought to be sensitive to empirical considerations, about human nature, interaction, social organization, etc., but they also have an irreducible normative component. A defense of rules and rights would need to defend this normative component. We would also want rules and rights that would provide a climate for moral growth toward a caring society.

Rules and rights do play an important role in my ethics of caring, but we should not forget that our primary responsibility is to care for. If this means that we are often unsure about just what to do, then we must live with this uncertainty. Discovering what to do requires that we listen carefully to the ones cared for. We should also recognize that it is often painful to be confronted by those in need, and even by those whom we could enrich. Appealing to rules provides a measure of security for ourselves, but we should not allow it to distance us from the objects of care.

VIII.   CARING AND OTHER ETHICAL THEORIES

As I argued in Chapter Two, caring as I describe it is not an ethical theory in any full-blown sense. I have just now argued that it is not an ethical theory in the sense of a set of rules to be rigidly applied. Still, one might wonder if it could be compared to virtue theory or what I call perspectivism.

Hume's influence is broad and obvious. I have adopted both his picture of what a moral philosophy should be (the art of suggesting and testing moral strategies in light of our real world experience) and his conviction that humans have a capacity for care and that this capacity explains the force morality has for humans (and perhaps other animals).

One might think that I am simply defending virtue ethics, but I don't believe so. Virtue ethics require that the virtue not enter into the deliberations of the virtuous person. The brave person does not do an act because it is the act that would be chosen by a brave person. She does it because she thinks it is the right thing to do and because she is more interested in the rightness of the act than the personal consequences of doing so. In Noddings's and my view, caring does and must enter into the deliberation of the caring person. The caring person must sometimes ask herself what her ideal caring self would do in the situation. Still, an ethic of care has much in common with virtue theory. They both emphasize the importance of habit and inclination. Neither pretends to provide a calculus for moral decision making; rather they insist that the context coupled with the character of the actor and some general rules of thumb will provide all the cues.

Nietzsche offers a model that is similar in some respects to an ethic of care. Both Nietzsche and an ethic of care suggest that we answer questions about how to live our lives by taking a particular perspective. He advocates taking an "eternal recurrence" perspective.[51] He invites us to imagine living our lives over and over again, eternally. We can then ask ourselves, "If I were to live this moment over, eternally, what would I have wanted to do?" An ethic of care invites us to take the perspective of our ideal caring selves. Both views share with the virtue tradition the belief that the ideal moral agent should internalize this perspective to a certain extent so that one's actions flow naturally from a settled disposition. Nietzsche's view is broader than an ethic of care because he is concerned with how we live our lives and not just how we make moral decisions.

The next ethic I wish to consider is the land ethic, first described by Aldo Leopold and recently elaborated and defended by J. Baird Callicott.[52] As Leopold puts it, "A thing is right when it tends to preserve the integrity, stability, and beauty of the biotic community. It is wrong when it tends otherwise."[53] An ethic of care is similar to a land ethic in two ways. First, they are both holistic ethics; second, they share a commitment to the sacredness of the natural world.

A land ethic is holistic in the following sense: the good of any part is defined in terms of the good of the whole. Callicott draws many implications from this view, one being that right now humans are a blight upon the earth because they are squeezing out other species. The land ethic's commitment to the sacredness of the natural world is shown by this definition of the good in terms of what is good for the whole, the whole being the natural world.

An ethic of care is holistic in two ways. First, it recognizes that we are embedded in connections of care and that our self-identity is, in large part, a function of our role in these complex interconnections. In this sense, we see ourselves as part of a larger whole, and inseparable from this whole. An ethic of care, as I conceive it, is holistic in a larger sense as well. It assumes an underlying picture of the earth as one body, and of ourselves as part of this body. It sees an attitude of awe as the appropriate response to the recognition that we are part of this sacred body. Not every version of an ethic of care need be holistic in this second sense. Nel Noddings, for example, is not committed to this. But I think it allows us to escape from the parochialism of an ethic of care that is grounded only in human attachments.

So, while both ethics are holistic, they are holistic in different ways. There is a second way in which they differ. A land ethic, as Callicott describes it, is indifferent to the value that humans put on other humans and certain animals.

Both a land ethic and an ethic of care are ethics for and from the perspective of humans. In this sense, neither can escape from human psychology. If an ethic is seen as providing guidance for living a good human life, then we must recognize important features of human psychology—the attachments of humans to other humans and certain animals, for example. While Callicott tries to ignore this, an ethic of care takes it as central.

IX. CONCLUSION

An ethic of care has many advantages. It allows us to reconceptualize, and thereby better understand, many moral quandaries, such as that of the porcupine and the moles. It strikes many, and women in particular, as a truer picture of their own moral intuitions. It assumes a theory of human nature that is an improvement upon abstract individualism. It generates a theory of moral education which focuses on the enhancement of the capacity to care. Finally, and most importantly, it might, if widely adopted, make the world a better place.

NOTES

1. Nel Noddings, *Caring: A Feminine Approach to Ethics and Moral Education* (Berkeley: University of California Press, 1984).

2. Hume argued that the task of moral philosophy ought to be to look reflectively at actual moral practice. This conception also can be seen, though to a

lesser extent, in Aristotle, and in Alasdair MacIntyre, *After Virtue* (Notre Dame, Ind.: University of Notre Dame Press, 1981).

3. Annette Baier argues forcefully that we should pay exclusive attention to reforming current moral practices. See *Postures of the Mind: Essays on Mind and Morals*, especially chapters 11–15 (Minneapolis: University of Minnesota Press, 1985).

4. Carol Gilligan, *In a Different Voice* (Cambridge, Mass.: Harvard University Press, 1982).

5. Marilyn Friedman and Margaret Urban Walker point out that there are two separate theses in Gilligan: that care and responsibility moral reasoning is extremely sensitive to context and that the appropriate response is care and responsibility. See Marilyn Friedman, "Care and Context in Moral Reasoning," in Eva Kittay and Diana Meyers, eds., *Women and Moral Theory* (Totowa, N.J.: Rowman and Littlefield, 1987) and Margaret Urban Walker, "What Does the Different Voice Say?: Gilligan's Women and Moral Philosophy," *The Journal of Value Inquiry* 23 (1989): 123–34.

6. Starhawk, *Dreaming the Dark* (Boston: Beacon Press, 1989) 44.

7. Richard Schubert, one of my creative and courageous colleagues, gives such assignments.

8. See my "The Random Collective as a Moral Agent" for a further discussion of collective action and obligation. *Social Theory and Practice* 11 (Spring 1985): 97–105.

9. Alasdair McIntyre, following Aristotle, made much of this notion of role responsibility. See *After Virtue*. See also Virginia Held, *Rights and Goods* (New York: The Free Press, 1984).

10. Noddings makes much of the requirement that caring requires an ongoing relationship. It is on this basis that she denies that we can have an obligation to care for the starving children in Africa, and animals. In an October 1988 talk to the Society for Women in Philosophy, she allowed that caring for does not exhaust our obligations, so we could have other obligations to the starving children in Africa. I would prefer to say that we have obligations to care for the starving children and animals, but that not all caring obligations require direct care.

11. MacIntyre, *After Virtue*, 105.

12. We can see how one would defend morality by appeal to divine law, and why such an appeal might fail. The *Meno* is a good example of such an appeal.

13. Karl Marx, "On the Jewish Question," in T. B. Bottomore, ed., *Karl Marx: Early Writings* (New York: McGraw Hill, 1964).

14. Elizabeth Wolgast, *The Grammar of Justice* (Ithaca, N.Y.: Cornell University Press, 1987), chap. 1.

15. Alison Jaggar, *Feminist Politics and Human Nature* (Totowa, N.J.: Rowman & Allanheld, 1983) throughout, but see Chapter Three.

16. Ibid.

17. Noddings, *Caring*, 174.

18. Ibid., 104.

19. David Hume, *An Enquiry Concerning the Principles of Morals*, sect. 3, L. A. Selby-Biggs, ed., (Oxford: Oxford University Press, 1962); *A Treatise on*

Human Nature, bk. 3, pt. 20, L. A. Selby- Biggs, ed. (Oxford: Oxford University Press, 1964).

20. Noddings, *Caring*, chap. 4.

21. Martha Nussbaum, "Finely Aware and Richly Responsible: Literature and the Moral Imagination," *The Journal of Philosophy* 82 (1985): 516–29.

22. Peter Singer, *Practical Ethics* (Cambridge: Cambridge University Press, 1979), 168.

23. This analysis is from Milton Mayeroff, *On Caring* (New York: Perennial Library, 1971).

24. Noddings, *Caring*, 14.

25. Ibid., 24.

26. Ibid., 86.

27. Ibid.

28. Ibid.

29. Ibid.

30. Ibid., 87.

31. Ibid., 89.

32. Noddings has since given up these consequences. See her response to critics, "A Response," *Hypatia* 5 (1990): 120–26.

33. Noddings, *Caring*, 86.

34. Ibid., 87.

35. Ibid.

36. Ibid.

37. For other discussions of abortion from the perspective of an ethic of care, see Janet Smith, "Abortion and Moral Development Theory: Listening with Different Ears," *International Philosophical Quarterly* 28 (1988): 31–51 and Celia Wolf-Devine, "Abortion and the 'Feminine Voice'," *Public Affairs Quarterly*, 3 (1989): 81–97.

38. The inappropriateness of slavish caring has long been a theme in feminist thought. Betty Friedan called thinking that one's role in life requires such caring "the problem that has no name." See *The Feminine Mystique* (New York: Dell Publishing Co., 1963).

39. Lawrence A. Blum, "Gilligan and Kohlberg: Implications for Moral Theory," *Ethics* 98 (April 1988): 472–91.

40. See Elizabeth Wolgast, *The Grammar of Justice*, chap. 3.

41. I reconstructed these arguments from comments that Noddings makes throughout, but especially in chapters one and two.

42. Seyla Benhabib, "The Generalized and the Concrete Other: The Kohlberg-Gilligan Controversy and Feminist Theory," *Praxis International*, 5 (January 1986): 402–24.

43. Noddings, *Caring*, chaps. 1 and 2.

44. Ibid.

45. Alfred H. Bloom, "Psychological Ingredients of High-Level Moral Thinking," *Journal for the Theory of Social Behavior* 16 (March 1986): 89–103.

46. Barbara Herman, "Integrity and Impartiality," *Monist* 66 (1983): 233–50; Marcia Baron, "The Alleged Repugnance of Acting from Duty," *Inquiry* 26 (1984): 387–405.

47. Barbara Houston, "Caring and Exploitation," *Hypatia* 5 (1990): 115–19.

48. Onora O'Neill, "Virtuous Lives and Just Societies," *Journal of Social Philosophy*, 20 (1989): 25–30.

49. Owen Flanagan and Kathyrn Jackson, "Justice, Care, and Gender: The Kohlberg-Gilligan Debate Revisited," *Ethics* 97 (1987): 622–37.

50. Held, *Rights and Goods*.

51. While I am inclined to see eternal recurrence as a normative principle, others have interpreted it differently. Bernd Magnus, for example, sees it as a description of a certain attitude, the attitude that an Ubermensch would take toward life. See *Nietzsche's Existential Imperative* (Indianapolis: Indiana University Press, 1978).

52. J. Baird Callicott, *In Defense of the Land Ethic* (Albany: State University of New York Press, 1989).

53. Aldo Leopold, *A Sand Country Almanac* (New York: Oxford University Press, 1949), 224–25.

Chapter Five

Caring for Persons

We have seen in Chapter Four that there are two important dimensions of an ethic of care. The first is methodological: an ethic of care is not an appeal to abstract principles but to the use of our moral imaginations, where our attention to the particulars of a situation is infused by our involved concern about the other(s). The second is substantive: while the practice involves moral imagination, this moral imagination is directed by a concern to advance the good of the other(s) in the context of a network of care.

An ethic of care takes as morally significant and morally problematic practices, attitudes, beliefs, and actions that rule-based accounts have often seen as marginal or insignificant. Kohlberg, for example, concedes that Gilligan has correctly identified relationships as a particular concern of women and girls, but argues that questions about relationships are not properly moral questions.[1] Second, whether it directs its attention to issues traditionally excluded from moral discourse or issues seen as morally weighty, the caring eye attends differently than the eye of traditional impartialist accounts of morality.

We see this in the examples I have chosen to discuss here.[2] Caring for children, for example, has received precious little attention from philosophers in large part because it was seen as morally and philosophically unproblematic, in addition to being seen as women's work. But even when the subject *is* broached (in Plato's *Republic*, for example), we see vague generalizations about child-rearing, but no discussion of how to care for individual children in a particular social context and little attention to the interests of the children themselves. I try to address this lack. I also hope to illustrate the focus of an ethic of care: the details that are

89

morally significant differ from those that are seen as foreground in impartialist accounts.

Finally, I hope my examples will help us to arrive at something like a wide reflective equilibrium between our moral intuitions and the commitment of an ethic of care.

I should say at the outset that I think that there are many kinds of caring relationships, and they differ in significant ways. But I suspect that an ethic of care as expressed in all caring relationships will have a shared core: an understanding of the situation of the other and a commitment to the good of the other, a recognition by the carer of the relationship between the carer and the cared for, and a commitment to an ideal of caring.[3]

In this chapter, I propose to examine caring in several different contexts. The first is interacting with children. The second involves caring for those either totally or relatively helpless. The third explores caring in the context of mentoring relationships characterized by differences in power. The fourth looks at caring between peers. Finally, I will look at caring in situations of conflict. This is certainly not an exhaustive list, but a set of what I take to be interesting and challenging illustrations of an ethic of care.

I. PARENTING: CARING FOR CHILDREN

Though parenting is one of the most morally significant experiences most of us will ever have, philosophers have had surprisingly little to say about it.[4] It is morally significant in two ways: one, because the potential for benefiting or harming our children is so great, and two, because our influence on our children's moral development is so profound.

I want to begin my discussion of parenting with two caveats. First, it is very difficult to say what is good and bad, or as I shall say, caring and uncaring parenting. Second, there is no one style of caring parenting; rather, one can be a caring parent within a wide variety of parenting styles. Still, in spite of this, there are some general guidelines.

Let me explain the first point. Child-rearing practices are deeply embedded in our social fabric. Most parents are unreflective about child-rearing and manuals of child-rearing are notoriously sensitive to social agendas, though they pretend to offer objective advice about the best way to raise children. Michel Foucault points out, for example, that the turn to therapeutic language and practice in child-rearing shared with the penal system the goal of more carefully and systematically disciplining people, creating the kind of children who would best fit in our world.[5]

But children must always grow up to live in a world not of their making. The role of the parent includes outfitting them for the task. Here we have two almost inevitably incompatible goals: to help them to fit in and thus survive, and to encourage them to fight for social change.

Before turning to a discussion of general guidelines for caring parenting, I want to discuss abuse briefly. Later in this chapter I will offer an analysis of partner (usually spouse) battering. The case for children is much worse. Adults are more likely to have a conception of what is appropriate behavior; they are more likely to enter relationships with some understanding of their own worth and what they can legitimately expect from their partners.[6] But children, especially very young children, have no independent sense of self; their only sense of self comes from their interactions with adults.[7] If their primary interaction is with abusive adults, they come to see themselves as deserving the abuse. And children are largely defenseless against abuse; even if they understood that they didn't deserve the abuse, they wouldn't know how to get help. So abused children are denied care and, at the same time, their developing sense of self is severely undermined.

I turn now to more ordinary ways of failing to care for children. Though styles of child-rearing differ greatly across culture and class, I shall limit this discussion to two common patterns of child-rearing. The first is the style of parenting that prevailed in my neighborhood when I was growing up, a relatively stable, mostly Irish Catholic, working-class neighborhood. In many of these families, the withholding of affection and sympathy is seen as normal. Most people are fairly inarticulate and unreflective about child-rearing, but if pushed, parents of this school would probably point to the consequences of "babying." How will the child learn to live in a basically hostile world if he/she is babied at home? The job of the parent is to toughen children up.

Along with this refusal to baby children goes a habit of belittling them when they are getting too big for their britches. Where verbal criticism did not suffice, physical punishment is often seen as the cure.

While I was growing up in the get-tough school, many of my friends were being shaped in the image of their parents. They worried about grades, about how they looked, about whether their parents would be disappointed if they did not get into the right college. Belittling was not unknown in these households, but the motivation was different; it was not done to puncture a puffed-up ego but to motivate the child to do what the parent wanted, and it was often coupled with a withdrawal of affection.

Alice Miller has written at great length about the problems of the second style of child-rearing; she argues that it creates a child who has little sense of his/her own needs and desires because he/she is so preoccupied with the needs and desires of his/her parents.[8] The first style of parenting too often results in children with a fragile sense of their own ability and worth.

I have described the worst cases of each style here, though I admit that there are variations on each theme. Both styles flourish in our society in part because they respond to social "manpower" needs: the first provides docile grunt workers; the second fills the ranks of middle managers.[9] But parents are not motivated solely by the desire to fill society's needs; most parents are concerned to do what is best for their children. Parenting styles survive because they fill social needs, and are adopted because they were deeply imprinted on generations of children who later became parents. Both styles of parenting allow for variations that could be described as motivated by an ethic of care, though I think that our social context limits our ability to be truly caring parents. Working-class parents do need to toughen their children up. Middle-class parents must inculcate attitudes and habits that impinge on self-expression if their children are to remain members of this class.[10]

I have sketched, then, two common ways in which we can fail to be genuinely caring parents. What does this tell us about how to succeed? First, we must recognize that there is no one right way to parent; our children will live in very different worlds, and we must do what we can to help them to survive.[11] Second, we must also recognize our commitments to an ideal of caring and to the other members of society. This requires that we try to raise our children to resist evil and to recognize their obligations to be caring persons.

Third, as Sara Ruddick argues, parenting should be governed by an interest in the "preservation, growth and acceptability" of children.[12] I agree with Ruddick, though I have some reservations about acceptability, which I will discuss shortly. Children are entrusted to our care, not by God, but by social institutions. In our society, with little support for children, parents are completely responsible for their children. If they are to grow up at all, it requires a great commitment on the part of their parents. (I am not restricting "parent" here to biological mother or father, but to those who are recognized by law as responsible for the child.) Parents of a healthy white infant can give up this responsibility by giving the child up for adoption, but parents of a child of color, of an older child, of a child with some disability, are often the only thing that stands between the child and the grave. Unfortunately, this is only a slight exaggeration. With this stark reality in mind, most parents see that their first duty to the child is seeing to its survival.

Seeing to the growth of a child is far more complicated. A child grows toward an ideal: committed, caring, connected, yet autonomous and self-reliant. It is not enough to understand what the child's immediate desires are and satisfy them, because doing so might undermine his/her growth. In satisfying and in thwarting desires, one must be sensitive to the child's possibilities. One should allow the child to develop a full range of potentialities and interests along with the capacity and will to actualize them, while at the same time helping the child to grow in emotional depth and relatedness to others.

But, in seeing to a child's growth, we are not technocrats; rather we should be devoted to this growth. As Milton Mayeroff puts it,

> This, then, is the basic pattern of caring, understood as helping the other grow: I experience the other as an extension of myself and also as independent and with the need to grow; I experience the other's development as bound up with my own sense of well-being; and I feel needed by it for that growing. I respond affirmatively and with devotion to the other's need, guided by the direction of its growth.[13]

In helping the child grow in relatedness to others, we must help the child to develop a sense of her interconnection with others while at the same time helping her to develop a full range of potentialities and interests. Amelia Rudolph, a choreographer, uses a weight-balancing improvisational dance both as a metaphor for this balancing and as a strategy for teaching it. In this dance, the two partners must stay connected at all times, alternating between the role of leader and follower, while they shift their weight back and forth. First, I lean on my partner, later my partner leans on me. The improvisation continues until we no longer are conscious of who is leading and who is following. At this point, we have achieved what Rudolph describes as a balance between assertion and receptivity.[14]

Nel Noddings offers a further description of how to teach receptivity to children. First, we must care for the child. Without a ground of being cared for, no child can grow into a caring adult. But if the child has had the experience of being cared for, we can encourage the growth toward receptivity by continuing a dialogue with the child. In this dialogue, we share with the child our own feelings and experiences of receptivity and caring. Next, we must offer them opportunities to practice receptivity and care. Finally, we must always attribute to the child the best possible motive, a motive compatible with receptivity and care.[15]

If seeing to the growth of the child is not hard enough, Ruddick argues that we must also work toward a second goal which is often, in practice, incompatible with the first—that of making the child acceptable. This might be seen as in the best interest of the child, since a child who does not fit in, even if filled with the sense of self-esteem based on a recognition of his/her own abilities and talents, will not be a happy child. Still, why should we ask our child to fit into a society that is unkind? Should we encourage our gay child to pretend an interest in the opposite sex simply to satisfy a homophobic society? I have a second concern about accept-ability and that is that even if it were in the interests of the child to fit in, it might not be in the interest of other members of society. Suppose, for example, I live in a racist society. Should I encourage my white child to scorn children of color?

I would prefer to see our parental practice guided by two goals: re-sponding to the interests of the child, developed insofar as they can be by the child, and responding to the moral demands of the society in which our child will live. I don't mean to suggest that we should accept the conventional demands of our society. Rather, our social critique should be guided by our ideal of caring. Where these two goals are in conflict, we must do some balancing.

II. CARING FOR THE HELPLESS

As children grow, they become more able to do for themselves. It is a happy coincidence that this emerging self-reliance is both good for their growth and compatible with the goal of accommodating everyone's inter-ests, since most parents are not interested in spending their lives caring for totally helpless creatures.

But infants are totally helpless creatures, and unfortunately, some adults are totally helpless as well. How can we best care for them? I think that in both cases, we should be guided by a sense of what is in their best interest. We know that most infants will grow up to be healthy adults with their own projects, connections, and so on. Our care of infants, even when they are totally helpless, is geared toward encouraging this growth. As we come to know more and more about infant capacities and development, it is clear that this growth can be influenced, either positively or nega-tively, at a very early age, and this recognition puts more pressure on today's parents.[16]

The care of helpless adults is much more difficult. I shall begin this discussion by telling two stories, one about my grandfather and one about a friend's father.

My grandfather lived to be eighty-seven and was never sick until the last year of his life. Even when he was in good health, he worried about his last days; he was afraid he would end up in a rest home. When he became ill, he made me promise that we would not put him in a rest home, that I would let him come and live with me if my grandmother was unable to care for him. He never did come to live with me, he went instead to a rest home, and his last days were not happy ones as he faded from life, and from our lives.

I would like to think that I would act differently if I had it to do over again, and I think an ethic of care would require that I respond differently. My failure was twofold: a failure to really see him in his last days and a consequent failure to respond.

Although I visited him twice a week, I rushed in and out and we didn't really communicate, except to exchange trivial comments about the weather, for example. He was as sharp as he had ever been, though I sensed his great disappointment that I hadn't brought him to live to me. Why hadn't I brought him to live with me? There were all the practical objections, there wasn't enough room, I wasn't home during the day, he required semiskilled nursing; but these weren't the primary reasons. As he became more and more ill, I became more and more distant. This was even more pronounced when other visitors were there—we talked to each other as though he were not there.

I think this is a fairly typical reaction, at least in our culture. We begin our grieving long before death comes, and we begin the task of severing relationships, of reweaving the tapestry of relationships, while the dying goes on. But the consequence of this grieving is that the person who is dying is deprived of his or her place in the network of care just when he/she needs it most.

The second story is about my friend's father. He slipped into a coma almost two years ago. His doctor says that it is clearly irreversible, but that he could survive another ten years in his present condition. At the moment, he has a trachial tube and a feeding tube. In the meantime, her mother has had to split their assets, leaving her with almost no reserve for her remaining years. My friend goes to see her father often, as do the other members of the family. But his lingering death has put them all in limbo; they have done most of their grieving, I suspect, but they cannot complete the reweaving while he is still alive.

I think these stories illustrate two things. One is that a response that focuses too strongly on the dying person's intimates blinds us to the needs of the one who is dying. The second is that a response that focuses too strongly on the dying person blinds us to the needs of the network of family and friends.

How should we respond as ones caring? First, if the adult is helpless but still able to understand what is going on, we must be sensitive not only to what we take to be in his/her best interest but to what he/she wants. In addition, we must give some thought to how best to carry these desires out. Obviously, we can draw here on the discussions of autonomy in medical ethics.[17] But an ethic of care is sensitive to the status of persons as related carers and not just as autonomous agents, hence it will also include a very different picture of what it is to be an autonomous agent than the picture presupposed by abstract individualism. In my view, commitments are not freely chosen but come from a menu given by the social context, nor are they to be evaluated solely with respect to how they affect us.

We can generalize to other medical cases. First, if we are an intimate of the patient, we can use our knowledge to help us decide what is in the best interests of the patient, to help us ascertain his/her desires. This is a necessary task even when the patient is conscious because the effect of illness and stress on a patient's ability to understand and consent are too often underestimated. It is not selfish or unreasonable to consider the effect of any decision on those connected to the patient through networks of caring, since they will be affected by any decision.

Perhaps we are not intimates of the patient, but medical caregivers with no strong prior attachments to the patient. When we see the patient as connected to others, as autonomous in a more limited sense, it seems reasonable to consult with his/her intimates; their desires are not irrelevant. Not only will we expect them to shed light on the desires and interests of the helpless adult, but we care about them in their own right; we understand how deeply they will be affected by actions taken with respect to the patient.

The prognosis is also an issue. Where a patient is not autonomous and not likely to ever become so, our obligations differ. We must now depend more on intimates; not only will we need their knowledge of the interests and desires of the patient, but now the effects on them of any decision are more important. It's not that the patient now lacks the only property that confers moral worth, autonomy, but that the patient is no longer the same person; the patient no longer has the capacity to relate to others. The relationships no longer exist in their earlier robust form; only the intimates are even aware of the relationship.[18]

III. CARING FOR THE RELATIVELY HELPLESS

Obviously, there are many who are unable to meet all their needs though they are far from helpless. The homeless come to mind here. The first thing to point out here is how the very expression "the homeless" serves to distance us from those who have no place to live. An ethic of care would require that we see people in all their particularity, not as mere shadows, identified only by the variety of their social distress.

A rights-based ethic, with its language of claims, makes it hard to talk about the issue of homelessness. When we are faced with a person who does not have a place to live, we are faced with a story of need, of despair, of personal and social failing. When we are forced to talk in a language of claims, much of the story is irrelevant. The only thing that matters is that this person has no home; this is the only fact that a right to shelter need acknowledge. The refusal of rights language to talk about needs— a refusal reflected in its insistence on the language of claims and positive rights—betrays and accepts a cultural bias against need. It is shameful to admit to a need, it is shameful to respond to a need.

An ethic of care is open to need; it acknowledges that we all have needs. We are not autonomous agents perfectly capable of taking care of ourselves, whose misfortune must then be blamed on our own lack of effort or inability to make demands. We are all needy; our relationships are based on a recognition of need and the commitment to fill need. And needs are not filled surreptitiously, but publicly and joyfully. We recognize our humanness and our connection in our reciprocal need. Take a barnraising, for example. We could talk about this in the language of rights: the barn builder has a right to have this barn built, and the helpers have a duty to respect this right, all other things being equal. But imagine the character of such a barnraising! Compare this to the barnraising done in response to a simple need for a barn where such needs are seen as the excuse for a party, a celebration of a community of need.

Finally, an ethic of care is sensitive to how needs are filled. Patsy Schweikart describes an interaction between ourselves and a person without a place to live. If we describe it in terms of rights, the homeless person can be said to demand a contribution. If we recognize the demand as legitimate, we respond. The homeless person is not grateful and is not expected to be so; we have merely done our duty. We feel no connection to this person, nor do we feel a sense of doing good. Rather, we both feel demeaned by the encounter. She invites us to reconceptualize this encounter in terms of an ethic of care: "Within the framework of an ethic of care, the beggar's approach will be read as an appeal—the presentation of a need, rather than the assertion of a right. He presents himself to me as one to be cared-for. Since there is nothing inherently disgraceful about vulnerability and dependency, about needing to solicit care, I can give him a dollar, and he can receive the gift, without either of us feeling shamed by the transaction."[19]

IV. CARING IN A MENTORING RELATIONSHIP

Being a teacher involves being in a mentoring relationship with students. This is not unique to teachers; such mentoring relationships are common in other callings as well. Since my experience has been in teaching, I will focus on teacher-student relationships, but what I say can shed some light on caring in other mentoring relationships as well.[20]

One of my friends confessed her fear at the beginning of each semester that her classes wouldn't go well, that the students wouldn't work well together or with her. This was not a worry about her student evaluations and prospects for advancement; she was already a full professor. I think that she understood that she was embarking on a relationship with her students, a relationship that mattered a good deal to them all, and a relationship that conferred special obligations on her as the teacher.

Contrast this with the view defended by Steven Cahn in *Saints and Scamps: Ethics in Academia.* In response to a suggestion that "a class has 'obvious affinities to a therapy group' and that good teaching has a 'kinship to therapy,'"[21] he writes:

> It is both foolish and dangerous for a person whose advanced degree is in English, economics, or engineering to attempt to act as a clinical psychologist. A student undergoing an emotional crisis should be sent to the school's counseling service, not treated by a medical tyro, however well meaning."[22]

He goes on to argue that faculty members should never be friends with students:

> When a student is graduated or no longer enrolled in the school, whatever personal relationship may develop with a professor is up to the two of them. But during the years of undergraduate or graduate study, the only appropriate relationship is professional. It is in everybody's interest to maintain these bounds.
>
> In sum, a faculty member ought to guide students through a field of study, not seek to be their psychiatrist, friend, or lover.[23]

Cahn's objections are couched in terms of what is good for the profession, the potential student-friend, and the other students. "Even the appearance of partiality is likely to impair the learning process by damaging an instructor's credibility, causing students to doubt that standards are being applied fairly."[24]

I disagree with Cahn; we must be open to the possibility of being friends with our students. To do otherwise is to refuse to see them as complete human beings, to see them merely as students.

We can describe the difference between my view and Cahn's view as rooted in our competing moral conceptions. Cahn is primarily concerned with the professor's responsibility to impartially give out grades and certify the students' competence. Here he is adopting an impartialist position. An ethic of care says that we must respond to each student as one caring. We must try to see each student in his or her particularity. This is not to say that it is easy or even possible to do this in a real classroom; the institutional barriers to meeting our students as one caring are daunting and, I fear, growing.

How do these views translate into action? As an example, I would like to tell another story. I had a student who seemed to have a learning problem. He clearly understood the material and was passionate about philosophy, but his responses on tests indicated that he memorized virtually the entire book. I had reservations about giving him an A in the class because I wasn't sure, on the basis of these tests, whether he really understood the material or simply memorized the book. He also wrote two papers, both of which were clear and insightful. But given the availability on campus of rather more extensive "editorial" assistance than I think helpful, I tend, at least in lower-division undergraduate classes, to put more weight on in-class essays. In the end, I gave him an A, in part because he needed it to stay in school.

Cahn would insist that the student's economic and educational difficulties would be simply irrelevant. The teacher would have to be clear about what the principle of grading would be and apply it to each case impartially. But this would be a sticky case, even for Cahn. If the standard was "the student gave the right answer," this student would get the A. If the standard was "the student gave the right answer, and it was clear that the student knew it was the right answer," then the teacher would not know how to grade this student.

An ethic of care would enjoin me to pay attention to this student, while recognizing that my other students mattered too. This student had formed a special relationship with me; I liked him and wanted the best for him. An ethic of care doesn't forbid these relationships, though I would be inclined to argue that the role of teacher requires that being open to forming this kind of relationship with students, subject to the teacher's needs and affinities. For example, I don't think that an ethic of care requires that I spend long hours in my office arguing with a neo-Nazi who likes me because I give him a run for his money.

Still, I did have a special relationship with this student. What was I to do? First, we should consider the effects of our actions on our students. Simply passing students on is not the best alternative, but neither is flunking out students who have already been seriously disadvantaged by the unequal and inferior educations offered in many primary and high schools. An institutional compromise would be the ideal solution: while we wait for high school to improve, we provide the time and financial support for students to gain the skills and confidence necessary to succeed in college.[25] Classes in four-year colleges would not be divided up rigidly into ten- or fifteen-week segments merely for administrative convenience, but

learning would proceed at the students' pace. In the absence of such an
alternative, what is the caring teacher to do? I think we do the best we
can, and we spend as much time as we can with these students. We give
them many opportunities to master the material. We let them write papers
over and over until they learn how to do it.

I would like to be able to say that I was a caring teacher in this case
and that the story had a happy ending, but sadly, this is not the case. I
do not know how this student is doing, and, in my reluctance to get involved and to violate the student's privacy, I did the minimum. I gave the
student the benefit of the doubt and the A, and I closed my grade book on
the incident.

This is evidence of how difficult it is to adopt an ethic of care in an
institution that is committed, where it is committed to any ethic at all, to
an ethic of impartiality. But it needn't be this way. Niara Sudarkasa, the
president of Lincoln University, gave a talk on campus during which she
explained the success of black colleges with black students: "We care about
them and we tell them they're great."[26]

Let me return to Cahn's claim that we should not counsel our students
but send them to the counseling center. He defends this in terms of the
student: a mere professor is likely to add to the student's problems, better
leave it to professionals. But how do we do this? I often have students
who share their problems with me, personal and academic. (It's not clear
to me that we can really separate these anyhow.) I like to think they do
this because they see me as a sympathetic listener. F. Scott Fitzgerald
opens *The Great Gatsby* with a description of such a listener:

> In my younger and more vulnerable years my father gave me some advice that
> I've been turning over in my mind ever since.
> "Whenever you feel like criticizing any one," he told me, "just remember that
> all the people in this world haven't had the advantages that you've had."
> . . . In consequence, I'm inclined to reserve all judgments, a habit that has
> opened up many curious natures to me. . . . The abnormal mind is quick to detect
> and attach itself to this quality when it appears in a normal person, and so it came
> about that in college I was unjustly accused of being a politician, because I was
> privy to the secret griefs of wild, unknown men. . . . Reserving judgment is a
> matter of infinite hope. I am still a little afraid of missing something if I forget
> that, as my father snobbishly suggested, and I snobbishly repeat, a sense of the
> fundamental decencies is parceled out unequally at birth.[27]

An ethic of care calls for this reserving of judgment, calls for a willingness to receive the other as he/she sees him/herself. But if you do
cultivate this reserving of judgment, you are likely to be privy to the griefs
of many, your students, in particular. What are you to do when they come

to you, clearly on the brink of unburdening themselves? You could pick up the phone and say, "It's been nice chatting with you, but I have work to do." But how will the student be affected by this response? I suspect that I would feel humiliated and rejected if I'd already begun to unburden myself and was then cut off. One way to avoid this might be to make sure that students never begin to unburden themselves.

A colleague from another department avoids these episodes by putting a sign-up sheet outside his office. He requires students to state their business in writing when signing up for an appointment, even during office hours. He explains this procedure to his classes at the beginning of the term, and he pointedly tells them that the business must be connected to the class. But isn't this a way of telling the students that you are really not interested in them as people? And doesn't this merely increase the pressure on teachers who are willing to talk to students even about things not connected to the course?

I do not want to be this kind of teacher. I want to take seriously the ethic of care; I want to be my ideal caring self, as often as I can and insofar as I am able. I don't agree with Cahn that in doing so I am risking harming my students. If my students see me as open to them as persons, they won't worry that my partiality will hurt them at final grade time. If my grading policies focus on mastery, and I allow every student to master the material and be graded on this mastery and not on how hard and how long it took to acquire this mastery, hopefully this worry won't come up anyway. I don't think that listening to my student's concerns and worries will push them over the deep end; nor do I think this attention constitutes practicing psychiatry without a license. I am free to refer them to a professional if I think they need it, but how will I even know that they need it if I don't first listen?

This is the kind of teacher I want to be, and I think an ethic of care would require me to do so as often and insofar as I am able. But again, the institutional barriers to this kind of interaction are formidable. Students in large bureaucratic institutions often feel like mere ciphers; they feel that no one cares about them, that they are not part of the institution but merely raw material. In such an institution, the needs of the students are great and their trust is small.

Finally, I return to the question of whether I can and ought to be friends with a student. Aristotle pointed out that true friendship can only exist between peers. My students and I are not peers in one sense; I have the power to organize instruction, to give grades, and the exercise of this power can make a real difference in the lives of students.

I agree that this difference in power affects our ability to be friends with our students. Although I don't share Cahn's worries about appearance of partiality, I have other concerns. I worry about self-deception on the part of the teacher, and how it can cause a teacher to forget the way in which they can affect students. The appearance of equality that comes with friendship can blind us to the influence we have over students, can cause us to forget that perhaps they see us not as friends but as role models. I worry that we will let them down if we begin to act like friends, to burden them with our concerns. I don't think that we should allow these worries to cause us to renounce all friendship with students, but we should always be careful about its effects on the students; we should be mindful of how they see the relationship.

I have one other worry about the possibility of true friendship between students and teachers: that our obligation to the department and the institution will require that we be silent about our true feelings on many issues. Students ask me what I think of Professor Y's class, and I don't know what to say because Professor Y is a colleague, perhaps even a friend. Perhaps I think that Professor X's class would be better for the student, but I know that Professor Y needs the enrollment or the class will be canceled. This is not just the usual conflict of interest that we face when we can't satisfy all our friends on some occasion. I have special and abiding obligations to the institution, obligations that rest on the commitment I feel to the shared project and to the web of relationships of which I am a part.[28]

I think that we can and should be open to the possibility of friendship with our students. At the very least, we should receive our students as individuals with lives and projects, connections and commitments beyond those of student. It is very difficult to do this in many of our bureaucratic institutions, but this is a criticism of our institutions, not of an ethic of care.

V. CARING FOR PEERS

I use "peers" to indicate relative equals. Peers may be involved in reciprocal relationships, or exploitive relationships, or they may be strangers and related only metaphorically (and metaphysically, in my view). Since there are many types of relationships between peers, I will divide this section into a discussion of caring for partners, family, friends, colleagues, and enemies.

A. Caring for Partners

I could further divide this section into caring for spouses, lesbian partners, and other intimate partners, but I don't think this is necessary. Though

I think there are likely to be great differences in these relationships, what is crucial is that these are partnerships between intimates who are relatively equal and committed to a continuing relationship of mutuality and intimacy.[29] Much of what I will say about partnership relationships is relevant only to partnership relationships in a particular social context. In our society, for example, there are many partnering relationships, and many of our needs for care, for intimacy, and for acceptance are only met within such relationships.[30]

In a caring partnering relationship, we can expect our partners to pay particular attention to us, to be accepting of our failings and sensitive to our needs. At the same time, we have reciprocal obligations to our partners. Both partners must recognize each other as individuals, with projects, commitments, and relationships independent of the partnering relationship, and both must act to support each other in pursuit of these projects, commitments, and relationships.

I don't think that monogamy, or even sexuality, need be a part of caring partnership relationships, though we must be sensitive to how social norms condition our expectations. This suggests that if we know that our partners would be deeply wounded by a refusal to be monogamous in the context of our relationship, we should, all other things being equal, either be monogamous or refuse to enter into such a relationship. I include the exception clause because many of the expectations of partners in our society, men in particular, are unreasonable. For example, though my partner may be conditioned to expect me to do all the housework, and would be deeply wounded by my refusal, seeing it as a sign that I did not really care for him, I have no obligation to meet this expectation. Doing all the housework would interfere with my pursuit of projects, commitments, and relationships that are important to me.

Some critics of an ethic of care have worried that abusive relationships would be accepted by an ethic of care.[31] Presumably, the fear is that if we are committed to sustaining relationships, we will support all existing relationships, even abusive ones. I think this worry is misplaced. An abusive relationship is not a caring one. Abusers in an abusive relationship do not have an understanding of their partners' good nor do they support their partners in pursuit of their projects, commitments, and other relationships.

In fact, an ethic of care allows us to develop a fuller critique of abusive relationships than the language of rights. The language of rights says that the abused partner's rights, perhaps to bodily integrity and liberty, are being violated by the abuser. The victim of abuse is justified in demanding that these rights be respected and acting to secure them. An ethic of care deepens the critique. It's not just that the abuser has violated the

rights of the victim of abuse; the victim of abuse is deprived of the care
that it was reasonable to expect in such a relationship. The jealousy of
the abuser and the subsequent isolation of the victim of abuse compounds
the abuse; the victim is deprived of care that is typically available only
in partnering relationships in our society, and at the same time is unable
to develop a partnership relationship that would satisfy the need for care,
intimacy, and acceptance.[32]

B. Caring for Family

There are especially intimate connections among family members, based
not just on their history but on the expectations of each other and the
effects of their interactions on the larger web of family connections. Though
there are many different kinds of families, my discussion here will focus
on the family as I experience it: a tightly woven group of parents, siblings,
their spouses and children, aunts, uncles, and grandparents.[33]

Children enter into families and come to learn about their place in these
families; they learn what to expect from other members, and they learn
what is expected of them. Later, they come to see both how fragile and
how enduring the family is: fragile in the sense that any disharmony re-
verberates through the entire web of relations, often causing ruptures far
from the site of the original disruption, enduring because such ruptures
mend and the family goes on. Often, it's a different family that goes on;
the rupture mends by creating different strands in the web. Families are
not self-sufficient bodies, immune to the larger world; rather their strength
and survival depend upon appropriate social institutions.

We can illustrate this point by looking at the effect of social security
on the extended family. Older members expect that social security will
allow them to meet their own needs; younger members plan their lives as
though they will have no financial responsibilities to their aging kin. Not
only does the style of family interaction change as society adopts policies
like social security, but the living arrangements change. In our society,
for example, we have moved into single-family units, often far from our
aging kin. This is likely to change as medical technology allows our aging
kin to live longer, though more fragile, lives, and as social security becomes a more and more threadbare blanket.

Though there is nothing universal about family structure or family
connections and obligations, there are special obligations in virtually all
families. These obligations are based on ties of affection, a shared history,
shared expectations, and the effect of disruptions on the web of interconnections that make up the family. Impartialist positions either deny special obligations or struggle to discover the source of special obligations,

including family obligations. Perhaps an implicit promise creates the obligations; perhaps utility is best maximized when we make use of the ties of affection common in families.[34]

An ethic of care points to the ties of affection themselves as a source of obligation. As Noddings puts it, natural caring creates an "I must." But natural caring does not always flow in us, even toward family members. Often, we are more aware of venom and spite. Perhaps I am contemplating a divorce. First, I imagine how I would respond as one caring; I think about the situation with moral imagination, becoming sensitive to the emotions that color my response, trying to understand the perception of the other and the effect on us both of any possible response. But now I recognize that it is not just we two or three, but we as members of a family. Now I must reflect on our shared history. This helps me to understand our present conflict. I try to become conscious of the expectations that color our reactions to this episode. Finally, I reflect on the effects on the larger family. All of this reflection takes place in the shadow of my commitment to caring as an ideal, and with the recognition of myself as deserving care.

No outcome is automatic, though I will be open to the possibility of a compromise that accommodates us all. As I suggested in Chapters Three and Four, compromise toward accommodation is not necessarily a joyless splitting of the difference. Often the very desire to compromise will let us see things in a new light; the compromise might then emerge as an exciting and satisfying new prospect for us all.[35]

But not all families are supportive; many families have tragic histories and unhappy expectations. This suggests that we must not be insensitive to the flaws in our family. Neither should we automatically respond to the expectations that happen to exist. Perhaps I am expected to marry at an early age, to have my five or six children, to work the afternoon shift at K-Mart, to volunteer at the church and school, though I dream of college and career. Perhaps I am expected to become a drug addict, to prostitute myself to provide money for drugs for other members of my family. In both cases, I must subvert expectations; I must risk a rupture of the family.

An impartialist position would see this perhaps in terms of obedience to abstract principles, or in terms of my rights. An ethic of care conceives my decision in terms that include me and my family. Leaving my family, if I feel I must, is not a liberation but a great tragedy, no matter how "dysfunctional" my family is. Leaving my siblings behind to face the terror is a terrible thing. In the best of all possible worlds, I can shift the expectations, and save my family and myself.[36]

C. Caring for Friends

In many ways, friends are like family. In the film *The Four Seasons*,[37] we see how the divorce and recoupling of the character played by Alan Alda affects the network of friendship that exists between these friends. Very close friends are like partners; Aristotle's perfect friends are partners in my sense. In both these cases, our caring response to our friends is similar, perhaps identical, to our response to family and partners.

But, as Aristotle points out, there are other kinds of friendship; he offers friendships based on pleasure and usefulness as two examples.[38] We have some friends because we simply enjoy their company, others because they are useful to us. Although I would be inclined to characterize these as acquaintances rather than friends, in what follows, I will follow Aristotle's categories.

When we are interacting with a partner or a family member, our obligation to "get it right" in caring is greater than it is with acquaintances. This is so because we know these people better; our moral imagination has a leg up here. Also, there are more complicated webs of relationships with partners and family members, and the larger network is affected by our interaction.

An ethic of care requires being open to the possibility of acquaintances becoming friends or family. This is simply a consequence of being open to the other, trying to see things as the other sees them, appreciating the other as unique. But when they are mere acquaintances, the response as one caring must take note of our relationship, in addition to being willing to receive the acquaintance, in the sense sketched above.

D. Caring for Colleagues

Academic departments are much like families; the tenure system creates this by isolating groups of people for so many years. In dealing with our colleagues, then, we must be sensitive to the web of relationships that make up the department. We must recognize when our actions undermine the solidarity that must exist if we are to be a functioning and happy department. But, like families, there are better and worse departments. When acting in "dysfunctional" departments, we should first be sensitive to their similarities with families. Our actions must then be colored by all the factors that I sketched in the discussion of family: our history, our shared expectations, the other members of the department, and the effect on the web of relationships that constitute the department.

One of the great shortcomings of many members of departments, and consequently of many departments, is to fail to see themselves as like families, to fail to see themselves as related in any significant way. In these departments, loyalty is not considered a virtue. This is apparent in the treatment of temporary faculty who are dealt with worse than strangers. I'm not suggesting here that they always get the next tenure track job that comes open (though I do think they have a prima facie case if they have been doing a good job) but that we recognize them as family. We should understand the hurt and disappointment that will accompany our unwillingness to take them seriously; we should recognize the effect of not seeing them as family on the web of relationships that make up the department.

Other departments are simply dysfunctional families. Temporary faculty are treated as illegitimate children, there to be abused. Junior faculty are treated as children to be pampered, abused, or ignored as the parent so desires.

There is a danger even in healthy families that strangers will be ignored or even sacrificed for the good of the family. This certainly happens in academic departments. The notorious resistance of many departments to admitting white women or people of color as faculty is a case in point. The solidarity of the current faculty might well be based on their similarity, and admitting faculty that are different in any way might well undermine this solidarity. (Of course, their decisions are never defended on these grounds, though I think self-deception is the best explanation for this.)

I recognize this as a challenge to an ethic of care. It seems to me, though, that this is a very shallow basis for relating, and consequently a fairly "thin" family. It also seems to me that this kind of a department is shamefully insular; while they recognize their obligations to each other, they fail to see how they relate, either as a department or as individuals, to the larger whole: to the students, to the school, to the university, and to the society at large, which subsidizes the university in countless ways.

E. Caring for Enemies

Does an ethic of care require us to turn the other cheek? Does an ethic of care allow us to have enemies? Iris Murdock suggests that if we give others "careful and just attention,"[39] we can change our opinion of them. Does it follow that our enemy can cease to be our enemy? Does an ethic of care require this careful and just attention?

The first thing to notice is the ambiguity in "enemy." It can refer to someone for whom you have abiding and personal animosity, a feeling that is typically returned by its object. It can also refer to someone whose beliefs and actions you feel obligated to resist. An ethic of care does challenge us to stop having enemies in the first sense, while it may require us to have enemies in the second.

Enemies in the first sense are often close to us. They become enemies as our disappointment and hurt at a real or an imagined injury festers and grows. An ethic of care requires that we try to understand the other, to see things through his/her eyes. When we do this, we become open to reconciling, to forgiving.

But our feelings of animosity need not be caused by the breach of an intimate connection. We might feel animosity because of the actions and beliefs of our enemy. In this case, an ethic of care would still counsel understanding, but wouldn't require ceasing efforts to resist the actions of our enemy. In fact, if our enemies' actions threaten care, we are required to resist.

VI. CARING IN CONFLICT

There are two principle ways in which conflict emerges as an issue for an ethic of care: obligations to care can conflict or two persons may be in conflict. I shall discuss both cases by looking at stories.

When I was thinking about where to go to graduate school, I faced an extremely difficult and painful decision. At the time, I was living in Boston, just getting ready to graduate from college. I was divorced and taking care of my two boys, then seven and nine. I was also helping to care for my elderly grandmother, shopping for her once a week and visiting her twice a week. I wasn't her only relative; my two brothers lived in town, and her son and his three children lived close by. But we had a special relationship. My grandmother is my model of an ideal caring person; she loved us without limit and shared her life and her worldly goods with us till the very end. Yet she had a strong sense of self; she had a busy and exciting life almost until she died. When I would visit her after my divorce, she would always insist that I take some money when I left, a dollar or two, sometimes more. I would always refuse; she lived on social security in a public housing project, and I worried that she needed the money more than I. But somehow the bills ended up in my sweater pocket or in my purse.

At the same time, my boys were suffering. My interracial family was battered by the racism which was always endemic to the city, but which was flaring because of the school busing controversy. To make matters worse, the Boston public school system was severely damaging my children.

I applied for graduate school in California. I chose the University of California at Riverside as the program that could best meet all our needs. They had excellent, well-integrated family student housing, and the school district assured me that they would have a program for my sons. As it turned out, all my hopes were met, and I regard my years at Riverside as among the happiest of my life.

But I agonized over my decision; I wanted to do what was best for myself and my sons, but I did not want to desert my grandmother in her old age. She had always been there for me, and I wanted to be with her until the end. She wouldn't go with me; she wanted to die as she lived, on her own turf, on her own terms. She made it all easier by insisting that I go. She even gave me money to help with the move. My grandmother died a few years later, and I was fortunately able to be with her just before she slipped into a final coma. But the last few months were extremely difficult for her, and I shall always regret that I wasn't there. Although I think I did the right thing, I still regard this as a tragedy.

This story illustrates three things. The first is that caring in cases of conflict like this requires a balancing. The factors to be balanced include the relationships and ties of affection involved, the needs of the parties, and the possibilities for meeting these needs. The second point is that doing the right thing is not a simple or all-or-nothing thing; even when we think we did the right balancing, we can still view our actions as tragic, we can still feel regret. Finally, there is no calculus to tell us what to do, no alternative to the anguished soul-searching that is involved in trying to meet our sometimes conflicting obligations as one caring.

I want to contrast this story with an example taken from medicine. Emergency rooms can sometimes be faced with more patients than they can handle. For this reason, each emergency room will have policies and procedures for handling this possibility. Urban areas may even have regional solutions to this dilemma. The Bay Area, for example, has a regional trauma policy with regional trauma centers and procedures for routing patients in the event of a major emergency. In this case, we cannot do without policies and procedures; a simple balancing is not sufficient. I take this to be evidence that we must sometimes construct general rules. These rules help assure patients of care even when they are not intimates of the ones caring, even when they are strangers. I don't think that this shows that we need to apply rules when dealing with intimates; it would have been truly heartless for me to triage my grandmother.

The second story is about my son. He has a band, which is very important to him. His band made a demo tape for distribution and sale, and this was a crucial part of their drive to succeed as a band. Each of the band members promised to pay his share of the cost of the tape, but when the tape was ready, one of the members said he could not come up with his share on time. I watched my son rage over this, and I tried to help him see how he might negotiate a solution. I was struck by his inability to see things in terms of negotiation; all he could say was, "But he was supposed to pay his share on time." His response was entirely appropriate from an impartialist position. Everyone promised to pay his share on time, and everyone else did. I was unable to help him see it from a care perspective, so I tried another tack. I suggested that he put aside the moral rightness or wrongness and simply try to figure out how to agree to an outcome that they could all live with. But his conviction that he was right stood in the way of even considering a negotiation.

I think this story illustrates two things. First, an impartialist position does not help us to see how to get past our assessments of praise or blame. Either we are right and they are wrong, or they are right and we are wrong. The focus is on trying to see where the right lies, and everything after that is anticlimactic. Second, the conflict would have been conceived very differently by an ethic of care, and this conception would have made negotiation both more natural and morally relevant.

Let me now reconceive this scenario from the perspective of an ethic of care. First, the relevant information would be different. The details about his friend's inability to pay on time would have been relevant: his other indebtedness, his difficulties in an intimate relationship would have been crucial rather than mere irrelevancies. If my son had viewed this from the perspective of an ethic of care, he would have seen himself as required to negotiate. As it turned out, they did negotiate and ultimately compromise, but my son's inability to see this from any position but an impartialist one undermined the trust that must exist for a band to thrive.

VII. SUMMARY

At this point, I want to look back at the claims I made at the beginning of this chapter. First, I suggested that an ethic of care takes as morally significant issues that are not seen as central in impartialist accounts. Second, I said that an ethic of care attends to different things than traditional impartialist accounts. Third, I hoped that looking at diverse and detailed examples would allow us to achieve something like a wide reflective equilibrium between our intuitions and the commitments of an ethic of care. I now want to see how well I have succeeded.

Let me begin with the discussion of caring for children. First, I think it is obvious that this has received very little attention in traditional impartialist accounts, though this need not be so. There is no reason why a Kantian or a consequentialist account of caring for children could not be developed. I suspect that the reason why no such accounts have been offered has to do with a conception of morality that underlies each account. Kant explicitly argues that morality begins where inclination leaves off. Mill suggests that the vast majority of life decisions are not moral ones. In both cases, the assumption might be that caring for children is one of those extra-moral areas. In any case, if these two impartialist views were to focus their attention on child-rearing, I suspect that they would look at it in a very different way than an ethic of care would. An ethic of care, which assumes that all our moral guidance flows from the actual situation in combination with our well-developed moral sentiments, looks at actual child-rearing practices within a given social context, and at real children and adults. No assumption is made that one value should be centrally significant in each case or that one set of principles should guide us in every similar case, though rules of thumb do arise from this careful look at individual cases.

The examples of caring for the helpless illustrate the focus of an ethic of care on the needs of the helpless in the context of a network of care. First, we see that autonomy is not the only, or even the most important, value. Second, we see that we cannot decide how best to respond without seeing how our actions effect the network of care which sustains all its members, including its most needy member.

Though all plausible accounts of morality must see homelessness as morally problematic, the example of the homeless illustrates the difference in perspective between an ethic of care and a rights-based ethic.

Though most moral philosophers today earn a living teaching, ethical issues in teaching have received little attention from moral philosophers. I have tried to help reverse that here. From the perspective of an ethic of care, our obligations as teachers emerge as morally central. Although I believe that Cahn represents the worst in impartialist accounts of the ethical issues involved in teaching, I think that he shares with other impartialists the emphasis on discovering or justifying the correct moral principles to guide us in this task. An ethic of care, on the other hand, focuses on individual students in a particular institutional context. Perhaps rules of thumb will emerge, but we must be guided by the needs of the student in the context of the network of care that binds us to our students.

Finally, in caring for peers, whether partners, colleagues, family, or friends, caring puts a special emphasis on relationship. Where most impartialist accounts deny special obligations, an ethic of care insists on them.

At this point, I would simply invite the reader to reflect on the fit between his/her intuitions and the commitments of care as expressed in these examples.

In this chapter, then, I've described how an ethic of care can inform some of our interactions with persons. I have focused on the importance of relationships, of ties of affection, of careful moral attention, and of the role of compromise and accommodation in dealing with conflict. The next chapter will turn to a discussion of caring for animals.

NOTES

1. Lawrence Kohlberg, with Charles Levine and Alexandra Hewer, "The Current Formulation of the Theory," in *The Psychology of Moral Development: The Nature and Validity of Moral Stages* (New York: Harper & Row, 1984), 212–319.

2. In some of these examples, we see caring used both to refer to a practice of giving care and to the ethical perspective of an ethic of care.

3. Virginia Held argues that mothering is just the right paradigm, since the experience of mothering or the social conditioning in preparation for mothering colors the moral experience of women. See "Feminism and Moral Theory," in Eva Kittay and Diana Meyers, eds., *Women and Moral Theory* (Totowa, N.J.: Rowman and Littlefield, 1987).

4. Laurence Thomas is a notable exception here. See *Living Morally: A Psychology of Moral Character* (Philadelphia: Temple University Press, 1989).

5. Michel Foucault, *Discipline and Punish: The Birth of the Prison* (New York: Vintage Books, 1979).

6. I have qualified this claim because many adults in abusive relationships lack such appropriate expectations; they grew up in abusive families and they have come to expect abuse. Worse, they think that this is an appropriate response; abusive parenting or the history of abuse by the partner has convinced them that they deserve no better. This is reinforced in women by a culture that treats all women with contempt, and as fit objects for men's violent aggression.

7. Thomas discusses this in some detail. See "Parental Love" in *Living Morally*.

8. Alice Miller, *The Drama of the Gifted Child* (New York: Basic Books, 1983).

9. Christopher Lasch talks about this at some length. See *The Minimal Self: Psychic Survival in Troubled Times* (New York and London: W. W. Norton & Co., 1984).

10. Barbara Erenreich points out that what she terms "professional middle class" (well-educated, engaged in jobs usually described as professional) parents cannot assure their children's continued membership in the class through inheritance, so they instead try to inculcate values that she sees as sometimes inimical to a healthy sense of self. See *Fear of Falling* (New York: Pantheon Books, 1989).

11. It might seem easier with very small infants; here it seems we need only respond to their physical needs. But even here, we can see the influence of different styles of parenting. Should we respond to the child whenever he/she cries, or should we try to put him/her on a schedule? Should we leave the child in the crib most of the day or should we carry it constantly?

12. Sara Ruddick, "Preservative Love and Military Destruction: Some Reflections on Mothering and Peace," in Joyce Treblicot, ed., *Mothering: Essays in Feminist Theory* (Totowa, N.J.: Rowman and Allanheld, 1983).

13. Milton Mayeroff, *On Caring* (New York: Perennial Library, 1971), 9–10.

14. Amelia Rudolph, "Our Inner Lives," a talk given at the 1991 Women's History Month Celebration, San Jose, Calif., March 27, 1991.

15. Nel Noddings, *Caring: A Feminine Approach to Ethics and Moral Education* (Berkeley: University of California Press, 1984), 120–24.

16. I confess to a certain skepticism here. Experts on infancy discover how much more care infants need just as more and more mothers are going into the job market. Still, I think the burden is on the parents to evaluate the research and to amend their caring practices accordingly. If infants need more stimulation than heretofore believed, then we should try to make their lives more interesting. Obviously, this is an obligation that falls on parents, and on the society at large, not just on mothers.

17. See, for example, James Rachel's discussion of euthanasia. Here, autonomy is one of the central concerns. *The End of Life* (Oxford: Oxford University Press, 1986).

18. Many feminist discussions of medical ethics adopt similar analyses. See, for example, the special issue of *Hypatia* "Feminist Ethics & Medicine" (Summer 1989); Daniel Dugan, "Masculine and Feminine Voices: Making Ethical Decisions in the Care of the Dying," *The Journal of Medical Humanities and Bioethics* 8 (1987): 129–40; Stephen Post, "An Ethical Perspective on Caregiving in the Family," *The Journal of Medical Humanities and Bioethics*, 9 (1988): 6–16.

19. Patsy Schweikart, "The Politics of Cultural Feminism," a paper delivered at the Midwest Radical Scholars and Activists conference, Loyola University, Chicago, October 1990, 9.

20. For a discussion of how feminist ethics influences the teaching of moral philosophy, see Deborah Slicer, "Teaching with a Different Ear: Teaching Ethics after Reading Carol Gilligan," *Journal of Value Inquiry* 24 (1990): 55–65; Tangren Alexander, "The Womanly Art of Teaching Ethics, or One Fruitful Way to Encourage the Love of Wisdom about Right and Wrong," *Teaching Philosophy*, 10 (1987): 319–28; John Waide, "Gilligan's Wake: Some Implications of Carol Gilligan's Work for Teaching Ethics," *Teaching Philosophy* 10 (1987): 305–18.

21. Steven M. Cahn, *Saints and Scamps: Ethics in Academia* (Totowa, N.J.: Rowman & Littlefield, 1986), 34–35.

22. Ibid., 35.

23. Ibid., 36.

24. Ibid., 35.

25. Mike Rose gives a moving account of the struggles of poor and minority students to succeed in college. He also offers suggestions for institutional reform. *Lives on the Boundary* (New York: Penguin Books, 1989).

26. Niara Sudarkasa, president of Lincoln College, address given at San Jose State University, Fall 1989.

27. F. Scott Fitzgerald, *The Great Gatsby* (New York: Charles Scribner's Sons, 1925), 1.

28. This problem may also come up with other colleagues, and with outside job candidates. I might disapprove of the department's handling of a particular issue, and yet I feel I must remain silent because I am part of the department, because I feel obligated to sustain the complicated relationships that must exist

if we are to be a department at all. But this sense of obligation sometimes leaves me feeling that I cannot be a true friend to someone who is being adversely affected by the department's policies.

29. Many feminists have argued that relationships between women and those between women and men are substantially different. See, for example, Andrea Dworkin, *Intercourse*, (New York: Free Press, 1987).

30. I am not assuming that these needs typically *are* met in such relationships; I'm merely describing what an ethic of care would require in such relationships. Further, it's perfectly possible to imagine a world in which no partnering relationships existed but rather more complicated relationships between other numbers of persons. Marge Piercy envisions such a world in *Woman on the Edge of Time* (New York: Fawcett Books, 1985).

31. See Claudia Card, "Women and Evil" *Hypatia* 5 (1990): 101–8.

32. Patsy Schweikart makes this point in "The Politics of Cultural Feminism," 6.

33. Germaine Greer's analysis of the traditional extended family suggests that an ethic of care could flourish in such a setting. See "The Fate of the Family," *Sex and Destiny* (New York: Harper & Row, 1984).

34. Bernard Williams pokes fun at Charles Fried's attempt to give an impartialist defense of special obligations. See Charles Fried, *An Anatomy of Value* (Cambridge, Mass.: Harvard University Press, 1970), 227, and Bernard Williams, "Persons, Character, and Morality," in George Scher, ed. *Moral Philosophy* (San Diego: Harcourt Brace Jovanovich, 1987).

35. Empirical research suggests that competition can often be defused simply by reconceptualizing the interaction as an attempt to negotiate a compromise. See D. G. Pruitt and S. A. Lewis, "The Psychology of Integrative Bargaining," in D. Druckman, ed., *Negotiations: A Social-Psychological Perspective* (New York: Halsted, 1977).

36. Much of the therapeutic work being done on substance abuse is an attempt to reform families: Al-Anon, Al-Ateen, Co-Dependency Anonymous. Although I disagree with much of the theory and am skeptical about the social policy, I applaud the effort to treat families and not just "rescue" members.

37. *The Four Seasons*, written and directed by Alan Alda, produced by Martin Bregman, 1981.

38. Aristotle, *Nichomachean Ethics*, bk. 8, chap. 3 (Indianapolis and New York: The Library of Liberal Arts, 1962).

39. Iris Murdoch, *The Sovereignty of the Good* (New York: Schocken Books, 1971), 37.

Chapter Six

Caring for Animals

I freely confess to being a bit tired of debates about animal rights. It seems to me that opponents of animal rights almost inevitably fall into the trap of begging the question against nonhuman animals and in favor of human animals.[1] Proponents spend so much of their time defending themselves against opponents that they don't get to spend enough time reflecting upon the real issues that confront us as we try to care for animals.[2] I am not criticizing the defenders of animals; I think that their work is crucial and effective.[3] I simply want to get on to the next stage.

In the first part of this chapter, I'm going to focus directly on concrete issues that confront us as we try to care for companion animals. I will not defend my descriptions of my companion animals' behavior, which rely on my assumption that they have a rich mental life. To those who object to my attributing intentional states to animals, I give the reply that Steve Sapontzis gives in his book on animal rights, go adopt a dog (or some other animal) and get to know it personally.[4] In section II, I will discuss other domestic animals, and in section III, I will turn to a discussion of wild animals. In each of these discussions, I will be looking to extend, clarify, and test the ethic of care that I have been defending. In the final section, I discuss the more general question of why we should care for any animals.

I. CARING FOR COMPANION ANIMALS

A. Don't Fence Me In

Looking like a cross between a Chihuahua and a pit bull, Thorp made his appearance one evening out at the barn where I boarded my horses. I continued to see him there scrounging food for a couple of days, but I resisted my son's pleas to take him home. Finally, my hand was forced. The owner of the barn got tired of seeing him hanging around and resolved to take matters into his own hands. When he locked him up in a cage by the office while he went to get his gun, my son and I sprung him and brought him home.

It didn't take long for us to discover that he was a confirmed roamer. No fence could keep him in. We got him neutered, expecting it to change his behavior, but it made absolutely no difference.

For ten years he has "belonged" to us. During that time, he has racked up hundreds of dollars in fines for not being confined, while we tried everything we could think of to crimp his style. I reinforced the fence, tied him up, even moved to a house on two-thirds of an acre to give him room to run, but nothing seemed to help, though he did learn not to come when the dogcatcher called. The only thing that seemed to work was to keep him on a chain, but this seemed terribly cruel. I resorted to it, for a time, when his roamings inevitably took him to my neighbor's front yard at 3 A.M. where he howled at passing deer.

Finally, I gave in and let him roam. I don't know how he spent his days and nights, but he came to visit us regularly. Sometimes he would spend most of his time with us, leaving for a day or two at a time. Later, he spent most of his time elsewhere, coming to visit us every couple of weeks and staying for a day or two.

This went on for a couple of years until one morning two little girls brought him home. He had an enormous swelling under his chin, and he was thin and miserable. I took him to the vet, who diagnosed him as having either a tumor or an abscess and who suggested exploratory surgery.

The surgery revealed an abscess, which the vet drained. Thorp was placed on two-week confinement while his wound healed. While Thorp was at the hospital, he got a present and a card signed by half the kids in the neighborhood. Later when he was able to go out for walks on a leash, he would be greeted by almost everyone we met. Obviously, he'd had a rich social life in his roaming days.

I have gone back to crimping his style. I reinforced the fence again, keep him tied up when I'm not here, take him running every day, and got him a puppy. It seems to be working, at least for the most part. He has escaped a few times, but he stays gone for only a day or so.

I'm still not sure I'm doing the right thing keeping him confined. This question does not come up with our horses, who are pathologically reluctant to leave familiar surroundings, nor does it come up with our other dog, who stirs herself only if you wave a leash under her nose. But there are real questions that I want to raise in connection with Thorp.

If we asked Thorp what he wanted, I am convinced that he would choose to roam. He is a very friendly dog and obviously values his time away from home enough to go to great lengths to escape. (He was once seen scaling a tree to vault over our six-foot chain-link fence.) He does display some conflict, though. When he makes his getaway right under your nose and you call him to come back, he looks over his shoulder and gives you a very guilty look as he keeps running, tail between his legs.

But caring does not require that we simply accede to the wishes of the one cared for.[5] Rather, we should respond in the interest of the one cared for, insofar as furthering that interest is compatible with our abilities and where this response sustains the network of care that connects us. In doing so, I should be sensitive to the relationship, and open to the possibility of compromise and accommodation.

The number of well-wishers who phoned or came by when he was sick convinced me that he had established many strong and loving relationships while he was living away from home. This concerned me, since three claims about relationships are relevant to our obligations to care. The first is that persons are, to a large extent, identified and self-identified by their relationships. This is a metaphysical view, which Michael Sandel calls the "embedded self" and which he contrasts with abstract individualism.[6] Second, whether or not the embedded-self picture is correct, persons can only thrive in relations with others. Finally, relationships with others place special obligations on us. I don't intend to defend these claims here; instead I want to see if they can be applied to dogs.

I don't know what to say about how dogs develop a sense of self. I am not even sure that they can be said to have a sense of self, though I do think we can say that they have selves in the sense of having a center of awareness. The effect of training on dogs and other animals suggests that this limited self is highly influenced by the context in which it develops.[7] Still, I am not sure whether this first claim about relationships should be applied to dogs.

The second claim—that persons can only thrive in relationships with others—can be applied to dogs who are essentially social creatures who are miserable if left alone for long periods of time. The question for Thorp, though, is not whether it is permissible to isolate him totally, but whether it is permissible to sever some of his existing relationships and limit his ability to fashion future new ones.[8]

I am inclined to take seriously the moral import of restricting Thorp's relationships, but on balance I think that this is a permissible restriction. My assessment depends, in large part, on my sense that he is relatively happy with his present life, even though it is more restricted that his earlier life.

It seems obvious that obligations are imposed by relationships. What is not obvious is what relationships create obligations. It is not even clear what counts as a relationship. I will return to this question when I discuss horses. Here, I want to focus on the obligations that I recognize as following from my relationship with dogs. I recognize an obligation to protect; to provide food, shelter, and companionship; to provide veterinary care. In so doing, I recognize an obligation to allow the dog to live a dog's life, a life that allows the dog to satisfy its desires and independently experience its life. This cuts to the heart of my dilemma about restricting Thorp. In doing so, I am concerned that I am thwarting both his desires and his ability to independently experience his life. On balance, I have decided that my obligation to protect him takes priority here, though that does not mean that my obligation to let him be a dog ceases.

It is fair to say that Thorp has some obligations too. This is a common view among people who raise what are called "working dogs." The dogs are expected to work in exchange for the care they receive, and in so doing, they are expected to display certain virtues, notably loyalty. This seems to be a fair exchange, especially in view of the evident pleasure working dogs get from discharging their obligations. The problem with Thorp is that he simply hasn't enough work to do. Serving vaguely as a watchdog does not sufficiently engage his interest. I do expect loyalty, though, and his wanderings display a lack of this virtue. If our arrangement—protection and care in exchange for some light work done with a keen sense of loyalty—is fair, then I think I am justified in enforcing its terms.

One might argue that it is not clear how a deal can be seen as fair when one of the parties is unable to refuse. To compound the problem, it is not even clear how dogs can be said to consent. I think that this objection underestimates the dog. I believe that dogs can refuse. They can run away and refuse to return and they do so. It is true that most dogs accept the deal and that they sometimes put up with terrible conditions rather than strike out on their own. I certainly do not want to deny that a dog can be broken, can lose its capacity to refuse, as can a human, but this does not show that all dogs are incapable of refusing.

The final two values for an ethic of care which are relevant here are compromise and accommodation, and these two values must be explained in terms of each other. A compromise that merely splits the difference and leaves no one satisfied is not worth making. The ideal compromise ends by accommodating everyone. The spirit of compromise and accommodation is generous and fair, and pleasure is taken in the satisfaction of the desires of others. With this spirit, compromise is often easy and pleasant. I recognize that it is often impossible to fully satisfy everyone in cases of conflict, but a compromise that accommodates everyone is less rare than we think.

A focus on compromise and accommodation reminds us that obligations are not an all-or-nothing thing. I don't discover that it is morally permissible to restrict Thorp's wanderings and give the matter no further thought, and it is not morally permissible to restrict his wanderings without regard to the means. For example, it would be wrong to keep him tied up twenty-four hours a day, or to keep him in a crate. When I restrict Thorp's wandering, I must do so in a way that accommodates him and me. I must strike a compromise.

B. Out to Pasture

When Champ was fifteen, I was faced with the need to retire him. I simply could not keep him comfortable enough to ride him. He had lived his entire life in a stall and paddock and would be content to live that way until he died. There were two problems, however. One was that constant light exercise is best for an aging, arthritic horse; living in a confined space only exacerbates arthritis. Second, a stall and paddock was more than twice as expensive as the pasture, and I wanted to be able to afford a horse that I could ride.

I was terrified about putting him out to pasture. It symbolized the end of our special relationship, it made me aware of his mortality, and I was afraid he would hate it. Being turned out in a field or arena is supposed to be horse heaven, but he always hated it. He would race up and down in a panic until I came to get him. I was afraid he would see being put out to pasture as abandonment, as being turned out and forgotten.

I was also afraid he would kill himself out there. Once, he had had an injury that required being turned out for six weeks. After less than a week he ran through the fence, and it took four hours to stitch him up. Clearly, he didn't want to be out in the pasture when he could be in the barn.

After agonizing over it for months, I finally turned Champ out. First, I made sure the pasture was as safe as a pasture can be. Second, I got a tranquilizer from the vet, who assured me that if I tranquilized him and put him out while he was still groggy, he would wake up out in the pasture and be fine. For five days, he raced around the pasture in a panic. The other horses beat him up, and they chased him away from the food and water.

Around that same time, I got back a twenty-year-old horse that had been leased out. Champ and Bernard had been stabled together for years, though they hadn't seen each other for at least four years. I made arrangements to put Bernard out in the pasture with Champ. To my great surprise, they remembered each other. When I unloaded Bernard from the horse trailer, he and Champ started calling to each other. When I turned Bernard out, he and Champ ran laps around the pasture together, and from that day on they were inseparable. There was only one fly in the ointment.

Champers is a very big horse, standing seventeen hands and weighing fourteen hundred pounds at his best weight. The other six horses in the pasture included my daughter's incredibly fat pony, Billy, who should weigh about seven hundred pounds tops, and five average-size horses who should weigh between nine and eleven hundred pounds. A horse's need for food depends upon his size, his metabolism, and his level of activity. Given his much larger frame and his metabolism, Champ needed almost twice as much food as the other horses, and four times as much as the pony. Unfortunately, in a pasture situation, you cannot separate the horses for feeding. Seven large flakes of hay were thrown to the horses twice a day. Champ, being at the absolute bottom of the pecking order, was getting thinner and thinner, while the horses at the top of the pecking order were getting fatter and fatter.

I found another stable which specialized in retired horses and brood mares, but I agonized over separating Champ and Bernard. I didn't want to move Bernard, because he was being used in lessons. Not only did it help to pay his way, but it kept him in shape, and this is very important for a twenty-year-old horse.

This story does have a relatively happy ending. I moved Champ. He is now out with one old mare, and he seems perfectly happy and healthy. Bernard has adjusted, though he does not have a best friend out in the pasture anymore. He is tolerated by the other horses, so his life is not unpleasant.

This story raises several questions. The first is whether it is permissible to confine horses. Champ is a perfect example of the folly of thinking that a natural environment is best for all horses. Horses in pasture live in herds, in which they establish a pecking order. Horses on the bottom are sometimes mercilessly hounded. Some dominant horses are fair and generous, ruling with benevolence. Others are nasty and cruel, creating a dog-eat-dog atmosphere. Champ experienced both types of leaders while he was out with a herd. The first leader, who was nasty and cruel, was deposed by a new horse who came to live in the pasture. Luckily, he was fair and generous and discouraged mayhem. Still, he did not protect Champ while he ate. He ate his own dinner and then did what dominant horses do—he chased the less dominant horses, including Champ, away from their dinners.

So a "natural" life is not always the best life for a horse. In a stall, a horse is protected from other horses; he gets to eat his meals in peace; he has a warm, dry spot to lie down in, and he has a soft bed to cushion him from the cold, hard ground.

Again, it is important to accommodate a horse. In keeping horses, we must be sensitive to their needs for companionship, for exercise, and for variety. A horse with a large stall and paddock, plenty of food and clean bedding, who can see and touch his stablemates while being protected from their biting and kicking, who is turned out regularly, and who is groomed and exercised several times a week is a happy horse. This type of horse-keeping accommodates a horse's needs for security, for comfort, and for movement.

This raises another question. If this is ideal horse-keeping, is it permissible to keep horses in less luxurious surroundings? In particular, am I cheating Champ of the comfortable retirement that he worked so hard to deserve? I must confess that I worry about this. I could have kept him in a stall and paddock and had him turned out during the day. But doing so would have meant that I would have nothing to ride, since I could not afford to have two horses living in this style. Eventually, my craving for a horse to ride overcame my belief that I should focus all my attention on Champ. I could plead "ought implies can" here, but instead I will just admit to being human; adopting an ethic of care does not eliminate weakness of will.

The final issue I want to address in connection with this story is friendship between animals. While I don't think that horses can have the same kinds of friendships as humans can, I think it is clear enough that they do have friendships.

Aristotle described friendship as consisting of mutual good will, recognized by both parties.[9] Perfect friendship requires mutual trust, in addition to mutual good will.[10] Although horses lack the mental capacity to understand each other's good in the full-blown sense required by Aristotle for human friendship, I think horses can be friends.

There are three components of horse pairing that justify describing these pairings as "friendship." First, horses engage in behavior that resembles the behavior engaged in by humans as part of a friendship. They choose to be together. They often protect each other against more dominant horses. They seem to take pleasure in each other's company and display distress when they are separated. Second, the best explanation for this behavior is that they feel affection for each other. Third, these ties of affection are not based on mere habit or instinct, but on preference.

The close attachments horses form with other horses is not just a matter of being thrown together. Horses who are stabled next to each other are as likely to hate each other as love each other. Friendship in horses seems to be based on affection, and the object of the affection is uniquely favored.

Horses in a pasture will usually group themselves into pairs. The pairing may or may not be between geldings and mares, so a biological explanation based on sexual attraction is not the explanation for all of these pairings. Horse pairs seem to enjoy each other's company, though it is not unusual to see a pair, often a gelding and a mare, where the affection seems to be all on one side. The gelding is either more dominant than the mare and forces her to put up with him, or so in love with her that he follows her around even though she makes it clear that she does not want his company. I suspect that these pairings are based on sexual attraction, but I don't think that is the explanation for all horse pairings. Champ and Bernard are both geldings, and it is not at all unusual for geldings to pair. These pairs are often deeply and mutually devoted, as Champ and Bernard are. They spend the entire day together, often protecting each other from more dominant horses.

I am sure that explanations based on instinct or self-preservation could be offered for these pairings, but this is also true of human friendships. Although in both cases there is a biological basis, horses and humans both being social animals, I would argue that the burden of proof is on the person who claims that friendship in either case is based on mere instinct. Most would agree that human friendship is not based merely on instinct, and I think that the preference shown by two horses for each other's company is sufficiently similar to the preference of two humans for each other's company to justify calling these horse pairings friendship.

Even if I am wrong about this, the fact that the horses want to be together and are clearly distressed when they are apart is a sufficient reason for some moral concern about separating horse pairs. Do we then have any obligations to accommodate horse friendships?

I want to suggest that we get some guidance here from our more settled intuitions about whether and when it is permissible to separate human friends. Since concerns about liberty cloud the issue in the case of competent adult humans, I propose that we look to our intuitions about the permissibility of separating children from their friends.

Changes in jobs or family situations, or a concern for the safety of the child, are perhaps the most common reasons for separating children from their friends. If we think that a child is a danger to another child, we will often act to separate the child from the danger. Parents are notoriously self-deceptive both about the real cause of the danger and the efficacy of the solution, but I think that we would all agree that in most cases we would be morally justified in separating a child from a friend if that friend constituted a danger, and the danger could be eliminated by avoiding the friend.[11]

The pursuit of career or changes in family arrangements create pressures to move, and moving often necessitates the sundering of childhood friendships. My intuition here is that the importance of the career move or the need to accommodate a new family arrangement ought to be balanced against the harm to the child. This harm can be measured by appeal to two factors. The first is the strength of the bond, and the second is the difficulty of establishing similar bonds after the move. Younger children seem to have an easier time establishing new friendships and seem to grieve less at the sundering of old friendships. Adolescents seem to find the experience particularly traumatic. Even if I am wrong about the relative ease with which children make a move, I think that this is the right criterion for deciding whether a move is sufficiently harmful to outweigh the considerations in favor of the move.

Horses resemble younger children more than they resemble adolescents with respect to friendship. They do seem distressed at being separated from a friend, sometimes profoundly so, but in most cases, as with young children, they will settle down as long as they can make a new friend.

In Champ's case, the need to protect him from the more dominant horses precipitated the move, and my desire to have Bernard continue in a relatively active life necessitated separating them. But again, we have not settled the case by deciding where the right lies. In doing the permissible or even the obligatory act, we must do it in the right way. We must compromise with an eye to accommodation. In this case, I felt obligated to make sure that both Champ and Bernard either found a new friend or at least an accepting gang. I first turned Champ out with one gelding. In two days, it became clear that this pairing would never be a friendship. Next, we moved him in with a very submissive gelding and mare. Champ beat up the gelding, so we moved the gelding and let Champ have the mare to himself. Within a few days, it was clear that Champ had bonded to the mare, and, though the mare seemed less than enthusiastic, she seemed to accept him. Without the responsibility of protecting Champ against the more dominant horses, Bernard slipped into the herd. Though neither of them has the same relationship with any other horse that they once had with each other, they seem to be doing reasonably well and Champ has put on weight.

C. The Old Gray Mare

When I decided to retire Champ, I began to look for another horse. Clover, an eight-year-old mare boarded in our barn, was for sale. She had raced for two years and then sustained a fairly serious injury. She was not given the recommended treatment, but instead turned out to a pasture. Luckily, the injury healed reasonably well on its own. Eventually, she found her way to an agent for sale. At first, Clover was a basket case, but the agent was a kind and patient woman who worked with her until she was relatively tame. She was sold to a beginner, but returned when she proved to be too green for the green rider. When I tried her out, she was a model of kindness and trust. I loved riding her. She was incredibly willing and responsive.

I had her on approval for two weeks before I had her vetted. Unfortunately, the vet discovered arthritic changes in her ankle that made her unsuitable for my purposes because he doubted that she would stay sound for long. Since I already had one lame horse, and I didn't want to gamble with having two, with great sadness I decided not to buy her. At this point, the agent realized that she would be hard to sell. The only thing the agent wanted was a good home for her, but even that was questionable with the diagnosis of unsoundness. Months went by. Every time I walked past her stall, I felt guilty. Eventually, someone bought her. I have no idea if she is still sound, or where she will end up if and when she does go lame, but I sincerely hope she is doing well.

Three questions arise here. The first is, is it morally permissible to use animals when the use poses a risk of injury or death? The second question, which also comes up in connection with my story about Champ, is, does an animal have a right to life and, if so, what does this entail? The third is, how and when does someone become responsible for the care of an animal?

Describing an interaction with an animal as a "using" implies that the animals have not clearly consented to the interaction. It doesn't follow that the animals resent the use or that they find it unpleasant. Some would argue that any use of an animal is wrong.[12] Though I have some sympathy for this view, I think that one consequence of ending all uses of animals would be to sever many of the relationships and ties of affection that exist between humans and animals. This would be a tragedy, not just for the humans but for the many animals who flourish in these relationships.[13]

Yet I worry about the moral status of riding horses, because I am aware of the potential for injury that this practice involves. Horses die in traumatic accidents or they are killed ("put down") when it is decided that the injury will never heal well enough to warrant continued use. The more common scenario is a stress injury, caused by continued stress on a bone or a joint. These injuries often leave horses unable to be ridden ("unsound"), and often in pain.

We can do a great deal to reduce the incidence of both traumatic and stress injuries, but we cannot prevent them entirely.[14] Although I think it very likely that we would greatly reduce the incidence of both types of injuries by not riding horses, even horses in pasture suffer both kinds of injuries. The only sure cure is to stop breeding horses. I think this would be a great tragedy both because horses make wonderful friends and because they are unique parts of the natural world. They are exemplars of majestic values: beauty, dignity, strength, courage, speed, endurance, and agility. Although these qualities would continue to exist in the wild horses who would likely continue to survive, we would have far fewer encounters with horses.

One could argue that horses are not only willing partners, but sometimes more committed to the endeavor than their riders. Race horses, for example, are often praised for their heart, for their desire to run. The tragic death of Go For Wand at the 1990 Breeder's Cup was described as caused, in part, by the filly's incredible desire to run in front.[15]

If caring for animals requires that we take their good as a starting point, that we respect them as partners in the relationship, then I think that we have to stop using them in ways that pose a clear risk of serious injury. The death of Go For Wand was not an anomaly. Horses die every day on tracks all over the country. We race two-year-olds whose bodies and minds are three years from maturity. We race them on good and bad footing, we race them when they are sore and we throw them away when we are through. There are good people in racing, people who love horses, but the industry itself leads to the death of far too many horses. The factors that lead to this include the great cost of keeping a horse in training, the industry's inability to oversee the many horses running and training, the technical difficulties in identifying the many and constantly new drugs given to horses, and the proliferation of lower-rung tracks. Horses that were once retired to a good life as riding horses now race till they are completely used up. At that point, if they are lucky, they are humanely destroyed.

If racing is clearly beyond the pale, then what about other horse sports? What do we say about eventing which requires tremendous efforts of horse and rider at the advanced level? What about show jumping, dressage, cutting, and endurance riding? Each of these sports poses a risk of injury to horse and rider.

It does seems to me that an ethic of care requires that we actively seek to avoid risk of injury insofar as we can. This might require that we refrain from all use except gentle trail riding. In any case, we can do much to reduce injury: training systematically and carefully, providing the best footing we can, shoeing our horses regularly, and not letting our horses get overtired and susceptible to injury. We should be sensitive to our horse's own talents and weaknesses. However, none of these precautions can prevent all injuries. In the event of an injury, we must provide for the appropriate care, in the best interests of the animal. Finally, we should never have a horse killed merely to save on the feed bill. A horse injured enough to be unsound through our use deserves a loving retirement.

This leads to my second question, does a horse have a right to life? If a horse does have a right to life, is it a negative or positive right?[16] Horses bred for human use are often unable to survive in the wild. They might have feet that require shoes, a body size that requires more food than forage alone could provide, a coat that must be supplemented by blankets. For these horses, any meaningful right to life must be a positive right. But meeting the needs of a horse is a demanding and costly enterprise.

An ethic of care would be silent about the abstract right to life, whether positive or negative, though it could shed light on particular cases. Our intuitions about these particular cases generate rules of thumb to help us think about similar cases. I want to think about Champ and Clover here.

I have no doubt that Champ is entitled to my care until his life is more painful than pleasant. I take it that I owe him this much, since he probably sustained his arthritic changes through my use. But I have no intention of letting him suffer; when I judge that he is no longer enjoying his life, I will put him down. I think that I must do this if my care for him is to be guided by what is in his interest.

Although I think Clover is also entitled to this kind of care when she is no longer sound, I am not convinced that I am obligated to provide it. Here I turn to my final question; when am I obligated to care?

The answer to this question turns on four factors—need, ability to fill needs, existence of other avenues for filling needs, and relationship. With Champ the need is clear. It is also clear that I can fill this need. Next, no one else is available to fill this need; no one in his/her right mind would be willing to take on an unsound horse who required so much care. Finally, Champ and I have a relationship; he matters to me and I think I matter to him. We have a history together. In this case, the need was caused, in part, by me, but this need not be the case. Horses get old even if they never become unsound. Even in those cases, the strength of the relationship creates an obligation to care.

Clover was a different case. Her situation was not so bleak; the vet was optimistic that she could do well as a trail horse. As a result, I was not the only person who could fill her needs. Finally, she and I did not have the same kind of relationship that Champ and I had. The difference turned, in part, on the absence of a ritual transferring her to me. In the case of horses, the ritual is the economic transaction involved in buying a horse: the prepurchase exam, the bill of sale, the check. This ritual has a significance among horse people; it conveys a new sense of responsibility toward the animal.

But a new question presents itself here: Why should I be sensitive to these rituals? Why should *I* care what they signify? This hints at the larger question: Why *should* I care about animals?

One might point to the similarities between some animals and human animals, and/or to the role of animal care in building human character. We see both of these appeals in the classic tradition of horsemanship, which has many contemporary spokespersons:

> First of all, horses are like people . . . . As a group, they are probably more generous, more forgiving, and less neurotic than people, but they are all different, and all living. This means that our relationship with each of them will be different from our relationship with every other, and that it will be a dynamic relationship, subtly or perhaps not so subtly changing every day.[17]
>
> When Alexander the Great tamed Bucephalus, he succeeded, not because of the Macedonian prince's firm seat, but because of his mental attitude, for he had thought his way into the horse's soul.[18]
>
> The attitude of an equestrian must change and grow to include patience, humility, tolerance, optimism, consistency and empathy with the horse . . . . Without them no outstanding achievement is possible in riding, which is a character-improving art form.[19]

A second reason might be that some animals, at least, are as valuable as humans, and thus legitimately entitled to care. Any one who thinks that humans are more valuable than horses, for example, needs to provide an account of what makes this so. I would be tempted to add that this account ought to make sense to my horse as well as to me. This account should include a list of characteristics a good creature ought to have. I suspect that such an account will not be forthcoming, because an account of what a good X is requires that we say what X's are about; what role they are asked to play in the natural world. If we spell this out, we can see how to talk about a good horse or a good person, but it is not clear to me that we will be able to say that a good person is more good than a good horse.

D. The Ethics of Magic[20]

I draw one general conclusion from these stories and that is that we need a new understanding of our place in the universe.[21] I see my place as a member of the natural world.[22] As such, I must face my fellow creatures with humility. I have already referred to this sense of connection to the natural world. Here I want to discuss and defend it in more detail. I am adopting Starhawk's use of the term "magic" to convey this sense of the place of humans in the universe.

"Magic" is a word that has been revalued and reclaimed in much the same way as "witch" has been revalued and reclaimed. Starhawk, a witch, feminist peace activist, and eco-feminist, describes magic thus:

> Magical techniques are effective for and based upon the calling forth of power-from-within, because magic is the psychology/technology of immanence, of the understanding that everything is connected. . . . Magic is art—that is, it has to do with forms, with structures, with images that can shift us out of the limitations imposed by our culture in a way that words alone cannot, with visions that hint at possibilities of fulfillment not offered by the empty word. And magic is will—action, directed energy, choices made not once but many times. . . ."[23]

Magic involves two elements. The first is the recognition that everything is connected, that the earth is a living body, that it and all its parts are sacred. The second is the way we come to this realization, and how we transmit it to others. Here, visions, rituals, and involvement with the natural world are the media.

Horses have been my teachers. Through my relationships with horses, I have come to see the world as a living body and I have come to view it as sacred.[24]

The destruction of the earth has been encouraged by images of the earth as a machine to be manipulated or as a woman to be raped. It is perfectly obvious that the animals do not enjoy being tortured and that the earth is a less lovely place now than it was before being raped. If we begin to think of the earth as a living body of which we are a part, we will not be able to continue with our policies of wanton destruction.

Starhawk, in a recent talk, invited the audience to think of our own bodies as our culture thinks of the earth.[25] Here is a spot on my back. I don't use it very much; I can't see it. I might as well use it as a sacrificial area and put out cigarettes butts here. How is this different, she asked, from setting aside a part of the earth as a repository for nuclear waste? If the earth is a living body, no parts will be sacrificial areas. When I practice magic, she said, I see the earth as a living body; I see it as sacred; I see its parts as sacred.

So far we have seen that companion animals matter to humans because we can have rich and complex relationships with them; relationships characterized by communication and ties of affection, relationships that deepen our sense of connection to the natural world. We have also seen why this sense of connection to the natural world is valuable. This provides further support of an ethic of care. Let us now turn to other domestic animals.

II. OTHER DOMESTIC ANIMALS

J. Baird Callicott argues that domestic animals, which he describes as human artifacts, have less value, all things considered, than wild animals.[26] This follows from his commitment to a land ethic, first articulated by Aldo Leopold, which holds that things are right when they tend to "preserve the integrity, stability and beauty of the biotic community."[27] Domestic animals are plentiful and in competition with wild animals for resources. I have already pointed out the crucial difference between a land ethic and an ethic of care: while both assume underlying and fundamental connection between all parts of the natural world, an ethic of care puts a premium on the relationships between humans and other members of the biotic community, both human and nonhuman.

As Mary Midgley points out and as I hope my examples illustrate, our relationships to some domestic animals are rich and complex and deepen our sense of connection and commitment to the rest of the biosphere.[28]

I think there are important differences between animals raised for food and animals that are primarily companion animals. My hunch is that tending cattle or pigs doesn't provide the same complex relationship and concern for nature that tending companion animals does. This is not to suggest that tending these animals always, or even usually, prompts a concern for nature. I also agree that watching wild animals can provide a powerful experience of connection with and concern for nature. But companion animals seem to matter to us in a more immediate way. This suggests that an ethic of care would provide a unique place for them in our moral universe. But does it give us any guidance about other domestic animals?

A. Eating Pismo

My sister and brother-in-law, who teaches agriculture, bought a piglet with the intention of raising it for food. They named it Pismo, and they and their three children took excellent care of it until it was time to slaughter it. Shortly after the deed was done, we came to visit. Gracing the dinner table that night was Pismo. As they ate, they commented on what a good pig Pismo was. They spoke of him with affection even as they lifted his flesh to their mouths.

I must confess that this only deepened my commitment to not eating meat, but the question I want to ask here is, is eating meat consistent with an ethic of care toward animals? Can I be acting to further the interests of an animal by killing it and eating it? I think the answer to this question is no. But I think it is possible to give an animal care that is sensitive to its interests up to the moment of slaughter. In this sense, Pismo was cared for.

In a world where humans needed meat to survive (and perhaps other animal products as well), this would not seem so paradoxical. I have in mind here some of the Native American rituals of slaughter. In such rituals, killing is entirely compatible with a sense of the sacredness of the animal, and a sense of connectedness to the animal. What is curious about the claim that Pismo was cared for even though he was destined for the freezer was that we know that we don't need meat to survive. Interestingly enough, they never raised another pig or any other "meat" animal. I take it that this is evidence of the difficulty of truly caring for an animal destined for slaughter.

III. WILD ANIMALS

A. The Cats in Golden Gate Park

One day while walking through the Japanese Tea Garden in Golden Gate Park, I came upon a very sick cat sitting in the middle of the path, shivering and drooling. I was afraid to pick it up because I suspected it had rabies, so I called animal control. They were shorthanded, so they suggested that I put it in a box and bring it in. In the meantime, the cat slipped back into the bushes and I was unable to find it. There are hundreds of cats in Golden Gate Park, and virtually every other park in the area has its share. They live on mice and trash and handouts from humans, and I suspect that their lives are much shorter and certainly much harsher than their domestic cousins. There are two questions I want to raise here. The first is, what makes an animal a companion animal as opposed to a wild animal? The second is, what are our obligations to wild animals?

Callicott argues that domestic animals are mere human artifacts, products of hundreds of years of selective breeding, too stupid to survive on their own. He concludes on the basis of this that they are less valuable than wild animals because they are too numerous and compete with wild animals for resources. Let us suppose that he is right that they are human artifacts. Doesn't this suggest that we have special obligations to domestic animals? After all, their stupidity and inability to get along without us is our fault.

According to Callicott's analysis, the cats in Golden Gate Park are domestic animals, since they or some of their ancestors are the results of human breeding programs. He would decide what to do with them by appeal to the land ethic: are they contributing to the integrity, stability, and beauty of the biosphere? Here we would need to ask how they affected the other species in the park. If it turned out that they were not contributing to the biosphere in the appropriate ways, then we should get rid of them. There is nothing in Callicott's view that suggests that we cannot do this humanely, of course, but we can assume that most of these "wild" cats will never be suitable for companion animals.

I think that it matters, from the perspective of an ethic of care, that these are descendants of companion animals and that we are in some sense responsible for their fate. The question is, what do we do with them? Do we treat them as wild animals? This brings us to my second question, what are our obligations to wild animals?

On one reading, the case of wild animals provides a reductio for an ethic of care. How can we maintain that our commitment is to an ethic of care and allow wild animals to exist in the cruel way they do in nature? In nature, animals often live short and painful lives. Predators prey on other animals, eliminating the old, the young, the sick, and the slow. Is this compatible with a vision of an ideal caring world? I shall begin to answer this question by telling another story.

B. The Wild Dogs

I recently watched a show narrated by Jane Goodall about her research on wild dogs of the African plain.[29] One of the wild dogs was a female who had a litter of puppies that were rejected by the pack. The mother tried to protect her puppies, but she was powerless against the pack. Finally, only one puppy was left. The pack moved on and the puppy, unable to keep up with the pack, was left behind. At this point, the Goodalls interceded and saved the pup. They were later able to successfully place the pup with another pack in the wild. I don't think that there was any question that the Goodalls were horrified by the killing of the puppies, but it did not occur to them to interfere. They explained this by pointing out that they did not know the significance of this event. Perhaps it was a way to protect the pack from overpopulation and the cruel deaths that could face them all if the pack grew beyond a manageable size. They were reflecting the sense of humility appropriate to a recognition of the vast ignorance that humans have about the natural world. But they were also expressing a hope that the natural world would "get it right," that somehow the way things worked out in nature were for the best.

I would give a similar answer to the criticism that an ethic of care provides counterintuitive advice about how we ought to treat wild animals. I don't think that an ethic of care requires that we interfere with nature, because we simply don't know the effects of such interference. Further, the attitude of humility and awe is the appropriate one to take toward the natural world. However, when we have some sense of how things will turn out, when we see the part we have played in creating cruelty in the natural world, then I think our intuitions are different. This brings me back to the feral cats. We think we know something about cats, having lived in very close proximity with them for perhaps thousands of years. Although we know they can survive, albeit in a limited way, in the wild, we feel some connection to them, and we feel responsible for their fate. Whether or not they are human artifacts (I favor the alternative explanation that we simply evolved together), our shared history creates a sense of obligation.

I don't mean to suggest that our obligations are exhausted by our attachments. Further, I recognize that there are many people who feel this same sense of attachment and obligation to other members of the natural world. The main point I want to make here is that an ethic of care is not incompatible with a respect for the workings of the natural world, even where they seem cruel.

IV. CONCLUSION

What follows from all this about my obligations toward the natural world? The first thing I want to point out is that there is something odd about putting the question this way. It suggests two things: first, that I am not part of the natural world, and second, that I am in a superior position vis-à-vis the natural world. I get to make the decision about what the appropriate moral relationship between humans and the rest of the natural world should be. I would want to put the question differently: given that I am part of the sacred body of the earth, how ought I to acknowledge the other parts of this sacred body? It seems to me that I must recognize them as sacred. This requires, first of all, that I recognize them, that I look and see the other creatures that make up the body of the earth, that I look and listen and find the earth. I think that the appropriate moral attitude is humility and care.

There are no transcendent moral principles that should govern our behavior. This implies a dualism that magic rejects. There is no absolute to contrast with our finite, no soul to contrast with body, no God to command. We are the sacred body, we shape the consciousness of this body. There are many things that we will not do if we are informed by this vision of our place in the universe, and the state of the body and the damage to its parts will guide our moral actions.

We could appeal here to the argument that Thomas Nagel gives for altruism.[30] Nagel invites me to see other persons as standing in a morally similar relation to me as my future selves stand in relation to my present self. If I see myself as part of the living body of the earth, I will see myself as connected to other persons, animals, and the earth itself in a way very similar way to my relationship to my future self.

I offered an argument for a general obligation to care in Chapter Four. We can extend this argument to defend an obligation to care for the creatures of the earth (and other things as well: communities, values, objects etc.), but if one is convinced of the truth of magic, then one is committed to treating the natural order as sacred. This is simply an implication of the view; if I do not treat the natural order as sacred, then I do not understand the concept of the sacred. But I am willing to admit that not everyone shares this sense of the earth as sacred. The pitiful state of the earth and her creatures is testimony that this view is not the dominant one. How then can we argue that this is the view that should be adopted?

One strategy is to suggest that the consequences of not doing so are frightening. The problem is that the consequences are not as frightening to someone who does not share this conception. Someone who views the earth as exploitable and who views humans as the rightful dominators of nature will be concerned about the possibility of diminishing resources and the effect on humans of the diminished carrying capacity of the earth, but any reference to the sacredness of the earth becomes simply a metaphor to encourage us to improve the situation of human inhabitants of the earth. This does not require that we see the earth as truly sacred.

I would be inclined to take a different tack, and I would argue that those who have had a relationship with animals, with the earth, become, through these relationships, aware of the sacredness of the earth. I am willing to admit that this moral epistemology runs the risk of being circular. Farmers might point out that they are in contact with the natural world every day and that they have never seen the sacredness of a pig. I don't want to deny that this is possible; indeed, I suspect it is a common attitude for exploiters of the natural world. I am willing to argue here that the exploitive activity interferes with the recognition of the sacred. In short, exploiters are not truly relating to the natural world. Having a relationship with an animal or some other natural object then is a necessary and sufficient condition for recognizing the sacredness of the earthly body, but recognizing the sacredness of the earthly body is a necessary condition for having a relationship with the natural world.

The important epistemological questions become: How do I know that the earth is sacred? How do I know how to live even if I know that the earth is sacred?[31] To the first question I would say that you will come to know this if you make the attempt to relate honestly with the natural world. To the second question I would say that choosing a style of life requires an understanding of your proper role in the universe and deciding what to do in concrete situations requires reflecting upon that larger commitment and carefully listening to the creatures who are with you in that concrete situation. In deciding, remember that you are part of the sacred body and that you are shaping the consciousness of this body with your decisions.

NOTES

1. R. G. Frey seems to be an example of this in assuming that the focus should be on whether animals have interests. See R. G. Frey, *Interests and Rights* (Oxford: Clarendon Press, 1980).

2. Peter Singer is a notable exception. His *Animal Liberation* (New York: Avon Books, 1975) was tremendously influential.

3. S. F. Sapontzis, *Morals, Reason, and Animals* (Philadelphia: Temple University Press, 1987), does an excellent job responding to criticisms of moral treatment of animals.

4. Ibid.

5. I needn't address the larger question of paternalism toward humans here since Thorp, being a dog, does not know about the dangers outside our yard and hence needs to be protected. He might have a better idea in some respects than I do of what's out there, having actually lived a dog's life on the streets. (During his convalescence, well-wishers told us stories of Thorp's life on the run, and he certainly found nice places to hang out. It appears that he had at least two other families in addition to ours. He wasn't eating out of trash cans.) Still, though I think he does understand cars, mean dogs, and the dogcatcher, he does not understand illness and injury. He didn't bring himself home knowing that he needed veterinary care. And veterinary care is not something that he can find for himself the way he can find food, water, and shelter.

6. Michael Sandel, *Liberalism and Its Critics* (New York: New York University Press, 1984).

7. For a philosophically rich discussion of animal training, dog and horse training in particular, see Vicki Hearne, *Adam's Task: Calling Animals by Name* (New York: Vintage Books, 1982).

8. I think that this is an important question for humans as well, and I think it is curious that restrictions on one's actions are seen only as restrictions upon liberty and not as restrictions on relating. It seems to me that the most painful thing about prison would be the severing of relationships. The restriction on

liberty might be merely instrumentally bad, in large part because it requires severing or crippling relationships.

9. Aristotle, *Nichomachean Ethics*, bk. 8, chap. 2 (Indianapolis and New York: The Library of Liberal Arts, 1962).

10. Ibid., bk. 8, chap. 3.

11. The qualification is important here, because the danger might be caused through no fault of the child. For example, suppose I live in a racist society in which attacks on interracial pairings were common, should I separate my white child from his/her African-American friend? I am inclined to say no, depending upon the age of the child and the severity of the attacks, but I think this is an enormously difficult issue.

12. Some eco-feminists defend this view. Marti Keel, for example, made this observation in conversation.

13. Mary Midgley describes in rich detail the relationships that can exist between humans and animals and asserts that our moral obligation to animals follows from the possibilities of such relationships. *Animals and Why They Matter* (Athens: University of Georgia Press, 1983).

14. Dr. James Rooney makes many suggestions for improving our horse management in order to reduce the incidence of injuries, especially on the track. See *The Lame Horse: Causes, Symptoms & Treatment* (North Hollywood, Calif.: Hal Leighton Printing Co., 1973).

15. *Sports Illustrated* describes the tragic death of Go For Wand in "Requiem at Belmont," November 5, 1990.

16. Although I use the language of rights here, I find it more natural to focus on my obligations to care. For a discussion that focuses on animals rights, see Tom Regan, *The Case for Animal Rights* (Berkeley: University of California Press, 1983).

17. William Steinkraus, *Riding and Jumping* (Garden City, N.Y.: Doubleday, 1961), 11–12.

18. Waldemar Seunig, *Horsemanship*, Leonard Mins, trans. (Garden City, N.Y.: Doubleday, 1960), 47.

19. Charles de Kunffy, *Creative Horsemanship* (South Brunswick and New York: A.S. Barnes and Company, 1975), 15.

20. This is the title of Chapter Three of *Dreaming the Dark* by Starhawk (Boston: Beacon Press, 1989).

21. John Passmore offers a history of philosophical (and other) attempts to place a value on the world. *Man's Responsibility For Nature* (New York: Charles Scribner's and Sons, 1974).

22. There is some tension here between my sense of self as member of the natural world and my sense of self as related to specific creatures. This tension is evident in the debate between animal rights defenders and environmentalists. See J. Baird Callicott, *In Defense of the Land Ethics* (Albany: State University of New York Press, 1989) for a defense of an environmental ethic that does not require vegetarianism. See also Aldo Leopold's classic defense of an environmental ethic, *A Sand Country Almanac* (Oxford: Oxford University Press, 1949).

23. Starhawk, *Dreaming the Dark*, 13–14.

24. Starhawk used this example in a talk at San Jose State, March 6, 1989.

25. Philosophers are understandably impatient with insights that are not discursive. Symbolic natural and artificial languages are the traditional language of philosophy. But here we face a dilemma. If we use magic, in speaking another kind of language with animals, in understanding our relationship with the earth, we must either say that we're not involved in an activity that can be characterized as philosophy and cannot even be discussed from a philosophical point of view, or we adopt the standards of philosophy and say that we are not really speaking with animals or understanding anything. But the second option has consequences. Philosophers like to think that they and they alone have the answers to many crucial questions: whether animals feel, whether they reason, whether the earth is a machine or a living body. These are not idle questions, for answering them tells philosophers whether these things have value. And, as the experts on these questions, philosophers speak for our culture.

It is no accident that we call upon our philosophers to answer such questions; their historical commitments to a certain kind of discourse spell doom for the animals and the earth. Animals do not speak to us in any sense that philosophers understand, they do not have those properties that philosophers have singled out as conferring value. Since it matters to me, to women, to animals and to the earth that we begin to see the creatures of the earth as valuable, I want to take up the cultural space of the philosopher; I want to speak to this issue and I want to practice magic.

26. Callicott, *In Defense of the Land Ethics*, chap. 1.

27. Leopold, *A Sand Country Almanac*, 225–26.

28. Midgley, *Animals and Why They Matter*.

29. *The Wild Dogs of the Serengeti*.

30. Thomas Nagel, *The Possibility of Altruism* (Princeton, N.J.: Princeton University Press, 1970).

31. Christopher Stone tries to answer this question in *Earth and Other Ethics* (New York: Harper & Row, 1987).

Chapter Seven

Should a Feminist Care?

"An ethic of care" and "feminist ethics" are often used interchangeably, though many feminists have challenged this identification.[1] One reason for describing an ethic of care as a feminist project is that describing it involves paying special attention to the experience of women. I found that I had a very strong personal reaction to an ethic or care; it seemed to express my own moral reasoning and moral ideals. Further, it does not seem to me that an ethic of care was incompatible with my feminist commitments. Obviously, I do not consider this the end of the story. There are compelling feminist and other critiques that deserve to be heard.

Much of the criticism of an ethic of care has come from feminists, and their central criticism is that it is not a feminist ethic. This chapter will address this objection. Since my response to this criticism is part of a seamless web of responses to criticism in general, I will focus more broadly on objections to an ethic of care and will sort out the criticisms into two categories, what I call the pragmatic criticisms and the foundational criticisms.

Hume's conception of the task of moral philosophy, as Annette Baier eloquently argues,[2] is that moral philosophers should concern themselves with designing ethics for practical application. The standards of adequacy of an ethic, in this view, are all pragmatic. Does the ethic work? Will it make the world a more pleasant place? Can we transmit it to our children? Much of the criticism of an ethic of care focuses on these pragmatic issues. The feminist critiques focus on the practical implication for women in particular.

Foundational criticisms, on the other hand, focus on more theoretical issues. There are two main lines of argument here. The first is that an ethic of care is insufficiently action-guiding. The second is that an ethic of care is insufficiently grounded.

In what follows, I will first grapple with the pragmatic criticisms and then turn to the foundational criticisms.

I. PRAGMATIC CRITICISMS

A. An Ethic of Care Requires Too Much of Women

The first criticism I will address is that an ethic of care requires too much of women. In this respect, an ethic of care idealizes the status quo, it is simply, as Ketayun Gould puts it, "old wine in new bottles."[3] There are, it seems to me, three concerns here. The first is that women are unfairly burdened when they adopt an ethic of care.[4] The second is that women are disadvantaged in conflicts with men if they adopt an ethic of care while the men adopt an ethic of justice. The third is that the ethic of care is devalued in our society, so anyone who speaks in the voice of care runs the risk of not being heard. I will first sketch these concerns and then respond to each in turn.

Women, socialized to see themselves as care-givers, are already overburdened by responsibilities to care, burdens that are not shouldered equally by men. Men, who are socialized to further their own projects, are inattentive to calls for care and oblivious to the amount of work by women that goes into their own care.[5]

Women who adopt an ethic of care will be at a distinct disadvantage in conflicts with men. If the woman holds an ethic of care, she will feel obligated to compromise, to attempt to accommodate the other. If the other holds a similar moral perspective, a compromise that accommodates both is possible. But if the other is male and is concerned only about his own projects, she will be the one who caves in. Someone who holds an ethic of care will also be at a disadvantage in a conflict with someone who holds an ethic of principles, since someone who cannot violate absolute principles cannot compromise when they are at stake. If Gilligan is right that women are more likely to hear the voice of care while men are more likely to hear the voice of justice, then the person with the care ethic is likely to be female while the person with the justice ethic is likely to be male.

What makes this even worse is that men often see the moral perspective of women as morally deficient. As Gilligan puts it, "herein lies a paradox, for the very traits that traditionally have defined the 'goodness' of women, their care for and sensitivity to the needs of others, are those that mark them as deficient in moral development.["6] If this is right, then speaking in the voice of care will be worse than ineffective, since the voice of care is often not recognized as a moral voice.

My first response to all these criticisms is that there is nothing in the ethic of care that requires that women be the only care-givers.[7] In fact, if we see obligations of care as implicit in relationships and an attitude of openness to care as part of what is best about humans, then it is obvious that this ethic applies to all humans. But this is not my final response, since I do think that the Humean project is the right one; moral philosophers should be concerned with the application of ethics, and an essential desideratum for any moral perspective is its workability. This requires that we be sensitive to how it would be applied in the world in which we live.

I too am concerned that women are unfairly burdened by care giving, and I recognize that this situation is unlikely to change anytime soon. I do worry that revaluing an ethic of care will result in increased feelings of obligation and guilt among already overburdened women. I worry that teaching an ethic of care will undermine the confidence that many young women seem to have that they can and should pursue their own projects. I worry that identifying an ethic as feminist or feminine will exacerbate the situation. And yet, I am terrified about a future in which no one cares about anything but his or her own projects, narrowly conceived. I guess I am willing to run the risk of rationalizing the status quo by proselytizing for an ethic of care, though I think it is extremely important to make it clear that this is an ethic for humans, not just for women.

I remain hopeful that we can avoid this dilemma, however. As Gilligan's research has shown, men already hear the voice of care. My survey confirmed the impression that I already had that men are becoming more and more sensitive to the demands of care. If this is true, then perhaps the concerns about the burden of care resting too heavily on women will be less real in the future. I must confess that I am not counting on this happening without a great deal of struggle, both personal and political, and I think that such struggle should focus some attention on equalizing the burdens of care.

At the same time, I suspect that we, as scholars, are much less powerful than we think. If an ethic of care gains currency, it will be primarily because our world has changed and not because we taught it and wrote about it.

Finally, I am bothered by the possible classism of this criticism. I grew up in poverty and raised my two boys in poverty until they were seven and nine. I can still remember the tremendous feeling of satisfaction I got from paying my bills. I relished my ability to care, to put a roof over their heads, to feed and clothe them. I think that many poor parents, and

mothers in particular, would be put off by the suggestion that they should
be protected from the demands of care giving when they want very much
to be able to give adequate care to their families.   I also think that many
poor people wish that they could have been more cared for as children.
Barbara Smith, an African-American, and Cenen, a black Puerto Rican,
discuss their longing:

> Barbara: "Oh, you mean you can come home from school and say "Someone hurt
> my feelings," and someone would say, "Oh honey..."? Cenen: "Or hug you, my
> goodness. Give me some warmth, you know. Touch me and say I'm all right.
> That's what I needed and I never, well I shouldn't say I never got it, but I didn't
> get it the way I needed it."[8]

I do not want to deny that poor women and women of color are also
unfairly burdened by care giving, but I don't think we should be blind to
the different perspectives on care giving that accompany differences in
economic class.

This is reminiscent of the differences between white women and women
of color on abortion.[9]   White women focus most of their attention on the
abortion issue, while women of color worry about forced sterilization and
their inability to have and decently raise the children they may want to
have.   This difference in perspective betrays a difference in experience.
Middle-class white children are wanted in our society, so many middle-
class white women feel pressured to procreate.   This explains their preoccupation with abortion.   Poor women and women of color, on the other
hand, are pressured not to procreate.   This pressure is often direct (e.g.,
coerced sterilization), but more often indirect.   They know their children
will not be welcomed; they know raising them will be a constant struggle;
they know that their children will suffer in our classist, racist, patriarchal
society.   Hence, these women, though certainly concerned about forced
pregnancy, are also very sensitive to the positive rights assumed in a full-
blown right to reproduction.

I now turn to the second feminist concern, that conflict between women
and men disadvantages women if they adopt an ethic of care.   I suspect
that conflict between men and women is less often conflict between two
moral voices than conflict between competing desires or between a moral
voice on one side and simple self-interest on the other.   Although a conflict
between an ethic of care and simple self-interest might be resolved to the
disadvantage of the holder of the ethic of care, this is not a peculiar criticism of an ethic of care.   Taking the moral point of view, which enjoins
us to consider the interests of others, often puts us at a disadvantage in
conflicts with others who are not taking this point of view.   This is true
regardless of what moral perspective we accept.

The more interesting conflict is between a holder of an ethic of care and a holder of an ethic of justice. The worry is that when the voice of justice and the voice of care make different decisions, the voice of care will be at a disadvantage. This is so because the voice of care puts a premium on compromise, while the voice of justice, appropriately conceived, does not. If the voice of justice whispers that a principle that is to be taken as absolute requires that we do X and the voice of compromise says do Y, which voice will be heard? Again, the worry is that the person who listens to the voice of care will do all the compromising.

I do not think it is obvious that the voice of care will give way. I distinguish between two judgments: "Adopt the compromise solution that will accommodate all" and "Compromise with those who judge the situation differently." Let me return here to the fable of the porcupine and the mole. Suppose we have a mole who listens exclusively to the voice of justice and thinks that the relevant principle should be: "Property rights should be respected." This mole interprets the case as one in which the moles have a property right to enjoy their burrow, which is being threatened by the porcupine. From this mole's perspective, while it would not be wrong to let the porcupine in, the moles would be justified in keeping him out. This mole feels justified in keeping him out. Another mole is listening exclusively to the voice of care, and it says: "Adopt the compromise that will accommodate everyone." This second mole interprets this as requiring the moles to let the porcupine in as long as the porcupine helps the moles enlarge the burrow. Now these two moles are in conflict. The first has a second-level concern with justice, the second with care. The first values standing up for principles, the second values compromise. It is not at all clear that the second mole will go along with the first mole's decision to throw the porcupine out. It depends upon whether the second mole values care over compromise. I want to argue that compromise as a response to conflict is a consequence of a commitment to care. It is because we see others as needing and deserving care that we compromise with them with the hope of accommodating everyone's needs. In this case, I would expect the truly caring mole to refuse to compromise with the first mole. The porcupine needs a place to live, the first mole does not need to be right.

The moral of the story is that the belief that one who hears the voice of care will always give way assumes that compromise is the only, or at least the primary, value of an ethic of care. I think this is simply a misinterpretation of an ethic of care.

The final specifically feminist concern is that women who listen to the voice of care will be disadvantaged when they try to speak in this voice. Since male society often does not see this as a moral voice, a women who speaks in the voice of care will not be in the conversation. If we assume that moral conversations have real consequences, then the exclusion of women from these conversations will disadvantage women and all those for whom they speak.

I think that this criticism is another version of the adage, "If you want to be successful in a man's world, act like a man." I agree that it is hard for women to be heard, but I don't think that the solution is to adopt a different voice but to speak louder and to be clear about the purpose and results of speaking. First of all, I am a bit skeptical about moral conversations; too many of them are veiled attempts to rationalize one's agenda. Second, we must spend more time speaking to each other, and this involves and allows developing our own vocabulary and revaluing language. Third, though I am inclined to be pessimistic about our power to effect change, we, as scholars and teachers, can take a leading role in this revaluing. Finally, we should learn to speak louder and to act when we are not heard.

B.   An Ethic of Care Requires Too Much of Us All

Even if I have succeeded in showing that an ethic of care need not require too much of women, one might argue that I have done so by describing an ethic that requires too much of us all. If we are obligated to respond to presented need, to adopt a caring attitude that requires us to be sensitive to all need, then we will be spending all our time giving care. But since there is so much need in our world, our efforts to care would only make a dent in the need. The result would be that the caring person would be exhausted by caring while at the same time guilty over not doing enough.

I will divide my response here into two sections. Since I think that this objection can be applied to any moral perspective, I will begin by discussing general responses to this objection. In the next section I will focus on particular versions of this objection as they apply to an ethic of care.

Any moral perspective must face the problem of how to limit one's moral obligations. In a perfect world, everyone would take morality seriously. It would be interesting to speculate about whether this world would be an improvement over ours, even if its resources were more limited. In any case, in our world, we suffer from a lack of moral commitment, and, at the same time, we are faced with a grossly unequal distribution of the world's resources. Meanwhile, the earth and all of its human and nonhuman creatures are in serious danger. Anyone who takes the moral point of view seriously faces an existential crisis: How is one to do the right thing—however the right thing is described—to adopt the right attitude, and still live a life of some relative comfort and security? One answer might be that relative comfort and security is simply incompatible with great need.   If self-sacrifice is called for by one's moral commitments, then self-sacrifice is morally required.   Moral philosophers have been reluctant to accept this response.[10]   I take it that there are roughly three other responses available to them.

First, "ought implies can" applies to an ethic of care as it does to all other moral perspectives.   If it is simply impossible for me to care for some particular other, I am not obligated to do so.   Obviously, logical and physical impossibility limit my obligations, but psychological impossibility is also a legitimate excuse.

The second option is to suggest that moral imperatives apply only to moral situations and that moral situations do not come up that often.   This is the tack that Mill takes in his responses to criticisms in *Utilitarianism*.[11] I don't think this is a satisfactory response, because there is no good account of the features of a distinctly moral situation.   One might argue that the distinction between morality and mere social convention is culturally specific.   Indeed, there is some empirical support for this view.[12]   I would argue that all situations have a moral dimension, that all life has a moral dimension.   As Cheryl Noble puts it:

> Moral standards arise as part of the structures of various cultures, economies, and social forms . . . if . . . what is good or right within some realm of life is a function of a wide variety of conditioning factors ranging from psychoanalytic to economic ones, then how could it also be possible that, nevertheless, taken as moral phenomena, they all stem from a common, relatively unitary source?[13]

The third response is that certain obligations are properly seen as supererogatory.   One needs an account of supererogation here.   Traditional accounts have focused on particular actions.[14]   Others have argued that the principle of supererogations operates over sets of duties.[15]   In either case, one might point out that my obligations to myself limit my duties.[16]   I take it that this is the point Bernard Williams makes in his criticism of utilitarianism.[17]   He argues that without my own projects, life ceases to have any meaning for me.   This is not just a utilitarian point, that I will stop living if my duties interfere with my projects too much and that my death will decrease the amount of utility in the world.   Rather, my moral integrity suffers as my sense of self-identity and agency diminishes.

I am inclined to agree that the right way to delineate supererogation is in terms of duties to self, but I think the story is more complicated, and will tell it by focusing on particular responses to concerns that an ethic of care requires too much.

The first thing to point out is that some ways of caring are simultaneously ways to care for oneself.   I was talking to my retired neighbor about the home improvement projects we were both involved in, and he said: "When you don't care about your house anymore it's all over."   I knew exactly what he meant.   When I embark on a home improvement project, it is a way of feathering my nest, of caring for myself.   I think there is a parallel in caring for persons.   When I care for persons, I am caring for myself in two ways.   First, my relationship is enriched by the right kind of care (appropriate to the relationship).   Second, I often get tremendous satisfaction from caring for the other.

One might argue here that the caring is either ethical caring or mere selfishness.   If it is ethical caring, then my motive must be other-directed. If my motive is to enrich my relationship, then I am not engaged in ethical caring.   My first response is that I do not think that the distinction be- tween moral motives and selfish motives is terribly clean.   I am inclined to agree with Williams that the Greek conception, which did not draw the distinction, is the right one.[18]   Second, even if I accepted the distinction, it is possible for one to act from other-directed motives even when one is quite aware that he/she will benefit from the act.

In response to the second point, that I get satisfaction from caring, one might argue that this is just the satisfaction of living up to norms inter- nalized in my youth.   But not every norm is good for me.   I might live in a society where women are expected to raise all the children and work outside the home while their husbands study.   (This is not an unusual arrangement in this country, where wives take care of the kids and work while their husbands are in graduate or professional school.) I might get real satisfaction in doing so, in spite of the fact that this satisfaction is in some sense inappropriate because it is gained at the expense of my other projects.

I am willing to grant that if this is the correct description of the situ- ation, then I am not caring for myself while caring for the other.   But I do not think that this exhausts the possibilities.   There are relationships of care where caring involves simultaneously caring for the self.   Second, caring for others can also be adopted as one's own project.   Third, this response does not explain the satisfaction that males feel in our culture when they are engaged in certain kinds of caring.   Most men (though there are obvious differences among men of different cultures and classes) in our culture were not socialized to care for children, and yet many of them do so and take tremendous satisfaction in doing so.

My second, and related, response to the objection that care requires too much is that some relationships of care are reciprocal.   Noddings focuses on the mother-child relationship and even describes caring for an infant as the paradigm of caring.   If we see this as the paradigm of caring, it is not unreasonable to worry about whether caring requires too much, since infants require almost constant care. At the same time, infants give very little back; they do not interact in any obvious way until the first smile at about two or three months. In the face of this tremendous burden, parents console themselves by reminding themselves that this period is over after two or three months. But if this is the paradigm of care, then I agree that it requires too much.

Thankfully, this is but a brief moment in the relationship with a child, and relationships with adults seldom require this kind of care. As I pointed out in Chapter Five, there are other kinds of relationships with persons which call forth a very different kind of care, and these relationships are reciprocal to different extents. In a reciprocal relationship, the care goes in both directions. Sometimes it will be my turn to be cared for, sometimes I will do the caring. At other times, our caring itself will be reciprocal as we do something to care for ourselves, such as when I take a vacation alone with my husband.[19]

Still, though some caring is reciprocal, and some caring involves caring for self as one cares for the other, there will be times when the burden of care is simply too much. For this reason, an ethic of care needs a way to limit the obligations to care for. But we also need a politics of care. It is not enough to decide when we are justified in saying no to need. We also need a political philosophy and action strategy that will make saying yes less personally draining.

So far, I have argued that an ethic of care is not as burdensome as it may seem, and thus the problem is not as serious as it may seem. Still, adopting an ethic of care without a corresponding way to limit obligations to care would be tremendously burdensome, especially in this post-Reagan era. The following is a sketch of some ways in which one can limit one's obligation to care.

Virginia Warren, in a paper on world hunger, argued that our obligations are not static.[20] Her idea is that taking the moral point of view seriously requires an attitude of concern for others, but that we can spread this obligation out over our lives. We can choose to pay special attention at certain times in life and pay less attention later. Perhaps we have a dissertation to do now, perhaps we have a sick parent or a young child. Our lives have an ebb and a flow; sometimes we are struggling with burdens of care, sometimes we are engaged in important projects. We have to recognize this and take some time to focus primarily on social and political issues. The ideal of caring requires that we try to make caring a reality for all the earth's creatures, and the practice of caring requires that we care for those to whom we are related and those in need, but our responses can vary. When the demands of the practice of caring overwhelm us, we may shift our focus away from political activity, as long as we recognize that our commitment to care for particular others does not exhaust our obligations. When we are engaged in important political work, on the other hand, we may refuse to take on any new relationships.

What we have to work for here is a balance. Our commitment to the ideal of caring grows out of our understanding of care as it flowers in particular relationships. We come to recognize the value of caring for others. In doing so, we begin to see that the others who are not in direct relation with us are also worthy of care. This is similar to Hume's argument that justice flowers as a virtue when we realize that strangers have much in common with our special others.[21] Perhaps we begin to see ourselves, as I have, as part of a sacred body which includes all creatures in our biosphere.

My next strategy to limit obligations to care is to point out that human psychology limits our ability to care. As we become more enmeshed in obligations to care, we may begin to burnout. Caring for children and sick elderly parents at the same time, now a common experience for many middle-aged women, can result in total collapse. I have found myself in this situation, as a single parent with two small children, elderly grandparents who depended upon me, and a sick relative who needed care. All the while, I was working thirty hours a week and going to school full-time. I couldn't give myself permission to cut down my caring. I don't regard this merely as a fact about me, but as a damning indictment of social policy in this country which leaves poor people struggling madly to keep their families afloat. Still, the effect on me was devastating. I eventually responded by taking my two children and moving across the country. I don't think this is an unusual story; caring burnout is a major factor in stress, especially for women.

There is a personal as well as a political response here. Even if I am not being sensitive to my obligations to myself, even if I do not think it makes sense to talk about obligations to the self, my obligation to care requires that I avoid caring burnout since it will undermine my ability to care, both now and in the future. The political response is to restructure our society so that caring is supported. I am not arguing here for impersonal state-run "caring" institutions, but I do think we could go a long way toward the goal of a caring society.

My next response is that I think we have obligations to ourselves. The ideal of care requires that we understand our fellow creatures as valuable, as worthy of care. Seeing ourselves as mere caretakers is incompatible with this ideal. We must, then, care for ourselves, see ourselves and our projects as worthy of our attention. I will cease to be me, in a very real sense, if I do not have my projects; they help define who and what I am.

Ignoring my own projects undermines the sense of agency and integrity that are required for genuine action.

Finally, I must confess that I find the preoccupation with limiting one's obligations a trifle bourgeois. The relatively privileged can choose their burdens, while poor and working-class people are overburdened by life. In the face of the glaring maldistribution of the world's resources and the resultant suffering of the world's poor, the complaint of the affluent that they are overburdened by obligations to care sounds suspiciously like whining. Maybe we should continue to feel and be genuinely overburdened for a while until the debts of imperialism and capitalism are paid. After all, our good fortune has been purchased at the expense of someone else's exploitation. Even if you don't accept this analysis, I think we would all agree that we didn't deserve to be born relatively privileged, and if we didn't deserve this bonus, and others are suffering its lack, sharing seems like a caring response.

C.   An Ethic of Care Is Parochial

Nel Nodding's analysis in *Caring* leaves her open to this objection.[22] She argues that the obligation to care for flows from the existence or real possibility of relationship.[23] Thus, the missionary on her way to Africa where she will likely run into a starving African child has an obligation to hungry children in Africa, while I, who do not contemplate such a trip, do not. I agree with Noddings that I cannot be obligated to care for strangers in the same way I care for those related to me, but I am inclined to see this as a consequence of "ought implies can." I simply cannot do this. I cannot stay up with a sick child who lives a continent away. But it does not follow that I have no obligations. Indeed, I would argue that my obligation as a caring person is toward an ideal of caring. I am obligated to respond in a caring way to presented need and to work for the increase of caring in the world, and I can certainly do this for the starving children in Africa.

Though we need not adopt Noddings's response, we still have a problem with parochialism. In a way, this objection follows from a strategy to limit one's obligations: if I am justified in refusing any additional obligations because I am already sufficiently burdened with caring for those to whom I am already related, then I will never get around to doing anything for strangers, no matter how dire their situation.

This is a real worry. I agree with Noddings that I have a special obligation to those to whom I am already related. I have three dogs and three cats right now. Two of the dogs and all three cats were strays. I responded to their presentations of need by taking them in. I understand my obligations to them as including giving them adequate food, shelter, affection, exercise, and veterinary care. But even routine vaccinations are costly. Under the circumstances, I have no intention of going to the pound to take in another animal whose need might be every bit as great as theirs was when I took them in.

The situation with my children is similar. I have three children. My two boys are nearly out of college, but my daughter is five. I feel sufficiently burdened by caring for them that I would not dream of becoming a foster mother, even though I know that there is a desperate need for foster homes in my county.

In neither case is my care excessive or extravagant. The cats and dogs eat generic food, the boys do all their own laundry and share in the chores. But the dogs and cats sometimes get sick, the boys sometimes need an ear, and my daughter, who has asthma and is often ill, needs a great deal of care.

I am not now as politically active as I would like to be. I am aware of the state of this country and the world, and I am greatly concerned about it, but my primary focus is on bringing this awareness and concern into my classroom. Am I a victim of parochialism? Worse, am I parochial and if I am parochial, is this a consequence of my commitment to an ethic of care? Is it easier to be parochial with an ethic of care than with some other moral perspective?

I distinguish between two senses of "parochial." Someone who is parochial in the first sense is concerned only about those closely connected to her/ him, is aware only of those facts that are of immediate concern to those others, and acts only in response to the needs and desires of those closely connected to her/him. I will call this strong parochialism. A particularly pernicious version of this I will call very strong parochialism. Very strong parochialism would include the belief that those not connected to oneself were inferior to those so connected, and hence not morally considerable in the same way. An ethic of care supports neither strong nor very strong parochialism; rather it includes an ideal of caring and an openness to future connection and presentations of need which are incompatible with strong or very strong parochialism.

But there is another sense of parochialism, which I shall call weak parochialism. One is parochial in this sense if one's response to concern prioritizes the needs and wants of one's circle of family, friends, and acquaintances. One can be parochial in this sense even if one is concerned, aware, and responsive toward the circumstances of those outside one's circle of family and friends.

One could imagine an ethic of care that placed no emphasis on existing relationships. This ethic might call for caring for those who are most in need. In this view, I might be forced to choose between my animals and children and some other creatures in need.   I would justify my choice purely on the basis of need.   If some other child had a greater need, I would respond to its need rather than the needs of my own child.   While I think we should respond in some way to the needs of other children before we respond to the idle whims of our own, I find this view appalling and I am convinced that the morally good person is not impartial to this extent.   Bernard Williams makes this point when he discusses the man who must stop and deliberate before rescuing his wife, who is drowning along with a stranger.   Luckily for his wife, the husband decides that he is justified in saving her rather than the stranger, but, as Williams points out, the husband is asking one question too many.[24]

I do not want to defend an ethic of care that does not allow us to pay special attention to those related to us. Ties of affection, trust, and loyalty matter.   It does not follow, however, that our obligations are exhausted by caring for our loved ones.   Need plays a role in this ethic, as well as our obligation to work for a caring world.   This is a world in which every creature is able to respond to his/her demands of care for self and other. It is a world in which suffering is alleviated.

Still, in the real world, it is difficult to say how to balance the responsibilities based on relationship with the responsibilities based on need, but then no moral perspective can tell us what to do in every situation.   A moral perspective that claims to do so assumes an overly simple picture of moral life.   An ethic of care presents one with the ideal of caring, an ideal that grows from caring in particular relationships.   Each agent must struggle to live up to this ideal in his/her life.

I want to make two final points before I leave the discussion of parochialism.   First, it is important to keep in the mind the account of moral psychology that is assumed by an ethic of care.   Our ability to respond morally, to see the moral dimensions of life, requires that we exist in sustaining networks of care.   We learn to care for strangers by first developing strong attachments to particular others.   If this is right, then weak parochialism is not an impediment to taking the moral point of view, but a necessary condition.   One might argue here that even if this account if correct, weak parochialism ought to be dispensed with as soon as moral sensibility is sufficiently engendered.   This argument makes two assumptions.   The first is that moral sensibility would continue to flourish even with the abandonment of weak parochialism.   The second is that this moral sensibility, which would include the requirement of impartiality, is morally better than the moral sensibility that would flourish with weak parochialism.   The first is an empirical question, and I defer to moral psychologists and other social scientists to instruct us here, though my suspicion is that weak parochialism cannot be abandoned without at the same time undermining moral sensibility.   If the second assumes some impartial perspective from which to evaluate moral sensibilities, then it is question begging: an impartialist moral sensibility is morally superior to a weak parochialist moral sensibility on impartialist grounds.   If it is not to be question begging, then some other argument must be provided, but it is not clear what this argument would be.   I am inclined to be a naturalist about questions of this sort, and this inclines me to look at human psychology and social interaction, but this takes us back to the empirical question I offered above.

Second, I sometimes wonder if defenders of impartiality are confused about the relative difficulty of caring for friends and family as opposed to caring for strangers.   To put this another way, one may focus on impartiality because one assumes that it is easier to respond to one's responsibilities to family and friends than it is to respond to strangers.   If this is right, we ought to focus, as morality itself does, on what is hard.   But this assumption about the ease of meeting obligations toward family and friends is questionable at best.

There are two ways in which one may describe responding to family and friends as easy.   In the first sense, it is easy because it is obvious what is to be done.   In the second sense, it is easy because what ought to be done overlaps with what I want to do.   However, in neither sense is it obvious that responding to one's family and friends is easier than responding to strangers.   Quite the contrary, one is often confused about how one ought to respond to one's family and friends.   How one acts or doesn't act is as important as what one does.   Conflicts between the needs and wants of family members and friends often conflict, and our natural responses may not be the correct ones:

To summarize, an ethic of care is parochial in a very weak sense.   It does allow us to pay special attention to obligations based on relationship, but it does not permit us to ignore the needs of strangers.   In this respect, it does not differ from other moral perspectives which must also allow for our human need for intimate relationships.   Utilitarians allow for this by arguing that allowing special relationships will ultimately maximize utility.   Deontologists focus on obligations based on promises and contracts. I think it is an advantage of an ethic of care that it doesn't need to justify these special relationships, that it doesn't ask one question too many.

D.   An Ethic of Care Is Not Liberatory

Another objection that is often given by feminists is that an ethic of care is not liberatory.[25]   I think there are three different theses here: first, that caring is incompatible with personal liberation; second, that caring undermines the liberatory struggle of oppressed people; and third, that caring is not possible for revolutionary heroes. I will deal with each of these criticisms in turn.

The concern that an ethic of care will unfairly burden women is an instance of the larger worry that care is incompatible with personal liberation, whether personal liberation is seen as defeating oppressive circumstances or overcoming a psychology rooted in oppression. Often, personal liberation requires both.

There are more and less radical accounts of oppression and more and less radical programs for overcoming oppression. Overcoming a psychology rooted in oppression is a necessary condition for overcoming oppression, though these two goals are often accomplished simultaneously. Some would argue that they must be accomplished simultaneously since a revolutionary consciousness arises out of revolutionary struggle. In any case, overcoming oppression takes time, energy, and, above all, conscious struggle. Depending upon one's circumstances, it may require a willingness to go to prison or even to die. This struggle cannot be achieved unless we clear the decks, unless we streamline our lives. There is no room in this struggle for the responsibilities of care.

The scenario that feminist critics see as the worst case is the dutiful wife and mother who puts her projects on the back burner in order to care for her husband and children. While this scenario is very familiar to us, I don't think that an ethic of care requires ignoring one's own projects. As I argued earlier, caring for others can be embraced as one's own project, and even if it is not seen as a project, we do have obligations to ourselves. But suppose I have eleven children and I live in utter poverty, what time do I have for my other projects if I am to care for my children? Unfortunately, this is the reality for many, perhaps most, women in the world. But an ethic of care is not to blame here. Rather, the culprit is oppression, patriarchy, and poverty. An ethic of care would support an end to all these practices.

Overcoming oppression can be either a serious challenge or a self-indulgent whim, depending upon the oppression. The bourgeois version of it is all too familiar to us. This is the version that men offer when they leave their wives and children in the middle of a mid-life crisis. And though the angst is very real and the struggle often difficult, the pursuit of it requires that someone else be available to take over the caring abandoned in pursuit of personal liberation.

There are also very real threats to personal liberation that must be taken seriously. In the film *The Fringe Dwellers*,[26] the main character, Trilby Comeaway, is a young Australian aboriginal woman. Her overriding desire is to escape the poverty and insularity of her aboriginal village. She longs to go to the city to continue her education. Unfortunately, she becomes pregnant. In a deeply moving scene, she kills her newborn infant. Her grief is very real, but so is the realization that for her it would be impossible to get away and keep the baby. She is not unmindful of the baby's interests here. She knows that escape is difficult and painful, but that going on is impossible, and she does not want her child to suffer this fate. In *Beloved* by Toni Morrison, one of the main characters faces a similar decision.[27] She kills her children rather than see them returned to slavery.

In both cases, we are struck by the awfulness of the decision facing these women. It should have been possible for Trilby Comeaway to have her baby, her family and friends, and her liberation. The obstacles in her way were political; the poverty of her family was a function of social policy and culture and the racism and sexism of Australian society. It should have possible for the mother in *Beloved* to have freedom for herself and her children.

I think the moral of the story is that personal liberation may sometimes require sundering ties of caring, but in doing so, one pays a price. The one who cuts him/herself off from a nexus of care in order to achieve liberation pays a price, and the ones left behind pay a price.

This suggests that personal liberation should not be seen as a goal independent of the liberation of an oppressed people. The question I now turn to is whether the liberation of an oppressed people is compatible with an ethic of care.

The focus on communal liberation causes us to see personal liberation in a new way. True personal liberation is impossible without communal liberation. I can escape, I can be a token, but the price will be high. It will require giving up my culture, cutting myself off from the only comfort I ever knew, sundering the relations of care through which I sustained others and was myself sustained. But this is an incomplete liberation. I am liberated from menial jobs, from poverty and despair, but I am also liberated from my history, my culture, my family, and my friends.

If I value my history and my community, I will see my personal liberation as bound up with communal liberation. Granted, this full-blown personal liberation is much more difficult to attain, and I think most settle for something in between. But when we begin to see personal liberation as a function of communal liberation, it is much less obvious that we should be leery of an ethic of care in struggling toward liberation. In fact, I think an ethic of care is required for communal liberation.

It is no accident that African-American people refer to each other in familial terms: brother, sister, mother, auntie. This practice became more conscious and overtly political in the struggle for liberation during the sixties. The Black Panther Party had a breakfast program for African-American children. They didn't do this just because they thought they would have better success at proselytizing early in the morning; they did it because they knew the children needed a good breakfast. Afro-centered elementary schools stress the school's role in transmitting values, and the value of care is given special prominence, both as historically important and politically necessary.[28]

Some people, especially those who believe that violent revolution is the only way to achieve liberation, think that the best way to end oppression is to take advantage of great misery. Some even argue for emiseration as a conscious revolutionary strategy. Others, and I count myself among them, think that the struggle must involve caring for our own. This caring not only makes it possible for people to survive, but it empowers them. The transformation from victim to agent requires that we reconceptualize our situations, that we begin to see ourselves as innocent of our own oppression and as agents in its demise. Obviously, the debate here is not merely empirical; different views about the morality of war and revolution might divide these two camps. The point I want to make is that care is required by the second view.

One might still wonder if an ethic of care is compatible with violent revolutionary struggle. Sara Ruddick, in defending what she calls "maternal practice," which assumes an ethic of care, argues that violence is incompatible with maternal practice.[29] Mothers are concerned to preserve the lives of their children and to rear children who will become healthy adults. Victoria Davion, on the other hand, argues that violence is not incompatible with maternal practice or, by extension, with an ethic of care.[30] She argues that passionate attachments to particular others can serve both as motivation and justification for violence. If she is right about this, then one might be justified in going to war to protect the interests of particular others. It follows, then, that violent revolutionary struggle against oppression might be justified in terms of an ethic of care.

Here is a final point about an ethic of care and communal liberation: Many critics of an ethic of care have stressed the role that moral language plays in political debates. Rights talk has been the traditional vehicle for making claims on behalf of oppressed people, they argue. If we must give up rights talk, then we lose a powerful weapon in the struggle for liberation.

First, I must reassert my skepticism about the impact of moral persuasion. Second, even if I granted that such language had some power, there is no reason why we couldn't adopt a language of rights to further the commitments of care. Indeed, the blossoming of the language of positive rights seems designed for this purpose.[31]

The final concern about liberation is that a revolutionary hero cannot adopt an ethic of care. There are three reasons for this: the first is that the revolutionary hero must be willing to take risks, to die if necessary, in the struggle for liberation; second, the revolutionary hero must be willing to inflict harm; third, the revolutionary hero must not have particular attachments, but a commitment to the people as a whole. These are not conceptual requirements; this picture of the revolutionary hero is in part a normative ideal, and in part an empirical generalization which stems from the task of the revolutionary in the struggle as we know it. I will discuss each in turn.

The task of the revolutionary hero is to be a leader in a people's struggle for liberation. The revolutionary hero is often contrasted with the re-former; the reformer sees the task as reforming the political process to include oppressed people, while the revolutionary either rejects the insti-tutions of the oppressor or doesn't believe that anything less than revolutionary struggle will open the doors of these institutions to oppressed peoples. The revolutionary hero need not be committed to violent struggle; Gandhi is an example of a pacifist revolutionary hero.

In any case, the revolutionary hero will be in great danger because he/she is challenging the status quo. There are two problems for the revo-lutionary hero with respect to an ethic of care. Ties of affection and obligations of care might undermine the commitment to struggle or dis-tract the hero from the struggle. Second, the hero brings danger home to his/her loved ones. In response to the first worry, I am not convinced that these ties of affection will undermine the struggle; they might inten-sify the commitment to struggle in order to liberate those to whom the hero feels ties. The question of risk, however, is a real worry. One response might be to refuse to form attachments, at least to those who are not in a position to defend themselves. Perhaps one's comrades must be the only family the hero can have. This suggests that a commitment to revolutionary struggle which requires such sacrifice is supererogatory, as indeed I think it is, assuming that both the struggle and the means are justified.

We have not yet shown that an ethic of care is impossible for the revo-lutionary hero. What we have shown is that it might be difficult, inad-visable, or immoral for the revolutionary hero to have certain kinds of attachments. In fact, the hero might appeal to an ethic of care in support of his/her decision to limit attachments. It is entirely possible to decide to limits one's attachments and at the same time to be committed to an ethic of care, to recognize the obligation imposed by need, to be committed to an ideal of caring.

Up to this point, I have accepted, rather uncritically, the revolutionary hero as an ideal. Now I want to suggest that the picture is more complicated. How does one limit one's attachments if one already has important attachments? Suppose I have young children, what do I do with them? The revolutionary hero depends upon the existence of others to do the actual caring. I don't want to suggest that the ideal is morally bankrupt; I am convinced that in the right cause and with the right strategy the revolutionary hero is indeed a hero. What I want to suggest is that we can't all be revolutionary heroes. We can't put aside the children, the ill, the elderly, and the animals until the struggle is over. Alison Jaggar has pointed out that this ideal is also gender biased since women have traditionally been left to do the caring.[32]

The second worry about caring and the revolutionary hero is that the hero must be willing to inflict harm. As Sara Ruddick argues, this requires objectifying the enemy, since we cannot kill someone we regard as a fellow creature. A telling scene from *All Quiet on the Western Front*[33] illustrates this point. A soldier stabs an enemy soldier who dies slowly and painfully during the night. The soldier is unable to maintain the fiction that he killed an enemy machine, because they are trapped together in the same foxhole. But this ability to objectify is not easily lost, nor is the trauma of combat easily overcome. The experience of the Vietnam veteran suggests that it never is, that it poisons all aspects of life, including the ability to make and sustain relationships. Even if the trauma can be overcome, the objectification of the other is itself incompatible with an ethic that requires that we see the other in all his/her complexity, that we receive the other as fully human. If this is right, then killing is not compatible with an ethic of care.

One might argue that these two are not incompatible. If I see the struggle as requiring killing, I may kill with the full realization that I am killing a fellow human. I may want my enemy to come over to my side, I may give him/her the chance, but if he/she does not take it, I must kill for the sake of my people. I am loathe to accept killing as morally permissible, but at the same time, I recognize oppression as evil and think we all obligated to fight against it. Thus I leave it as an open question whether an ethic of care is incompatible with violent struggle, at least in certain cases.

All this applies to violent struggle. If the struggle is nonviolent, if the harm inflicted is political and economic, it is easier to show that the willingness to inflict harm is compatible with caring relationships. An ethic of care does not require that we accept everyone's projects as our own, that we respond to every need. We are free to rank needs, to balance them with our projects, to give priority to our circles. Though we may understand the desire of the capitalist to amass profits, we are not compelled to respond to this desire. Indeed, where this desire conflicts with a presented need that seems more compelling, we are obligated to respond to the need before the desire. This raises crucial questions: How do needs confer obligation? If needs are in conflict, how should we respond? If the needs of our circle conflict with the needs of strangers, how do we respond?

I think needs confer obligations in an ethic of care in part because becoming a caring person involves becoming more sensitive to others. This, in turn, requires recognizing need, since the desire to satisfy needs is so important to humans. This ideal is intimately connected with our human nature; when we feel loved and cared for we naturally respond with sympathy to presentations of need. When needs are in conflict, we should, *ceteris parabus*, respond on the basis of the strength of the need and our ability to respond. The *ceteris parabus* clause includes our own sense of self and integrity as these are expressed in our projects and attachments.

If I am right about this, then an ethic of care is compatible with inflicting harm, if doing so is required for responding to some more basic need.

The final worry about the revolutionary hero is that the hero cannot have the interests of the people at heart if he/she has particular attachments. This is the argument that Gandhi gives.

> If we look at it from the standpoint of ahimsa (non-violence), we find that the fulfillment of ahimsa is impossible without utter selflessness. . . . If a man gives his love to one women, or a woman to one man, what is there left for the world besides? . . . As a faithful wife must be prepared to sacrifice her all for the sake of her husband, and a faithful husband for the sake of his wife, it is clear that such persons cannot rise to the height of Universal Love, or look upon all mankind as kith and kin. For they have created a boundary wall round their love. The larger their family, the farther are they from Universal Love. Hence one who would obey the law of ahimsa cannot marry, not to speak of gratification outside the marital bond.[34]

This cannot be right. Obviously, we cannot be involved in intimate networks of care with an extremely large number of persons, though we can respond in a caring manner to every person we meet. In this sense, caring for particular others in the context of intimate relationships cannot be extended to all people. But this would be impossible anyway; giving up existing intimate relationships will not allow us to have intimate relationships with everyone.

Existing intimate relationships do take time and focus our attention inward toward our circle of intimates. It is also true that our ties of affection for a particular other will incline us to take their needs more seriously than the needs of strangers. But this is both an unavoidable fact about humans and one that instructs us morally. We should be sensitive to particular others; our ability to make and sustain intimate relationships is one of the best things about humans and other animals.

Still, I suspect that ties of affection to concrete others do interfere with a commitment to "the people" conceived as abstract other. What I want to contest is whether the commitment to "the people" conceived of as abstract other is defensible. It is not clear to me how this attitude is conducive to liberatory struggle. Rather, I suspect that it can result in revolutionaries fighting for "the people" being too willing to sacrifice particular others in the struggle. This is analogous to the danger of fighting for abstract principles that Ruddick discusses.[35] When our eyes are on abstract principles, we are more willing to send people in to die to defend them.

An ethic of care would enjoin us to see people as particular others, any one of whom is in potential relation with us. Our response to this is to be open to the possibility of relationship and to care about the fates of strangers.

E. An Ethic of Care Is Incompatible with Blame

If an ethic of care is committed to an attitude of engrossment in the other, to a response of accommodation in cases of conflict, then what becomes of the concept of blame? Blame is appropriate when we believe that someone has transgressed some moral limit and that the transgression was deliberate, or perhaps at least intentional, and not done in pursuit of some larger moral goal. Blame serves a function; it conditions behavior to a certain extent. But if I am to be forgiving and open to others, how can I blame them for their shortcomings, no matter how grievous?

Sarah Hoaglund has argued that women should dispense with blame, at least in their interactions with other women.[36] She argues that blame is counterproductive. Instead of looking to fix blame, we should be looking to better understand the agent and her motivations. Others have argued that blame is a necessary component of our moral lives.[37]

Though I concede that an ethic of care would prescribe a commitment to understand others, it is not incompatible with blame per se. It is only incompatible with a blame that looks through the transgressor to the crime, that fixes blame independently of the circumstances that led the actor to commit the "crime." In fact, I would argue that an ethic of care is sensitive to aspects of moral crimes that other moral perspectives might overlook; an ethic of care blames one not just for acts and omissions, but for failing to do these things or doing them in uncaring ways.

II. FOUNDATIONAL CRITICISMS

A. An Ethic of Care Is Not Sufficiently Grounded

One worry is that an ethic of care does not tell us why we should care about anyone.[38] Both Hume and Noddings point to the naturalness of caring. Hume goes on to point out that reflection will tell us to extend our actions, even if we cannot extend our sympathies, to strangers. Noddings exhorts us to care for others, even in the absence of natural caring, in order to become more caring persons. But neither provides an answer to the person who is genuinely puzzled about why he/she should care about anyone at all.

My first response is to say that we should not be concerned with satisfying such a person. If they are genuinely puzzled, no amount of argument will persuade them to become caring persons. If the question comes instead from someone who is curious about the foundation of moral life, then we can phrase an answer. Still, I am suspicious of all such projects because I think that they are ultimately question begging; the answers are too often a more or less complicated rephrasing of the moral perspectives themselves. Having stated these reservations, I do intend to offer something by way of an answer. I shall begin by looking at the answers given by the rights tradition and by utilitarianism.

The rights tradition answers the question "Why should I respect anyone's rights?" by describing persons as inherently valuable. This description is accompanied by and defended in terms of a picture of the individual that Alison Jaggar describes as abstract individualism. I have already discussed this picture in Chapter Four, so I won't rehash that discussion here, but even if we think that this picture is a bit too harsh, I think we would agree that the liberal rights tradition puts a special emphasis on the possible or actual autonomy of persons. If persons are genuinely autonomous, capable of guiding their actions by appeal to internal standards, then, so the argument goes, we should respect their dignity. This general obligation is fleshed out in terms of respecting various rights. This picture works more naturally for the negative rights tradition; it gets a bit dicey when we use it to defend positive rights. Here the usual argument says that exercising rights may sometimes require the cooperation of others and not merely their noninterference. If this is so, then respecting persons as autonomous individuals requires that we actively cooperate in helping them to secure at least some of their rights.

It seems to me that an ethic of care might be able to adopt a similar strategy. Obviously, we need to reject abstract individualism in favor of a picture of connected selves, and autonomy will not be the only characteristic of these selves that confers moral worth. Perhaps we could point to their capacity for caring attachment. In any case, we could argue that persons deserve to be cared for in virtue of their moral status. I would be inclined to argue that this provides a better grounding for positive rights claims than the rights tradition itself.

We might also try adapting the strategy Mill uses in *Utilitarianism*.[39] I would reconstruct the famous proof this way: The only evidence of the value to humans of anything is that it is valued by humans. Happiness is valued by all humans, whatever else they value. Therefore, happiness in the only thing inherently valuable to humans. We could then go on to defend caring: In caring, we are guided by our sense of how best to help another creature achieve happiness. So caring is instrumentally valuable, as a way of achieving happiness.

This defense of care must not run aground on the classic objections to utilitarianism. In particular, it must allow for the primacy of relationships, something that classic utilitarianism has a notoriously difficult time doing. But I think we could make something of a case for grounding care in a conception of human happiness.

However, I do not want to adopt either alternative, in part because they have great difficulty accommodating animals or other creatures. Instead, I want to appeal to the holistic philosophy described by Starhawk; we are part of a connected whole and the proper response to this whole and its parts is to see it and them as sacred. My obligation to care follows from my recognition that I am part of this connected whole and that its parts are also sacred.

Not everyone would be happy with this option, in part because of its metaphysics, in part because of its refusal to enthrone humans, but a large part of the problem will be that they see it as insufficiently action-guiding. This leads to the final foundational criticism.

B. An Ethic of Care Is Not Sufficiently Action-Guiding

I must confess that I used to find this objection compelling, now I simply find it puzzling. Obviously, we want some guidance from a moral perspective, but why should we want it to serve as a road map with all the exits plainly marked? Is it because we are afraid that without such a map we will do the wrong thing? Instead of binding ourselves by a moral code, why can't we simply trust the commitment to do the right thing that a willingness to bind ourselves implies? I suspect this is less a matter of wanting to do the right thing than knowing what the right thing is. But no calculus is going to help us here, because no calculus can capture the complexity of moral life. At best, a moral perspective can point the way, can suggest what variables are morally most significant. An ethic of care is perfectly capable of doing this, though it clearly fails as a calculus. So much the better for an ethic of care.

There is a related objection here, and that is that even if I don't think I need a calculus to decide what to do, I need something like a calculus to fight evil. Not everyone will agree with me, not everyone will want to do the right thing or have the moral imagination to know what to do, but if I am to have some power against evil, against indifference, against ignorance, I need an ethic with the roads clearly and plainly marked.

I have already responded to this objection in Chapter Two, so here I will merely summarize. I freely grant that the language of rights and utility has more currency than the language of care. I also think that when it is sufficiently embellished by a list of rights or utility calculations, it appears to be more of a calculus than an ethic of care. If we want to converse in the dominant language, we must be fluent in rights talk and utility calculation. But I am not convinced that rational persuasion is terribly powerful, and even if I were, I am not convinced that rights talk and utility calculations will give us the right spin on all the things we wish to discuss. Elizabeth Wolgast argues that the language of rights and utility cannot help us to understand or argue for defensible positions on pornography or maternity leave, for example.[40] I quite agree. Further, I think that it is time that we learned to hear and speak in our own voices. And finally, if you think that a calculus will help someone you believe to be morally deficient, then by all means offer a calculus, but don't assume that the moral defective's need for exquisitely detailed guidance tells us anything at all about an ethic for the morally mature.

III.   CONCLUSION

Throughout this book I have sketched and defended an ethic of care with these features: moral attention, response, and concern for networks of care. Moral attention involves two characteristics: an fine awareness of the features of a particular situation, including possible scenarios for its resolution and the effects of such scenarios, and a sympathetic identification with all the creatures in the situation. Richard Rorty describes this in terms of imagination and sensitivity: "the imaginative ability to see strange people as fellow sufferers . . . sensitivity to the particular details of the pain and humiliation of other unfamiliar sorts of people."[41]

Our response is often given through the process of applying our moral attention to the situation. When this does not happen, we must try to accommodate the interests of all the parties where interests are spelled out in terms of preservation and growth, contentment, expressed (and unexpressed) desires, and a concern to nurture, create, or sustain networks of care. An understanding of interests in terms of preservation and growth requires an analysis of preservation and growth. Briefly, preservation refers to the protection of the current status of the creatures involved, and growth refers to their movement toward the fulfillment of their potentialities. It is important to stress that our response must be colored by a concern to nurture, create, or sustain networks of care. This concern is motivated by a belief in the intrinsic value of such networks and an understanding that the solution to conflict and need must be seen in terms of strengthening such networks.

In the introduction, I distinguished between morality, normative ethics and metaethics. Here, I will summarize an ethic of care, as I perceive it, in terms of these rough but useful distinctions.

A morality can be described by appeal to its practices and conventions. One does not need to understand the underlying commitments to describe or even practice a particular morality. As a morality, an ethic of care is characterized by an attention to individual persons seen as connected by networks of care where these networks are created by existing or future relationships or presented need. In cases of conflict, the goal is on compromise with an eye toward accommodating everyone, insofar as that is possible.

When we look at an ethic of care as a normative ethic, we begin to see the underlying commitments and to understand the important concepts in more detail. First we see that the attention focused on the individual(s) has two features: the first is a recognition of all the relevant facts about the situation and a sympathetic understanding of possible outcomes; the second is a willingness to engage the other on an emotional level, to feel the other's pain, for example.

An individualistic ethic is likely to see the focus on compromise and accommodation as a strategy for satisfying no one, but an ethic of care sees individuals as parts of a network of care. Compromise is both necessary to sustain these networks and as a strategy for creating a new outcome that might make everyone concerned better off while strengthening the network of care.

An ethic of care, as I conceive it, is committed to two metaethical claims. The first is that morality should not be a matter of appealing to rigid rules. Rather, an ethic of care makes its first appeal to the concrete situation, the needs and interests of those involved and the networks of care that connect them.

This does not mean that an ethic of care is a prescription for moral chaos; it is not the case that anything goes. Rather than focusing on the correct moral rules, an ethic of care focuses on the right moral perspective—an engaged moral attention to the other which seeks to sustain and enrich networks of care.

I see an ethic of care as motivated by a holistic metaphysics which recognizes relationships as ontologically primitive, which sees each individual as part of the sacred whole.

A. Some Advantages of an Ethic of Care

My sense of the task for moral philosophy is both modest and ambitious—modest since I don't think it need discover and justify the one correct ethical theory, ambitious because I think it must engage the world. It must do this in two ways: first it must understand and speak in the moral language spoken in its world; second, it must use this language, appropriately understood, clarified, and enriched, to transform the world.

Two advantages of an ethic of care mirror these goals. The modest goal, understanding and clarifying moral language, can be furthered only if we learn to speak in the voice of care since this is a voice that is widely heard and spoken and it is a voice that moral philosophy has only begun to investigate.

If Gilligan is right, and I suspect she is, that the voice of care is more often heard and spoken by women, then our responsibility as feminists to take the experience of women seriously requires that we take an ethic of care seriously.

The transformative task of moral philosophy begins with its more modest task; if we are to affect the world we must learn to be part of the conversation and not merely umpires. Advancing the conversation requires that we listen and attempt to understand what is being said and not just set standards for completeness and correctness. It also requires a rich moral vocabulary including the language of care.

But beyond its advantages as a moral language, there is an additional advantage. Individualistic moral language, with its focus on claims and rights, has clear limits. We can see this in the case of homelessness discussed earlier. It is not merely that the homeless person is denied a right to a home; rather, a much more systematic wrong has occurred. A sense of place, of belonging, is missing in many cases, as well as a home of one's own. The tent cities that spring up in vacant lots are a testament to the need of homeless people to be connected to others, to be surrounded by caring others. Our failure to provide homes and communities for all our citizens is evidence of our insularity in the face of the needs of strangers, our undervaluing of community, and our inability to see ourselves (and to be) parts of a vibrant and caring community. This description of the problem and its related resolution can best be made in the language of care.

This leads me to the next advantage of an ethic of care: its conceptualization of individual and community. Individualistic ethics have difficulty defending communities: communities are instrumentally good or bad depending upon how the humans who constitute them flourish or suffer as a result of their membership in them. But communities that are conceptualized as mere aggregates of individuals have no intrinsic value. So we are left defending affirmative action, for example, by appeal to injustices done to individuals rather than as of a strategy for strengthening and reaffirming communities that have suffered. Indeed, in an individualistic ethic, it is even difficult to make sense of the notion of a suffering community. An ethic of care conceptualizes individuals as essentially communal, as existing and flourishing only within networks of care. According to this view, communities are not mere aggregates of individuals, but networks of relationships, practices, values, and ways of life.

B. New Directions

I have only scratched the surface in this book, but I hope I have inspired others to extend and clarify the analysis and to apply it in new ways. Here, I would like to suggest some avenues for future work.

I have discussed caring teachers, but this analysis could well be extended to other professions as well. This has already begun to happen in nursing,[42] but what about doctoring? Does the obligation to seek informed consent tell us anything about how to inform? Does a caring journalist have any obligation to rape victims? Should a caring lawyer always put the client first? Business ethics, which up to this point has been analyzed almost exclusively in Kantian and utilitarian terms, would benefit from an analysis from the perspective of care. What is a caring banker like? Do current banking practices undermine or sustain caring relationships?

I hinted at an environmental ethic of care in my discussion of wild animals, but obviously one could go much further here.

One could also pursue other implications of an ethic of care for persons. Co-dependency, for example, is a fascinating topic for analysis from the perspective of care. The central questions would be: When is caring appropriate or inappropriate? How do I know the difference? How is caring for self a requirement for appropriate caring?

Finally, I would like to see parallel work in political philosophy. A politics of care could give us a new and invigorating account of many issues. I have already discussed individual and community, homelessness, and affirmative action, but others spring to mind as equally fruitful avenues for work: immigration, managing growth, democracy in an age of increasing voter apathy and cynicism, taxation, obligations to emerging countries.

I plan to pursue some of these avenues, and I encourage any readers who have come to agree with me about the importance of an ethic of care to join me in this challenge.

NOTES

1. Alison Jaggar sees feminist ethics as much broader than a discussion of the pros and cons of an ethic of care. See "Feminist Ethics: Some Issues for the Nineties," *Journal of Social Philosophy* 20 (1989): 91–107.

2. Annette Baier, "Hume, The Women's Moral Theorist?" in Eva Kittay and Diana Meyers, eds., *Women and Moral Theory* (Totowa, N.J.: Rowman and Littlefield, 1987).

3. Ketayun H. Gould, "Old Wine in New Bottles: A Feminist Perspective on Gilligan's Theory," *Social Work* (1988): 411–15. See also Paul Lauritzen, "A Feminist Ethic and the New Romanticism—Mothering as a Model of Moral Relations," *Hypatia* 2 (1989): 29–44. Lauritzen worries that if we romanticize motherhood in a pernicious way then an ethic of care supports the status quo. He thinks that an ethic of care can provide a powerful social critique as long as we conceive mothering appropriately.

4. Betty Sichel, "Women's Moral Development in Search of Philosophical Assumptions," *Journal of Moral Education* 14 (1985): 149–61.

5. See Sarah Lucia Hoaglund, "Some Concerns About Nel Noddings' *Caring*," *Hypatia* 5 (1990): 109–14; Claudia Card, "Women's Voices and Ethical Ideals: Must We Mean What We Say?" *Ethics* 99 (1988): 125–35; and Joan C. Tronto, "Beyond Gender Difference to a Theory of Care," *Signs* 12 (1987): 644–63.

6. Carol Gilligan, *In a Different Voice* (Cambridge, Mass.: Harvard University Press, 1982), 19.

7. Noddings makes this point in a reply to critics. "Response," *Hypatia* 5 (1990): 120–26.

8. Cenen and Barbara Smith, "The Blood—Yes, The Blood: A Conversation," in *Home Girls* (New York: Kitchen Table: Women of Color Press, 1983).

9. Angela Davis, "Racism, Birth Control and Reproductive Rights," in *Women, Race And Class*, (New York: Vintage Books, 1981).

10. Peter Singer is an obvious exception here. See his *Practical Ethics* (Cambridge: Cambridge University Press, 1979), for example.

11. John Stuart Mill, *Utilitarianism* (Indianapolis, Ind.: Bobbs Merrill, 1977), 25.

12. See Mordecai Nisan, "Moral Norms and Social Conventions: A Cross-Cultural Comparison," *Developmental Psychology* 23 (1987): 719–25.

13. Cheryl Noble, "Normative Ethical Theories," in Stanley Clarke and Evan Simpson, eds., *Anti-Theory in Ethics and Moral Conservatism* (Albany: State University of New York Press, 1989), 51.

14. See Rawls's discussion of supererogation in *A Theory of Justice* (Cambridge, Mass.: Harvard University Press, 1971).

15. Russell Jacobs, "The Price of Duty," *Southern Journal of Philosophy* 17 (1981).

16. Rita Manning, "'Ought Implies Can' and the Price of Duty," *Southern Journal of Philosophy* 19 (1981): 117–21.

17. Bernard Williams has long been a critic of utilitarianism. See, for example, the discussions throughout *Ethics and the Limits of Philosophy* (Cambridge, Mass.: Harvard University Press, 1985).

18. Ibid.

19. Michael Katz pointed this out to me.

20. Virginia Warren makes this point in an unpublished paper.

21. David Hume, *An Enquiry Concerning the Principles of Morals*, L.A. Selby-Biggs, ed., (Oxford: Oxford University Press, 1962), sect. 3; *A Treatise on Human Nature*, L.A. Selby-Biggs, ed., (Oxford: Oxford University Press, 1964), bk. 3, pt. 2.

22. This objection has been made by Card, "Women's Voices," and Tronto, "Beyond Gender." See also N. Katherine Hayles, "Anger in Different Voices: Carol Gilligan and *The Mill on the Floss*," *Signs* 12 (1986): 23–39. She argues that the repression of anger required by an ethic of care is evident in Gilligan's work.

23. Noddings, *Caring: A Feminine Approach to Moral Education* (Berkeley: University of California Press, 1984), chap.4.

24. Bernard Williams, "Persons, Character and Morality," *Moral Luck* (Cambridge: Cambridge University Press, 1981).

25. Dianne Romaine makes this point. See "Care and Confusion," in *Explorations in Feminist Theory* (Indianapolis, Ind.: Indiana University Press, 1992). See also Barbara Houston, "Caring and Exploitation," *Hypatia* 5 (1990): 115–19, and Hoaglund, "Some Concerns."

26. *The Fringe Dwellers*, directed by Bruce Beresford, 1986.

27. Toni Morrison, *Beloved* (New York: Knopf, 1987).

28. *Chicago Tribune*, October 17, 1990.

29. Sara Ruddick, "Preservative Love and Military Destruction," in Joyce Treblicot, ed., *Mothering: Essays in Feminist Theory* (Totowa, N.J.: Rowman and Allanheld, 1984).

30. Victoria Davion, "Pacifism and Care," *Hypatia* 5 (1990): 90–100.

31. See, for example, the essays collected in *Philosophical Issues in Human Rights*, edited by Patricia Werhave, A. R. Gini, and David T. Ozar (New York: Random House, 1986).

32. Alison Jaggar, *Feminist Politics and Human Nature* (Totowa, N.J.: Rowman and Allanheld, 1983), chaps. 4 and 5.

33. *All Quiet on the Western Front*, directed by Delbert Mann, produced by Norman Rosemont, 1939.

34. M. K. Gandhi, *Non-Violent Resistance* (New York: Schocken Books, 1961), 43.

35. Ruddick, "Preservative Love."

36. Sarah Lucia Hoaglund, *Lesbian Ethics* (Palo Alto, Calif.: Institute of Lesbian Studies, 1988), 217–21.

37. Barbara Houston, in a paper given at the Midwest Radical Scholars and Activists Conference, Loyola University, Chicago, October 1990.

38. Julie Ward, in a paper given at the Midwest Radical Scholars and Activists Conference, Loyola University, Chicago, October 1990, and in conversation.

39. John Stuart Mill, *Utilitarianism*, chap. 4.

40. Elizabeth Wolgast, "Wrong Rights," *The Grammar of Justice* (Ithaca, N.Y.: Cornell University Press, 1987).

41. Richard Rorty, *Contingency, Irony, and Solidarity* (Cambridge: Cambridge University Press, 1989), xvi.

42. See, for example, Sara T. Fry, "The Role of Caring in a Theory of Nursing Ethics," *Hypatia* 4 (1989): 88–103.

Bibliography

Addlelson, Kathryn Pyne. "Moral Passages." In *Women and Moral Theory.* Eva Feder Kittay and Diana T. Meyers (eds.). Totowa, N.J.: Rowman and Littlefield, 1987.

Alexander, Tangren. "The Womanly Art of Teaching Ethics, or One Fruitful Way to Encourage the Love of Wisdom about Right and Wrong." *Teaching Philosophy* 10 (1987): 319–28.

Allen, Jeffner. "Motherhood: The Annihilation of Women." In *Mothering: Essays in Feminist Theory.* Joyce Treblicot (ed.). Totowa, N.J.: Rowman & Allanheld 1984, 315–30.

Allen, Paula Gunn. *The Sacred Hoop: Recovering the Feminine in the American Indian Tradition.* Boston: Beacon Press, 1986.

Aptheker, Bettina. *Woman's Legacy: Essays on Race, Sex and Class in American History.* Amherst: University of Massachusetts Press, 1982.

Baier, Annette. "Doing Without Moral Theory?" In *Anti-Theory in Ethics and Moral Conservatism.* Stanley Clarke and Evan Simpson (eds.). Albany: State University of New York Press, 1989.

———. "Hume, The Women's Moral Theorist?" In *Women and Moral Theory.* Eva Kittay and Diana Meyers (eds.). Totowa, N.J.: Rowman and Littlefield, 1987.

———. "The Need for More than Justice." In *Science, Morality and Feminist Theory.* Marsha Hanen and Kai Nielsen (eds.). Calgary: University of Calgary Press, 1987.

———. *Postures of the Mind: Essays on Mind and Morals*. Minneapolis: University of Minnesota Press, 1985.

Baron, Marcia. "The Alleged Repugnance of Acting from Duty." *Inquiry* 26 (1984): 387–405.

Benhabib, Seyla. "The Generalized and the Concrete Other: The Kohlberg-Gilligan Controversy and Feminist Theory." *Praxis International* 5 (1986): 402–24.

Bloom, Alfred H. "Psychological Ingredients of High-Level Moral Thinking." *Journal for the Theory of Social Behavior* 16 (1986): 89–103.

Blum, Lawrence A. "Gilligan and Kohlberg: Implications for Moral Theory." *Ethics* 98 (1988): 472–91.

———. "Kant's and Hegel's Moral Rationalism: A Feminist Perspective." *Canadian Journal of Philosophy* 12 (1982).

———. "Particularity and Responsiveness." In *The Emergence of Morality in Children*. Jerome Kagan and Sharon Lamb (eds.). Chicago: University of Chicago Press, 1987.

Brink, David O. *Moral Realism and the Foundations of Ethics*. Cambridge: Cambridge University Press, 1989.

Cahn, Steven M. *Saints and Scamps: Ethics in Academia*. Totowa, N.J.: Rowman & Littlefield, 1986.

Callahan, Daniel. "Moral Theory: Thinking, Doing, and Living." *Journal of Social Philosophy* 20 (1989): 18–24.

Callicott, J. Baird. *In Defense of the Land Ethics*. Albany: State University of New York Press, 1989.

Card, Claudia. "Women's Voices and Ethical Ideals: Must We Mean What We Say?" *Ethics* 99 (1990): 125–35.

———. "Women and Evil" In *Hypatia* 5 (1990): 101–08.

Cenen and Barbara Smith. "The Blood—Yes, The Blood: A Conversation." In *Home Girls*. New York: Kitchen Table: Women of Color Press, 1983.

Christ, Carol. *Laughter of Aphrodite: Reflection on a Journey to the Goddess*. San Francisco: Harper & Row, 1987.

Daly, Mary. *Gyn/Ecology: The Metaethics of Radical Feminism*. Boston: Beacon Press, 1978.

Davion, Victoria. "Pacifism and Care." *Hypatia* 5 (1990): 90–100.

Davis, Angela. "Racism, Birth Control and Reproductive Rights." In *Women, Race and Class.* New York: Vintage Books, 1981.

DeWolfe, Thomas E., Lee Jackson, and Patricia Wintergerger. "A Comparison of Moral Reasoning and Moral Character in Male and Female Incarcerated Felons." *Sex Roles* 18 (1988): 583–93.

Dien, D. S. "A Chinese Perspective on Kohlberg's Theory of Moral Development." *Developmental Review* 2 (1982): 331–41.

Deinerstein, Dorothy. *The Mermaid and the Minotaur: Sexual Arrangements and Human Malaise.* New York: Harper & Row, 1977.

Dixon, Vernon. "World Views and Research Methodologies." In *African Philosophy: Assumptions and Paradigms for Research on Black Persons.* L. M. King, V. Dixon, and W. W. Nobles (eds.). Los Angeles: Fanon Center Publications, 1976.

Donenberg, Geri R. and Lois W. Hoffman. "Gender Differences in Moral Development." *Sex Roles* 18 (1988): 701–17.

Dugan, Daniel. "Masculine and Feminine Voices: Making Ethical Decisions in the Care of the Dying." *The Journal of Medical Humanities and Bioethics* 8 (1987): 129–40.

Eisengerg-Berg, Nancy. "Development of Children's Prosocial Moral Judgment." *Developmental Psychology* 15 (1979): 128–37.

Eisler, Riane Tennenhaus. *The Chalice and the Blade: Our History, Our Future.* San Francisco: Harper & Row, 1987.

Erenreich, Barbara. *Fear of Falling.* New York: Pantheon Books, 1989.

Flanagan, Owen and Kathryn Jackson. "Justice, Care, and Gender: The Kohlberg-Gilligan Debate Revisited." *Ethics* 97 (1987): 622–37.

Flax, Jane. *Thinking Fragments: Psychoanalysis, Feminism, & Postmodernism in the Contemporary West.* Berkeley: University of California Press, 1990.

Foot, Philippa. *Virtues and Vices.* Berkeley: University of California Press, 1978.

Foucault, Michel. *Discipline and Punish: The Birth of the Prison.* New York: Vintage Books, 1979.

Fraser, Nancy and Linda J. Nicholson. "Social Criticism Without Philosophy: An Encounter between Feminism and Post-Modernism." In

Feminism and Postmodernism. Linda J. Nicholson (ed.). New York: Routledge, 1990.

———. "Toward a Discourse Ethic of Solidarity." *Praxis International* 5 (1986).

Frey, R. G. *Interests and Rights*. Oxford: Clarendon Press, 1980.

Fried, Charles. *An Anatomy of Value*. Cambridge, Mass.: Harvard University Press, 1970.

Friedan, Betty. *The Feminine Mystique*. New York: Dell Publishing Co., 1963.

Friedman, Marilyn. "Care and Context in Moral Reasoning." In *Women and Moral Theory*. Eva Kittay and Diana Meyers (eds.). Totowa, N.J.: Rowman & Allanheld, 1987.

Fry, Sara T. "The Role of Caring in a Theory of Nursing Ethics." *Hypatia: A Journal of Feminist Philosophy* (1989): 88–103.

Gibbs, J. C. and K. F Widaman. *Social Intelligence: Measuring the Development of Sociomoral Reflection*. New York: Prentice Hall, 1982.

Gilligan, Carol. *In a Different Voice*. Cambridge, Mass.: Harvard University Press, 1982.

——— and S. Pollak. "Images of Violence in Thematic Apperception Test Stories." *Journal of Personality and Social Psychology* 42 (1982): 159–67.

Gould, Carol C. *Rethinking Democracy: Freedom and Social Cooperation in Politics, Economy and Society*. Cambridge: Cambridge University Press, 1988.

Gould, Ketayun H. "Old Wine in New Bottles: A Feminist Perspective on Gilligan's Theory." *Social Work* (1988): 411–15.

Greer, Germaine. "The Fate of the Family." *Sex and Destiny*. New York: Harper & Row, 1984.

Griffin, Susan. *Women and Nature: The Roaring Inside Her*. New York: Harper & Row, 1979.

Harding, Sandra. "The Curious Coincidence of Feminine and African Moralities." In *Women and Moral Theory*. Eva Kittay and Diana Meyers (eds.). Totowa, N.J.: Rowman and Littlefield, 1987.

———. *The Science Question in Feminism*. Ithaca, N.Y.: Cornell University Press, 1986.

Harmon, Gilbert. "Ethics and Observation." In *The Nature of Morality: An Introduction to Ethics.* Oxford: Oxford University Press, 1977.

————. "Is There a Single True Morality?" In *Morality, Reason and Truth.* David Copp and David Zimmerman, (eds.). Totowa, N.J.: Rowman & Allanheld, 1984.

Hayles, Katherine N. "Anger in Different Voices: Carol Gilligan and *The Mill on the Floss.*" *Signs* 12 (1986): 23–39.

Hearne, Vicki. *Adam's Task: Calling Animals by Name.* New York: Vintage Books, 1982.

Held, Virginia. "Feminism and Moral Theory." In *Women and Moral Theory.* Eva Kittay and Diana Meyers (eds.) Totowa, N.J.: Rowman and Littlefield, 1987.

————. *Rights and Goods.* New York: The Free Press, 1984.

Herman, Barbara. "Integrity and Impartiality." *Monist* 66 (1983): 233–50.

Hill, Thomas E., Jr. "The Importance of Autonomy." In *Women and Moral Theory.* Eva Kittay and Diana Meyers (eds.). Totowa, N.J.: Rowman and Littlefield, 1987.

Hinman, Lawrence. "Emotion, Morality, and Understanding." In *Moral Dilemmas.* Carol Gibb Harding (ed.). Chicago: Precedent Publishing Co., 1985.

Hoaglund, Sarah Lucia. *Lesbian Ethics.* Palo Alto, Calif.: Institute of Lesbian Studies, 1988, 217–21.

————."Some Concerns About Nel Noddings' *Caring.*" *Hypatia* 5 (1990): 109–14.

Houston, Barbara. "Caring and Exploitation." *Hypatia* 5 (1990): 115–19.

Hursthouse, Rosalind. *Beginning Lines.* Oxford and New York: Basil Blackwell in association with the Open University, 1987.

Jacobs, Russell. "The Price of Duty." *Southern Journal of Philosophy* 17 (1981).

Jaggar, Alison. "Feminist Ethics: Some Issues for the Nineties." *Journal of Social Philosophy* 20 (1989): 91–107.

————. *Feminist Politics and Human Nature.* Totowa, N.J.: Rowman & Allanheld, 1983.

Johnston, D. Kay. "Adolescents' Solutions to Dilemmas in Fables: Two Moral Orientations—Two Problem Solving Strategies." In *Mapping the Moral Domain*. Carol Gilligan, Janice Victoria Ward, Jill McLean Taylor (eds.). Cambridge, Mass.: Harvard University Press, 1988.

Keller, Mara Lynn. "The Eleusinian Mysteries: Ancient Nature Religion of Demeter and Persephone." In *Reweaving the World: The Emergence of Ecofeminism*. Irene Diamond and Gloria Feman Orenstein (eds.), San Francisco: Sierra Club Books, 1990.

King, Ynestra. "Healing the Wounds: Feminism, Ecology, and the Nature/Culture Dualism." In *Reweaving the World: The Emergence of Ecofeminism*. Irene Diamond and Gloria Feman Orenstein (eds.). San Francisco: Sierra Club Books, 1990.

Kheel, Marti. "Ecofeminism and Deep Ecology: Reflections on Identity and Difference." In *Reweaving the World: The Emergence of Ecofeminism*. Irene Diamon and Gloria Feman Orentstein (eds.) San Francisco: Sierra Club Books, 1990.

Kohlberg, Lawrence. *The Philosophy of Moral Development*. New York: Harper & Row, 1981

————. "Stage and Sequence: The Cognitive-Developmental Approach to Socialization." In *Handbook of Socialization Theory and Research*. D. A. Goslin, (ed.). Chicago: Rand McNally, 1969.

————, with Charles Levine and Alexandra Hewer. "The Current Formulation of the Theory." In *The Psychology of Moral Development: The Nature and Validity of Moral Stages*. New York: Harper & Row, 1984.

Larmore, Charles E. *Patterns of Moral Complexity*. Cambridge: Cambridge University Press, 1987.

Lasch, Christopher. *The Minimal Self: Psychic Survival in Troubled Times*. New York and London: W. W. Norton & Co., 1984.

Lauritzen, Paul. "A Feminist Ethic and the New Romanticism—Mothering as a Model of Moral Relations." *Hypatia* 2 (1989): 29–44.

Leopold, Aldo. *A Sand Country Almanac*. New York: Oxford University Press 1949, 224–25.

Longino, Helen E. *Science as Social Knowledge: Values and Objectivity in Scientific Inquiry*. Princeton, N.J.: Princeton University Press, 1990.

Lonky, Edward, Paul A. Roodin, and John M. Rybash. "Moral Judgment and Sex Role Orientation as a Function of Self and Other Presentation Mode." *Journal of Youth and Adolescence* 17 (1988): 189–95.

Lovibund, Sabina. *Realism and Imagination in Ethics.* Minneapolis: University of Minnesota Press, 1983.

Lyons, Nona. "Two Perspectives: On Self, Relationships, and Morality." *Harvard Educational Review* 53 (1983): 125–45.

Ma, Hing-Keung and Wing-Shing Chan. "The Moral Judgments of Chinese Students." *The Journal of Social Psychology* 127 (1987): 491–97.

McGraw, Kathleen M. and Jeremy Bloomfield. "Social Influence on Group Moral Decisions: The Interactive Effects of Moral Reasoning and Sex Role Orientation." *Journal of Personality and Social Psychology* 53 (1987): 1080–87.

MacKinnon, Catharine A. *Feminism Unmodified: Discourses on Life and Law.* Cambridge, Mass.: Harvard University Press, 1987.

MacIntyre, Alasdair. *After Virtue.* Notre Dame, Ind.: University of Notre Dame Press, 1981.

Magnus, Bernd. *Nietzsche's Existential Imperative.* Indianapolis: Indiana University Press, 1978.

Manning, Rita. " 'Ought Implies Can' and the Price of Duty." *Southern Journal of Philosophy* 19 (1981): 117–21.

———. "The Random Collective as a Moral Agent." *Social Theory and Practice* 11 (1985): 97–105.

Mayeroff, Milton. *On Caring.* New York: Perennial Library, 1971.

Meyers, Diana T. "The Socialized Individual and Individual Autonomy: An Intersection between Philosophy and Psychology." In *Women and Moral Theory.* Eva Kittay and Diana Meyers (eds.). Totowa, N.J.: Rowman and Littlefield, 1987, 139–53.

Michaels, Meredith W. "Morality Without Distinction." *The Philosophical Forum* 17 (1986): 175–87.

Midgley, Mary. *Animals and Why They Matter.* Athens: University of Georgia Press, 1983.

Miller, Alice. *The Drama of the Gifted Child.* New York: Basic Books, 1983.

Morrison, Toni. *Beloved.* New York: Knopf, 1987.

Murdoch, Iris. *The Sovereignty of the Good.* New York: Schocken Books, 1971.

Nagel, Thomas. *The Possibility of Altruism.* Princeton, N.J.: Princeton University Press, 1970.

Nielsen, Kai. *Why Be Moral?* Buffalo, N.Y.: Prometheus Books, 1989.

Nisan, Mordecai. "Moral Norms and Social Conventions: A Cross-Cultural Comparison." *Developmental Psychology* 23 (1987): 719–25.

———. "A Story of a Pot, Or a Cross-Cultural Comparison of Basic Moral Evaluations: A Response to the Critique by Turiel, Nucci and Smetana (1988)." *Developmental Psychology* 24 (1988): 144–46.

Noble, Cheryl. "Normative Ethical Theories." In *Anti-Theory in Ethics and Moral Conservatism.* Stanley Clarke and Evan Simpson (eds.). Albany: State University of New York Press, 1989.

Noddings, Nel. *Caring: A Feminine Approach to Ethics and Moral Education.* Berkeley: University of California Press, 1984.

———. "A Response." *Hypatia* 5 (1990): 120–26.

———. *Women and Evil.* Berkeley: University of California Press, 1989.

Nussbaum, Martha C. "Finely Aware and Richly Responsible: Literature and the Moral Imagination." *The Journal of Philosophy* 82 (1985): 516–29.

———. *The Fragility of Goodness.* Cambridge: Cambridge University Press, 1986.

Okin, Susan Moller. *Justice, Gender and the Family.* New York: Basic Books, 1990.

O'Neill, Onora. "Virtuous Lives and Just Societies." *Journal of Social Philosophy* 20 (1989): 25–30.

Passmore, John. *Man's Responsibility For Nature.* New York: Charles Scribner's and Sons, 1974.

Piercy, Marge. *Woman on the Edge of Time.* New York: Fawcett Books, 1985.

Post, Stephen. "An Ethical Perspective on Caregiving in the Family." *The Journal of Medical Humanities and Bioethics* 9 (1988): 6–16.

Potter, David M. "American Women and the American Character." *Steton University Bulletin* LXII (1962): 1–22.

Pruitt, D. G. and S. A. Lewis. "The Psychology of Integrative Bargaining." In *Negotiations: A Social-Psychological Perspective.* D. Druckman (ed.). New York: Halsted, 1977.

Purdy, Laura M. "Feminists Healing Ethics." *Hypatia* (1989): 9–14.

Rabuzzi, Kathryn Allen. *Motherself: A Mythic Analysis of Motherhood.* Bloomington: Indiana University Press, 1988.

Rachel, James. *The End of Life.* Oxford: Oxford University Press, 1986.

Rawls, John. *A Theory of Justice.* Cambridge, Mass.: Harvard University Press, 1971.

Regak, Ariska. "Toward a Womanist Analysis of Birth." In *Diamond,* 165–72.

Regan, Tom. *The Case for Animal Rights.* Berkeley: University of California Press, 1983.

Rest, James. *Development in Judging Moral Issues.* Minneapolis: University of Minnesota Press, 1979.

———. *Moral Development: Advances in Research and Theory.* New York: Praeger, 1986.

Romaine, Dianne. *"Care and Confusion."* In *Explorations in Feminist Theory.* Eve Browning Cole and Susan Coultrap McQuinn, (eds.). Bloomington: Indiana University Press, 1991.

Rorty, Richard. *Contingency, Irony and Solidarity.* Cambridge: Cambridge University Press, 1989.

Rose, Mike. *Lives on the Boundary.* New York: Penguin Books, 1989.

Rothbart, Mary K., Dean Hanley, and Marc Albert. "Gender Differences in Moral Reasoning." *Sex Roles* 15 (1986): 645–53.

Sagoff, Mark. *The Economy of the Earth.* Cambridge: Cambridge University Press, 1988.

Sandel, Michael. *Liberalism and Its Critics.* New York: New York University Press, 1984.

Sapontzis, S. F. *Morals, Reason, and Animals.* Philadelphia: Temple University Press, 1987.

Shaw, William. "Intuition and Moral Philosophy." *American Philosophical Quarterly* 17 (1980): 127–34.

Sher, George. "Other Voices, Other Rooms? Women's Psychology and Moral Theory." In *Women and Moral Theory.* Eva Kittay and Diana Meyers (eds.) Totowa, N.J.: Rowman and Littlefield, 1987.

Sichel, Betty. "Women's Moral Development in Search of Philosophical Assumptions." *Journal of Moral Education* 14 (1985): 149–61.

Singer, Peter. *Animal Liberation.* New York: Avon Books, 1975.

————. *Practical Ethics.* Cambridge: Cambridge University Press, 1979.

Slicer, Deborah. "Teaching with a Different Ear: Teaching Ethics after Reading Carol Gilligan." *Journal of Value Inquiry* 24 (1990): 55–65.

Smith, Janet. "Abortion and Moral Development Theory: Listening with Different Ears." *International Philosophical Quarterly* 28 (1988) 31–51.

Sommers, Christina Hoff. "Filial Morality." In *Women and Moral Theory.* Eva Kittay and Diana Meyers (eds.) Totowa, N.J.: Rowman and Littlefield, 1987.

Song, Myung-Ja, Judith G. Smetana, and Sang Yoon Kim, "Korean Children's Conceptions of Moral and Conventional Transgressions." *Developmental Psychology* 23 (1987): 577–82.

Spretnak, Charlene. "Ecofeminism: Our Roots and Flowering." In *Reweaving the World: The Emergence of Ecofeminism.* Irene Diamond and Gloria Feman Orenstein (eds.) San Francisco: Sierra Club Books, 1990.

————. *The Spiritual Dimension of Green Politics.* New Mexico: Bear & Co., 1986.

Starhawk. *Dreaming the Dark.* Boston: Beacon Press, 1988.

Stone, Christopher. *Earth and Other Ethics.* New York: Harper & Row, 1987.

Swimme, Brian. "How to Heal a Lobotomy." In *Reweaving the World: The Emergence of Ecofeminism.* Irene Diamond and Gloria Feman Orenstein (eds.) San Francisco: Sierra Club Books, 1990.

Thomas, Laurence. *Living Morally: A Psychology of Moral Character.* Philadelphia: Temple University Press, 1989.

Tietjen, Anne Marie. "Prosocial Reasoning Among Children and Adults in a Papua New Guinea Society." *Developmental Psychology* 22 (1986): 861–68.

Toulmin, Steven. "How Medicine Saved the Life of Ethics." In *New Directions in Ethics: The Challenge of Applied Ethics.* Joseph DeMarco and Richard M. Fox (eds.) New York: Routledge, Chapman and Hall, 1986.

Treblicot, Joyce. "Dyke Methods or Principles for the Discovery/Creation of the Withstanding." *Hypatia* 3 (1988): 1–13.

Tronto, Joan C. "Beyond Gender Difference to Theory of Care." *Signs* 12 (1987): 644–63.

Turiel, Elliot, Judith G. Smetana, and Larry P. Nucci. "A Cross-Cultural Comparison About What? A Critique of Nisan's (1987) Study of Morality and Convention." *Developmental Psychology* 24 (1988): 140–43.

Valeska, Lucia. "If All Else Fails, I'm Still a Mother." In *Mothering: Essays in Feminist Theory.* Joyce Treblicot, (ed.) Totowa, N.J.: Rowman & Allanheld, 1984.

Waide, John. "Gilligan's Wake: Some Implications of Carol Gilligan's Work for Teaching Ethics." *Teaching Philosophy* 10 (1987): 305–18.

Walker, Alice. *In Search of Our Mothers' Gardens.* New York: Harcourt, Brace, Jovanovich, 1983.

Walker, L. J. "Sex Differences in the Development of Moral Reasoning: A Critical Review." *Child Development* 55 (1984): 677–91.

Walker, Margaret Urban. "Moral Understandings: Alternative 'Epistemology' for a Feminist Ethic." *Hypatia* 4 (1989): 15–28.

———. "What does the Different Voice Say?: Gilligan's Women and Moral Philosophy." *The Journal of Value Inquiry* 23 (1989): 123–34.

Warren, Virginia L. "Feminist Directions in Medical Ethics." *Hypatia* (89): 73–87.

White, Charles B. "Age, Education, and Sex Effects on Adult Moral Reasoning." *International Journal on Aging and Human Development* 27 (1988): 271–81.

Williams, Bernard. *Ethics and the Limits of Philosophy.* Cambridge, Mass.: Harvard University Press, 1985.

———. "Persons, Character and Morality." *Moral Luck.* Cambridge: Cambridge University Press, 1981.

Wolf-Devine, Celia. "Abortion and the 'Feminine Voice'. " *Public Affairs Quarterly* 3 (1989): 81–97.

Wolgast, Elizabeth. *The Grammar of Justice.* Ithaca, N.Y.: Cornell University Press, 1987.

Wong, Daniel. *Moral Relativity.* Berkeley: University of California Press, 1984.

Young, Iris Marion. "The Ideal of Community and the Politics of Difference." In *Feminism and Postmodernism.* Linda J. Nicholson (ed.) New York: Routledge & Kegan Paul, 1990.

————. *Stretching Out: Essays in Feminist Social Theory and Female Body Experience.* Bloomington: Indiana University Press, 1990.

Index

abortion, 14, 72, 86n37, 140
abstract individualism, 66–67, 84, 96, 117, 158
abuse: in partnership relations, 103–4, 112n6; of child, 91; of self, 91
Aesop, 35, 141
Allen, J., xvin3
altruism, 133
American liberalism, 4
animals: and magic, 127–29, 132, 136; as children, 123; as food, 129–30; as human artifacts, 129, 130, 132; as partners, 125; as sacred 132–33; as social creatures, 117; Champ and Bernard, 119–22; friendship, 117, 120, 121–23, 125; intentional states, 115; interference with in wild, 131–32; levels of interaction with, 124, 126, 135; needs vs. desires, 116–19, 121; obligation to protect and provide for, 118, 121–23, 125, 147; rights of, 71, 115, 124, 126, 135n16; sense of self, 117, 135; Thorp, 116–19, 134n5; using, 124–26, 130
applied ethics: as women's work, 9–11; ranking in profession, 9;

relating to applied science, 9–10; vs. theoretical, 7–12, 28
Aristotle, 14, 19, 26, 84n2, 85n9, 101, 106, 121
autonomy, 96–97, 111, 158–59

Baier, A., 21, 22, 34, 61, 85n3, 137
Baron, M., 80
Beloved, 151–52
Benhabib, S., 78, 79
Bentham, J., 1, 2
Bloom, A., 79
Blum, L., 18n24
Boldizar, Wilson, and Deemer, 49, 59n23
Brink, D., 31
Bucephalus, 127

Cahn, S., 98, 99, 100, 101
calculus—moral, 2, 21–22, 160
Callahan, D., 30
Callicott, J., 83–84, 129, 130–31, 135n22
care: burnout, 72–73, 76–77; capacity to, 64, 67, 70, 76, 82–83; continuous, 69; dimensions of, 61–62, 89; disposition to, 61–62, 76; ethical, 68–69, 70, 112n2; ideal of, 62,

About the Author

Rita Manning is an associate professor of philosophy at San Jose State University, teaching courses in ethics, social and political philosophy, and feminist philosophy (usually all at the same time). She is continuing to reflect on an ethic of care, paying particular attention to the nature and role of general principles in moral discourse, and the politics of care.